doing business with

Lithuania

GLOBAL MARKET BRIEFING

doing business with

Lithuania

CONSULTANT EDITOR:
MARAT TERTEROV

LITHUANIAN DEVELOPMENT AGENCY

KOGAN PAGE

This first edition published in Great Britain and the United States in 2003 by Kogan Page Limited.

Kogan Page Limited
120 Pentonville Road
London N1 9JN
UK

Kogan Page US
22883 Quicksilver Drive
Sterling VA 20166-2012
USA

Website: www.kogan-page.co.uk

ISBN 0 7494 3843 6

British Library Cataloguing in Publication Data

A CIP record for this book is available from the British Library

---

Library of Congress Cataloguing-in-Pubication Data

Doing business with Lithuania / consultant editor Marat Terterov.
p. cm. -- (Global market briefing)
Includes index.
ISBN 0-7494-3843-6
1. Lithuania--Commerce--Handbooks, manuals, etc. 2. Lithuania--Economic conditions--1991--Handbooks, manuals, etc. 3. Investments, Foreign--Lithuania--Handbooks, manuals, etc. I. Terterov, marat. II. Series.
HF3639.9.Z6D65 2003
330.94793--dc21

2003008889

Typeset by JS Typesetting Ltd, Wellingborough, Northants.
Printed and Bound in Great Britain by Biddles Ltd, Guildford and King's Lynn.
www.biddles.co.uk

Contents

Foreword

Lithuania, an open and rapidly advancing country of 3.5 million people, has everything in place to capitalize on its strategic location in the centre of enormous European markets and those of the Commonwealth of Independent States. It has made a great leap forward in just over a decade of independence and is now at an advanced stage of transformation. Development has been fast. Investment bank Goldman Sachs called it the 'Ballistic Baltic' in a recent report, stating that 'it is a rising star and a launch pad to profitable growth'. Along similar lines the International Monetary Fund stated Lithuania's economic achievements as a 'success story'.

Lithuania is also a great place to live and work as the attributes of a modern European lifestyle have enriched its long history and charming natural environment. With regard to the quality of life it offers, among 215 towns world-wide assessed by Mercer Human Resource Consulting, Vilnius is in third place in Central and Eastern Europe.

Lithuania started negotiations regarding accession to the European Union (EU) later than some other EU candidates; however, the catch-up strategy that was applied has proven to be successful. Lithuania's strong progress toward membership of the EU and NATO has won broad recognition, while the process of EU accession has helped the country to improve its legal, tax and customs systems – all of which is great for business. It is also a boon for investment, as investing in Lithuania becomes an integral part of EU-wide business development strategies.

Many leading international firms have established themselves in Lithuania over the last few years. Foreign direct investments are rising sharply (calculated at 24 per cent in 2002), with more and more reinvestment. As of 1 January 2003, cumulative foreign direct investment exceeded 3.8 billion euros. Major investors in Lithuania are Sweden, Denmark, Germany, the USA and the United Kingdom.

Why are so many companies coming here and expanding? Lithuania, an open export economy, has managed to accelerate growth while keeping inflation very low. Gross domestic product increased by 6.7 per cent in 2002 and is projected to rise an annual 5–6 per cent in the coming years. The Government gives priority to financial discipline, absolute currency stability and other business-friendly policies.

Lithuania, with its highly-educated and quality-oriented labour force and competitive wages, good geographic location, proximity to big markets, excellent infrastructure and low operating and living costs, is an excellent base for bringing extremely competitive goods and services to global markets. Plant capital here and watch it grow – life in Lithuania is on the fast track!

Algirdas Mykolas Brazauskas
Prime Minister of the Republic of Lithuania

List of Contributors

The Association of Financial Analysts (FAA) is non-for-profit professional organization established in January 1999, while its initiative group has been active since 1997. Currently, there are almost 30 regular members and a wide network of interested finance and investment professionals. The focus of FAA activities is to raise members' awareness of the current topics in the Lithuanian economy and other issues of interest through a series of discussions with guest speakers, advocates on professional ethics and best practices, comments on draft laws and other important events in Lithuanian financial markets. Finance and investment professionals, as well as a group of leading journalists and reporters, covering finance and economic topics, also take part in FAA discussion series.

Deloitte and Touche Tohmatsu is one of the world's largest auditing and consulting organizations. More than 92,000 people in over 130 countries serve nearly one-fifth of the world's largest companies as well as large national enterprises, public institutions and successful, fast-growing companies. Its internationally experienced professionals deliver seamless, consistent services wherever its clients operate. Deloitte and Touche has offices in Lithuania, Latvia and Estonia, covering business for its clients in the Baltic markets.

Kevin R Smith is Managing Director of **AWS Structured Finance Ltd**. AWS acts as an advisor to companies on most financing and accounting matters including raising trade and project finance, debt and equity but has particular expertise in Central and Eastern Europe and the Former Soviet Union.

Law Firm Lideika, Petrauskas, Valiūnas ir Partneriai was founded in 1992 and is currently the largest business law firm operating in Lithuania. The firm's principal office is in Vilnius, and from 1998 the branch office has been successfully operating in Lithuania's main seaport Klaipeda. The firm has 30 lawyers, a tax adviser, an adviser on competition matters and a patent attorney, who are supported by strong administrative staff including assistant-lawyers, translators and secretaries. The lawyers and the staff can communicate in Lithuanian, English, German and Russian.

Lideika, Petrauskas, Valiūnas ir Partneriai has a sound reputation for offering a full range of quality legal services (from initial investment advice with tax consultations to everyday corporate counselling) to both domestic and international business clients. The firm is best known for its representation of foreign clients in major M&A, privatization and financial projects in Lithuania. International clients constitute approximately 80 per cent of the firm's client base, which comprises a solid portfolio of renowned multinational corporations, financial institutions, international law and audit firms and local Government institutions.

The firm counts among its lawyers the leading specialists in the major areas of commercial and corporate law, M&A, competition, labour, banking and finance, intellectual property, IT and telecommunications, real estate, energy and natural resources, litigation and alternative dispute resolution. Through a team approach combined with the specialization of individual lawyers in different fields of law, the firm has a remarkable capacity for working with large projects and providing high expertise counselling.

Lideika, Petrauskas, Valiūnas ir Partneriai is a member of the world's major international lawyers' associations. The firm's strong co-operative links with leading law firms in Latvia, Estonia and other countries allow it to ensure that its clients receive quality legal counselling in all Baltic States and other foreign countries.

The Lithuanian Development Agency (LDA) is a professional public sector organization whose main functions are to promote foreign investment and Lithuanian exports. Investment, Export and Information and PR Departments offer a wide range of services to meet the needs of investors and exporters alike.

The Investment Department takes investors through various steps to facilitate their setting up and functioning in the country. It provides initial information, sets up contacts, offers legal advice, helps find partners and green-field sites. In addition, the Agency is in close co-operation with regional and local governments across Lithuania to service the needs of investors on a local basis.

The Export Department is the main source of information for outsourcing suppliers and finding business partners in Lithuania. Its staff organizes sector studies and works with foreign clients in promoting exports of Lithuanian products and conducts training programmes to make local firms efficient exporters.

The Information and PR Department provides first hand information about the general economic situation and business climate, carries out market research and analyses and publishes and distributes promotional materials. As a member of the Euro Info Centre Network it is ready to provide information and advice to SMEs on EU *acquis communautaire*, co-operation programmes or help to find business partners. The LDA has two representative offices in Germany that are engaged in both export promotion and investment attraction activities. LDA's website is www.lda.lt. It has been ranked by *Euromoney* publication as the best in the world among investment promotion agencies.

Lithuanian Free Market Institute (LFMI) is an independent non-profit organization established in 1990 to advance the ideas of individual freedom and responsibility, free market and limited government. The Institute's team pursues its mission by conducting research on key issues of public policy, developing conceptual reform packages, drafting and evaluating legislative proposals, submitting policy recommendations at the legislative and executive levels, and conducting educational work. LFMI's activities also include sociological surveys, publications, conferences, workshops, and lectures. Since its inception, LFMI has addressed a variety of core issues confronting the reform process. Not only has LFMI helped set the terms of debate but has also played a key role in helping to craft and refine legislative proposals.

Prime Investment is a leading Lithuanian investment banking company established in 1997. The company provides services in three major areas: Fund Raising, Mergers and Acquisitions and Strategic Advisory. Since its foundation, Prime Investment has carried out a number of successful projects in various industries, some of which were among the largest and most complex projects of their kind in Lithuania. Its core competences embrace IT and Telecommunications, Transport and Logistics, and Manufacturing. Prime prides itself on building and maintaining long-term relationships with the top corporate decision-makers in the country and serving as their trusted financial and strategic advisors. From its headquarters in Vilnius, Lithuania, Prime Investment operates across the Baltic countries and Belarus.

Prime Real Estate is a real estate advisory company providing a broad array of commercial real estate advice, real estate M&A and restructuring, fund raising, buy and sell-side advisory and brokerage services to clients of whatever size or business sector. Founded as a real estate practice of Prime Investment, Lithuania's leading investment banking company, Prime Real Estate combines the skills, experience and network of investment banking professionals and real estate experts. Consistent with the firm's emphasis on building and maintaining corporate partnerships, Prime Real Estate enjoys outstanding working relationships with major Lithuanian and international real estate developers, retail companies, hotels and real estate holders. Having established a wide network of professional contacts with companies and state institutions, Prime Real Estate has a proven ability to successfully represent the interests of our clients in Lithuania, Latvia and Belarus.

Suprema, Evli Group was founded in 1993 and was one of the first Lithuanian brokerage houses. In 1997, the majority of the shares were sold to the Estonian investment company Talinvest, forming a pan-Baltic securities and corporate finance house, Talinvest Suprem Securities, with a presence in Tallinn, Riga and Vilnius. A management buy-out was executed in 1999 and subsequent renaming as Suprema Securities took place, transforming the house from a single parent ownership to that of a highly-motivated partnership. Full merger with Finish Evli Bank plc took place in October 2002, forming the only Baltic investment bank with physical presence in Scandinavia. Suprema is the largest dedicated investment bank in the Baltic region, recognized by local and foreign investors. Key milestones are: winning the Award of 'Best Baltic Investment Bank' by Euromoney in 2000, EUR 1.2 billion worth of transactions arranged since 1997, largest non-bank equity broker in the region, Award of 'Best Broker in Estonia' by Central European in 1999, Award of 'Best Broker in Lithuania' by Central European in 1999, Award of 'Best Broker in Latvia' by Central European in 1998 and 1999 and being the largest Baltic pension fund manager.

Suprema offers a full range of investment banking services in the Baltic countries and employs 30 professional staff. Involvement in private equity takes place through affiliate Baltcap Management OY, the largest Baltic dedicated private equity fund manager, with EUR 85 million under management.

Map 1 Lithuania and its neighbours

Map 2 Vilnius and surrounding districts

Introduction

Lithuania has come a long way in adopting the major institutions of a market economy as well as a civil, democratic society since the country acquired independence from the collapsing Soviet Union just over a decade ago. Lithuania today stands on the verge of accession to the European Union (EU), is a member of the World Trade Organization, and is regarded as one of the most open market economies of the greater Baltic region.

The country has attracted substantial foreign investment and enjoys a fairly attractive rating from agencies accredited by the international business community. It has a diversified, well-managed and growing economy with a number of prominent sectors including forestry, electronics, information technology and engineering. Vilnius, the capital, is one of north-eastern Europe's historical gems, and with its newly-thriving commercial sector is increasingly the scene of consumer confidence typical of many of Eastern Europe's accelerating economies. However, the majority of older Lithuanian natives will recall that the country's recent history with economic and political development was not always nearly as benign as the position the country enjoys at present.

Annexed by the Soviet Union in 1940, in what was then a process of dividing up territorial spheres of influence between the Russian and German regimes, Lithuania was forcibly incorporated into Soviet political and economic space. There is no need to remind the reader of the manner in which Lithuania's economy and civil society were restructured for the purposes of serving the highly-centralized Soviet system. The suppression of any notable form of political expression, the reorganization of the social system based around Moscow's administrative bureaucracy, the incorporation of the economy into the state-owned enterprise sector and the relegation of private entrepreneurship to an all but marginal (or black market) role, were all dominant social formations during the years of Soviet rule.

It should be noted, however, that prior to its annexation by the Soviets, Lithuania was a country with a very rich tradition of its own independent national character and, itself, had once been a regional power competing for political prominence with the Tsarist Russian empire and the Polish kingdoms. As was the case with a number of states in Eastern and Central Europe during the 1930s, Lithuania was consolidating its post-Versailles sovereignty and the country was developing its early phase of industrial capitalism by embracing institutions of a nascent market economy and democratic methods of governance.

Most native Lithuanians understandably recall the incorporation of their country into the Soviet Union as a dark, regressive turning-point in their national history. The five decades of Moscow's domination of Lithuania was never accepted by many Lithuanians, whether they were resident inside the Soviet Union or in exile abroad, nor by much of the international community. To the country's nation builders and proponents of its national sovereignty, the era of the Soviet Republic of Lithuania was indeed a period lost to history. It therefore would come as little surprise to individuals familiar with Lithuania to appreciate just how enthusiastic the country's political elite must have been to re-establish a sense of Lithuanian nationhood once the imploding Soviet state accorded them the opportunity to do so at the end of the 1980s.

The remaining vestiges of Soviet domination were quick to depart from a newly-independent Lithuania after 1990. With Lithuania admitted to the United Nations in 1991 and seeing the last Russian troops leave the country in 1993, its first freely-elected president, Algirdas Brazauskas, and the remainder of the country's political elite appeared set to relaunch the work of their forefathers of the 1920s and 1930s in building the framework for a properly functioning market economy.

Today, a decade on, Lithuania is generally perceived as one of the more advanced transitional economies. Annual growth in GDP has averaged between 3.8 per cent and 5.9 per cent since 2000, the country's monetary and macro-economic indicators have been largely positive and, on the housekeeping side, the current centre-left coalition Government has been met with high levels of domestic and international approval.

Privatization of Government enterprises is at a fairly advanced stage, although some work still faces the Government – particularly in the energy sector. Inflows of foreign direct investment (FDI) have been coming noticeably into Lithuania during the 1990s and cumulative FDI stood at almost 4 billion euros in the summer of 2002. With a comparatively large population of some 3.5 million people, however, Lithuania still lags behind Latvia, and also Estonia, in terms of FDI inflows per capita. This alludes to scope for further market opportunities; many high-profile multinationals (including IBM, Motorola, Philips and Siemens) and other foreign companies have already invested in Lithuania, often attracted by the country's favourable investment climate, well-educated workforce and good access to regional markets. It seems now to be the case, with Lithuania likely to accede to the EU in May 2004, that the present time is a particularly attractive one to strongly consider business opportunities with this significant Baltic country.

This is our first attempt at compiling a significant volume on the topic of doing business with Lithuania. The book is designed for all parties contemplating Lithuania as a market in which to do business and is primarily divided into four sections. In Part One, we provide a general background to the Lithuanian market, where our two contributing authors – the Lithuanian Development Agency and the Lithuanian Free Market Institute – provide a discussion overviewing the Lithuanian economy, foreign trade patterns and the foreign investment climate. The very topical issue of Lithuania's pending accession to the EU is also discussed.

In Part Two, Lithuania's largest business law firm *Lideika, Petrauskas, Valiūnas ir Partneriai*, provides the reader with 11 in-depth chapters that discuss the crux of the legislation relevant to the conduct of commerce in the Lithuanian market. Special attention is also given to the themes of corporate governance and competition law, both of which are highly significant topics for informed observers of business in the transitional economies.

In Part Three, our authors discuss topics relating to the fiscal and financial sectors in the Lithuanian economies, providing overviews of the country's banking system, regulation of the financial markets, taxation, auditing and accounting. Also discussed is the Lithuanian experience with privatization and the mergers and acquisitions market.

In Part Four, we take an in depth look at the highly diversified Lithuanian economy from a sectoral perspective – our authors introduce no less than 13 different industries central to the country's economic activity. This part of the book will prove to be of major interest to foreign investors not deeply familiar with the structure of Lithuania's economy. Our authors not only cover the country's well-renowned industries such as electronics, textiles and woodworking; but also less prominent sectors such as metalworking, plastics and chemicals as well as booming sectors like telecommunications, retail and the commercial real estate sector.

At the end of the book some appendices analysing the level of business risk associated with the Lithuanian market are provided, together with a list of contacts that will hopefully prove useful to investors perhaps not previously familiar with doing business with this Baltic country.

Marat Terterov
Oxford, England
April 2003

Acknowledgements

In this, my first attempt at putting together a business publication about Lithuania, I am particularly grateful to all of the individual authors in Lithuania and in the UK who provided editorial articles of an extremely high quality and within the confines of the deadlines I set for their submission. I am also particularly grateful to Mr Laimonas Skibarka, of *Lideika, Petrauskas, Valiūnas ir Partneriai*, who encouraged me to fit in a trip to Vilnius during my Baltic tour in the autumn of 2002 and subsequently hosted my visit to this wonderful historical city. Mr Laimonas made my task as commissioning editor a much less burdensome one than it could have been when compiling a publication such as this, since he recommended many well-qualified authors who all contributed numerous quality articles to the book, which the reader now has the opportunity to review.

Marat Terterov

Part One

The Economy and the Business Environment

Dear reader,

The Lithuanian Development Agency (LDA) is a professional public sector organisation, founded by the Ministry of Economy and the European Committee, whose main goals are to promote Lithuania as an attractive market for foreign investment and business and encourage Lithuanian exports. Investment, Export and Information and PR Departments offer a wide range of services to meet the needs of investors and exporters alike.

The Investment Department takes investors through various steps to facilitate their setting up and functioning in the country. It provides specific information on tax regime, investment incentives, infrastructure, general business climate, etc., sets up contacts, helps find partners and green-field sites, In addition, the Agency is in close cooperation with regional and local Governments across Lithuania to service the needs of investors on a local basis.

The Export Department is the main source of information about outsourcing suppliers and finding business partners in Lithuania. Its staff organises sector studies and works with foreign clients in promoting exports of Lithuanian products, offers consultancy support to make local firms efficient exporters.

The Information and PR Department provides first hand information about general economic situation and business climate, carries out market research and analyses, publishes and distributes promotional material. As a member of the Euro Info Centre Network it is ready to provide information and advice to SMEs on EU *acquis communautaire,* cooperation programmes or help to find business partners.

The LDA has two representative offices in Germany and one in Italy that are engaged in both export promotion and investment attraction activities.

LDA's website was ranked #2 IPA website in Europe by Strategic Direct Investor Magazine in 2002. We invite you to visit our website "Advantage Lithuania", **http://www.lda.lt** to get comprehensive and detailed information about trade and investment opportunities.

If you have any questions about Lithuania, don't hesitate to contact us and we will be pleased to provide you with the services and information you need. In most cases our services are gratis.

Sincerely Yours,

Remigijus Kabečius
Director General

LITHUANIAN DEVELOPMENT AGENCY

Šv. Jono 3, LT-2600 Vilnius
Tel.: (370 5) 262 7438, fax: (370 5) 212 0160
Homepage: http://www.lda.lt

1.1

Country Profile

Lithuanian Development Agency

Lithuania is an open and rapidly advancing country of 3.5 million people, with everything in place to capitalize on its strategic location in the centre of three enormous markets. It has made a great leap forward in just over a decade of independence and is now at an advanced stage of transformation. Development has been fast. Investment bank Goldman Sachs called it the 'Ballistic Baltic' in a recent report – it is a rising star and a launch pad to profitable growth. Lithuania is also a great place to live and work, as the attributes of a modern European lifestyle have enriched its long history and charming natural environment.

Lithuania's strong progress toward membership of the European Union (EU) and NATO has won broad recognition, while the process of EU accession has helped the country to improve its legal, tax and customs systems – all of which is great for business. It is also a boon for investment, as investing in Lithuania becomes an integral part of EU-wide business development strategies.

Many international firms have established themselves in Lithuania over the last few years. Foreign direct investments (FDIs) are rising sharply, with more and more reinvestment. Cumulative FDI as of 1 July 2002 reached 3.9 billion euros. Major investor countries in Lithuania are Denmark (580 million euros or 16.6 per cent of total FDI), Sweden (568 million euros or 16.2 per cent), USA (357 million euros or 10.2 per cent) and Germany (336 million euros or 9.6 per cent).

Why are so many companies coming here, and expanding? Lithuania, an open export economy, has managed to accelerate growth while keeping inflation very low. Gross domestic product rose by 5.9 per cent in 2001 (soared to 6.8 per cent in the third quarter of 2002) and is projected to rise an annual 5–6 per cent in the coming years. The Government gives priority to financial discipline, currency stability and other business-friendly policies.

Lithuania, with its good geographic location, proximity to big markets, excellent infrastructure, low operating and living costs, and highly educated labour force with competitive wages, is an excellent base for bringing extremely competitive goods and services to global markets.

Country background

Landscape and climate

- Lithuania is the largest of three Baltic States, the other two being Latvia and Estonia;
- The territory of Lithuania (65,300 square kilometres) is larger than that of Belgium, Denmark, the Netherlands, or Switzerland;
- 70 per cent of Lithuania's territory is arable land and 27.6 per cent is forest. The countryside consists of lowland plains and hilly uplands. More than 2,800 lakes occupy 1.5 per cent of the country and 722 rivers run through the region. Lithuania also has 99 kilometres of Baltic Sea coastline used for recreation and nature preservation;
- The climate is midway between maritime and continental. The average daytime temperature in January is –5°C (23°F), in July +23°C (80°F). The growing season varies between 169 and 202 days;
- Major cities include Vilnius (542,300 inhabitants), Kaunas (378,900), Klaipeda (192,900), Šiauliai (133,900) and Panevėžys (119,700).

Population and language

- The population of the country is 3.5 million with 66.9 per cent living in urban areas and 33.1 per cent in rural areas. Population density is 53.5 people per square kilometre;
- The population's ethnic composition is 83.5 per cent Lithuanian, 6.7 per cent Polish, 6.3 per cent Russian with the remaining 3.5 per cent people being of other nationalities (eg Belarussian, Ukrainian, Latvian);
- The official state language is Lithuanian which is derived from Sanskrit and belongs to the Baltic family of Indo-European languages;
- The main religion is Roman Catholicism.

Recent history

11 March 1990 – Lithuania re-establishes independence

17 September 1991– Lithuania is admitted into the United Nations (UN)

14 February 1993 – Algirdas Brazauskas becomes the country's first freely elected president

31 August 1993 – Last Russian troops leave Lithuania

4 January 1994 – Lithuania becomes the first Baltic State to apply for NATO membership

12 June 1995 – Lithuania signs a Europe (Associate) Agreement with the EU

October–November 1996 – Parliamentary elections result in a pro-business governing coalition comprising the Conservative and Christian Democratic parties

4 January 1998 – Valdas Adamkus, a former high-level US Environmental Protection Agency official, is elected president

1 February 1998 – Lithuania becomes an Associate Member of the EU

December 1999 – Lithuania is invited to start negotiations for joining the EU

February 2000 – Start of the negotiations for the accession to the EU

October 2000 – Parliamentary elections take place, after which a new Government is formed by the new policy coalition consisting of liberals and social-liberals

31 May 2001 – Lithuania becomes the 141st member of the World Trade Organization

July 2001 – A shift to the left – a new coalition of social democrats and social liberals forms a new Government

9 October 2002 – Lithuania is recommended for EU membership by the European Commission

21 November 2002 – Lithuania is invited to start the accession negotiations with NATO

5 January 2003 – Rolandas Paksas, a former businessman, professional pilot and the leader of the Liberal Democratic Party is elected president

Currency

Lithuania's local currency is the litas (LTL), equal to 100 Lithuanian cents. On 2 February 2002 Lithuania re-pegged the litas to the euro at the rate of 3.4528 litas to the euro, thereby ending the litas–US dollar peg, which had lasted for almost eight years. The litas will remain in circulation for a few more years with a view to replacing it with the euro in 2007–2008.

Official state holidays

1 January – New Year's Day

16 February – Independence Day

11 March – Restoration of the Lithuanian State

Easter – Sunday and Monday

1 May – Labour Day

First Sunday in May – Mothers' Day

6 July – Coronation of King Mindaugas

15 August – St Mary's Ascension Day

1 November – All Saints' Day

25–26 December – Christmas

Political system

The Republic of Lithuania is an independent democratic state. The foundation of the social system is enforced by the Constitution of the Republic of Lithuania adopted in 1992 by referendum, which also establishes the rights, freedoms, and duties of citizens. Under that law, sovereign state power is vested in the people of Lithuania and is exercised by the *Seimas* (parliament), the President of the Republic, the Government, and the courts. Lithuania was able to grant full citizenship rights to all ethnic groups in Lithuania soon after the restoration of its independence. This initial effort by the Government to involve all Lithuanian citizens in the political process has contributed to the stable political and ethnic environment.

The *Seimas* is a one-chamber parliament which:

- considers and enacts amendments to the Constitution;
- passes laws;
- adopts resolutions for the organization of referenda;
- announces presidential elections;
- forms state institutions provided for by law;
- appoints and dismisses chief officers of these institutions;
- approves or rejects the candidature of the prime minister proposed by the president;
- considers and approves the Government programme submitted by the prime minister;
- establishes or abolishes ministries on the recommendation of the Government;
- appoints judges to the Constitutional Court and the Chairperson of the Constitutional Court;

- appoints and dismisses the State Controller as well as the Chairperson of the Bank of Lithuania;
- announces local Government elections;
- approves the state budget and supervises its implementation;
- approves state taxes and other obligatory payments;
- ratifies international treaties to which the Republic of Lithuania is a party;
- considers other issues of foreign policy.

The *Seimas* consists of 141 MPs who are elected for a four-year term. The *Seimas* elects its Speaker and his/her deputies.

The President is the head of state and performs all duties that he/she is charged with by the Constitution and the law. The citizens of the Republic of Lithuania elect the President of the Republic of Lithuania on the basis of universal, equal and direct suffrage by secret ballot for a five-year term. In January 1998, Lithuania again made history by being the first European country to elect an American citizen as its president. Mr Valdas Adamkus – a Lithuanian-born former high-ranking US Environmental Protection Agency official who had lived in the USA for almost 40 years and advised two US presidents – won a narrow election victory and renounced his US citizenship before being inaugurated. He emphatically reiterated Lithuania's two main foreign policy goals (NATO and EU membership) and during his term in office Lithuania was recommended for EU membership by the European Commission and invited to start the accession negotiations with NATO.

The Government is the highest authority of executive power. It comprises the prime minister and the cabinet of ministers. The President of the Republic of Lithuania, with the approval of the *Seimas*, appoints the prime minister. Ministers are appointed by the President of the Republic on the nomination of the prime minister. Lithuania is divided into ten regional administrative districts or counties, with county governors appointed by the cabinet of ministers.

Labour force

Total population – 3.5 million

Labour force – 1.7 million, over two-thirds employed in the private sector

Employee skills – 20.3 per cent with university degrees, 24.4 per cent with specialized education (ie technical certificates)

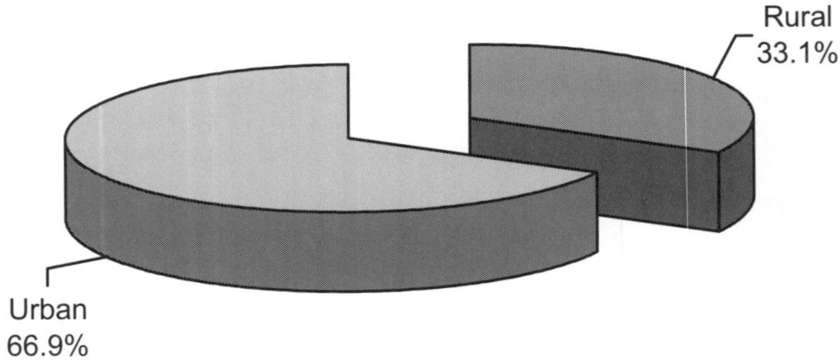

Figure 1.1.1 Proportion of urban and rural labour force

Source: Lithuanian Department of Statistics

Locality of labour force – Of the total labour force, 66.9 per is located in urban areas while the remaining 33.1 per cent is located in rural areas (see Figure 1.1.1).

Lithuania boasts a high-skilled, very efficient and competitive workforce. According to a survey conducted by the Lithuanian Development Agency (LDA) in February 2000 most major foreign investors cite the high quality and productivity of the workforce as one of the main reasons for investing in Lithuania.

Wages

Lithuania's labour costs are among the most competitive in Central and Eastern Europe. As of 1 October 2002, the minimum monthly salary was 430 litas (125 euros). The average gross monthly wage in the third quarter of 2002 was 1,141 litas (331 euros).

Labour unions

Trade unions exist in Lithuania, but are not very active. Since all trade unions were associated with the former Soviet Government, many disbanded after independence was restored. It is estimated that less than 10 per cent of workers belong to some form of workers' organization. Lithuanian citizens and persons without Lithuanian citizenship permanently living in Lithuania and working under employment contracts have the right to enter into trade unions, but it is not obligatory. Since the re-establishment of independence, Lithuanian unions have been pragmatic; little or no labour unrest has been reported. With or without labour unions, employers must follow current legislation of the Republic of Lithuania, which governs all social security issues including, among others, minimum wages and obligatory social insurance by the employer.

Education

Lithuania has one of the best-educated workforces in Central and Eastern Europe. According to the Lithuanian Department of Statistics its proportion of graduates is one of the highest with 3.3 university graduates a year per 1,000 inhabitants. All five major cities in Lithuania now have their own universities. A breakdown of the specializations studied at university is given in Figure 1.1.2.

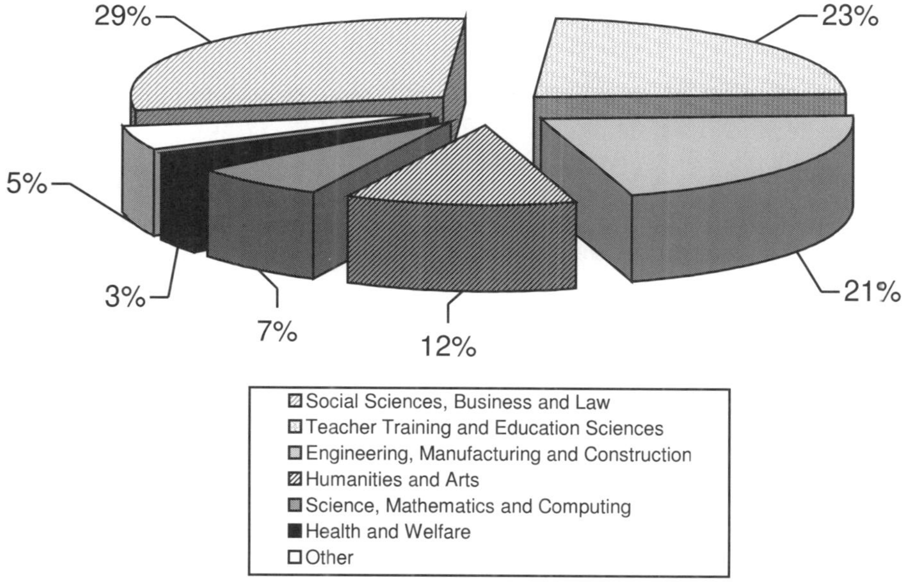

Figure 1.1.2 Breakdown of specializations studied at university (total number of graduates 18,947)

Source: Lithuanian Department of Statistics

Most education institutions are run by the state although several private gymnasiums, lycées and other education institutions (including private business schools) have recently been established. At present there are 19 institutions of higher education with a total enrolment of 117,290 students.

Elementary, primary and secondary education

The current system of secondary education comprises:

- elementary school (grades 1 to 4)
- primary school (grades 5 to 9)
- general education secondary school (grades 1 to 12) including four years of gymnasium which provides a more intensive education in humanities or sciences in grades 9 to 12
- special education institutions for children with special needs
- youth schools which provide basic education
- adult education institutions (centres, adult education divisions in schools of general education)
- programmes of secondary education in a number of colleges.

At the beginning of the 2001–2002 school year, there were 2,159 schools of general education, attended by a total of 576,377 pupils.

Compulsory education lasts until the age of 16. Since 1991 all teaching materials used in elementary and secondary education have been replaced due to changes in the social, economic and political life of the country.

Vocational training

Vocational training is provided by vocational and trade schools. There were 84 vocational schools in the 2000–2001 school year, 82 of which were run by the Ministry of Education. A total of 47,000 pupils attended vocational schools in 2000–2001. The duration of studies varies between two and four years. Students who have reached the age of 14 years are admitted to vocational schools. Studies in vocational schools are at four levels, which gives pupils the opportunity to choose a programme according to their present education and in order to acquire secondary education.

One of the most important tasks of professional education reform is the expansion of the curriculum. Narrow specialization is being rejected and replaced with a wider scope of training. Many vocational schools have ties to places of employment and offer pupils study programmes adapted to changes in the labour market.

In 1991, special secondary schools were abolished and replaced by specialized colleges. College programmes are designed for individuals who already have secondary education and studies last for three to four years. Colleges prepare specialists for employment in all branches of the Lithuanian economy and culture.

Higher education

Currently there are 22 state institutions of higher education in Lithuania: 15 state universities and 7 state colleges as well as 4 private universities and 9 private colleges. Higher education can be pursued by individuals with a secondary school graduation certificate or an equivalent document. Approximately 10,000 secondary school graduates (or 40 per cent of all graduates) are accepted by institutions of higher education each year.

The *Seimas* approves all funds for academies and higher education institutions. Research and higher education reforms are targeted toward the international recognition of the programmes of Lithuanian higher education institutions and activities of research institutes, so that study programmes, degrees and academic titles are recognized abroad, especially in the countries of the EU.

In 1994, Lithuania signed the UNESCO Convention on the Recognition of Courses, Diplomas and Degrees in the European Region. In reforming higher education and modernizing study programmes, many higher education institutions are successfully participating in the European Commission's Tempus, Leonardo and Socrates programmes.

Lithuania's infrastructure

Lithuania has the best infrastructure in the region according to investors and international organizations. The country has four international airports, an ice-free seaport and a satellite-based telecommunications system. Its already extensive road network is being upgraded with the assistance of the EU, the European Bank for Research and Development (EBRD) and the European Investment Bank. The EU has recognized Lithuania as the prime transport centre in the region linking the EU with the East. The EU's transportation commission designated two routes (I and IX) running through Lithuania – a north–south road and a rail route connecting Scandinavia with Central Europe and an east–west route linking the huge eastern markets with the rest of Europe – as among the ten most important in Europe.

Lithuania is strategically located in the gateway between the EU and the Commonwealth of Independent States (CIS). Parallel to the Pan-European Transport Corridor II which connects Russia, Belarus, Poland and Germany, a sea route connecting Belarus, Lithuania and the Baltic Sea can serve as another arterial road between the East and the West. At present, the port of Klaipeda handles cargoes that go to and come from Russia, Kazakhstan at one end, and Germany, the Netherlands, the USA, then South America and Asia at the other.

Port of Klaipeda – expanding to meet growing cargo flows

The port of Klaipeda has been designated the EU's regional priority port – the only port in the region to receive funding from the EBRD and the European Investment Bank to finance major expansion projects. The port has steadily increased cargo handling over the past four years from 14 to over 17 million tonnes (Figure 1.1.3) and handles 20 per cent of the cargo passing through all the eastern Baltic ports. Once current upgrades of modern container handling facilities are completed, the capacity of the port will grow to 40 million tonnes annually.

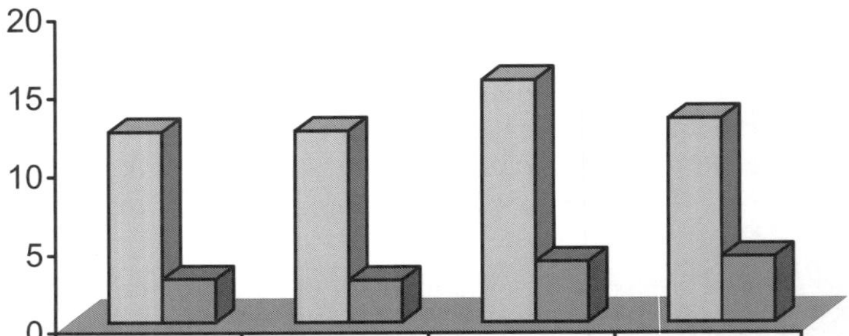

	1998	1999	2000	2001
Loaded	12.209	12.261	15.488	13.018
Unloaded	2.793	2.711	3.908	4.218

Figure 1.1.3 Cargo turnover of Klaipėda seaport (thousand tonnes)

Source: Klaipėda State Seaport

There are regular cargo-ferry lines including rail and Ro-Ro ships between Klaipeda and Hamburg, Bremen, Flensberg, Mukran and Kiel (Germany), Ahus (Sweden), and Copenhagen and Fredericia (Denmark).

Air travel and cargo services

Vilnius International Airport is located just minutes outside the city centre. Lithuania has two national airlines: the soon-to-be privatized Lithuanian Airlines and Air Lithuania. Main destinations include most major cities in Eastern and Western Europe as well as some direct destinations in the Middle East. Lithuania's other passenger airports are located in the cities of Kaunas and Palanga.

Kaunas airport is the busiest cargo airport in Lithuania handling two-thirds of the country's air cargo. It is located near Corridors I and IX and accepts all types of aircraft without any take-off weight limits. The former military airbase at Šiauliai has gone through a major modernization implemented by Philips of the Netherlands. The airport is the only one in the Baltics able to handle the largest cargo planes without any restrictions.

Modern rail and road system

Railways

Railways are one of the most important means of transport in Lithuania for long-distance freight transport. The rail system has good connections with the rail networks of the Baltic States and CIS. The main route between Russia and the Kaliningrad district passes through Lithuania. The total length of the railways is 1,905 kilometres (the density is 29.2 kilometres per 1,000 square kilometres). Among the most commonly transported commodities are crude oil and refined oil products, peat, metals, agricultural machinery, cars and other vehicles, chemical and mineral fertilizers, and coal. In 1993 a direct rail link with the Polish rail system was opened after the extension of a European standard-gauge railway line from the Polish border to the town of Šeštokai and Lithuania now has 334 kilometres of railways of the Crete Corridor I (Warsaw–Mockava–Šeštokai–Kaunas–Riga–Tallinn–Helsinki). Lithuanian railways are also used by Latvian, Estonian, Russian, Belarussian and Ukrainian passenger transit trains, or separate carriages belonging to these states. Lithuania is linked by direct rail routes with Russia, Belarus, Latvia, Poland and Germany.

Lithuanian shippers have taken advantage of the country's modern rail and road system resulting in total transport flows that are among the busiest in the region.

Since 1994 the average traffic density on Lithuanian roads has increased by 15–20 per cent per year. Lithuanian freight operators have increased their international shipments almost 16-fold from 1993 to 1997. In 2001 they reached 45 million tonnes. Between 1995 and the end of 2001, traffic on Lithuanian railways went up by 12.3 per cent (up from 26 to 29.2 million tonnes). Of traffic, 51.9 per cent is transit cargo.

Gas and oil pipeline network

The supply network consists of a gas main with branches and one oil pipeline. Natural gas is imported from Russia through a 1,400 kilometre main pipeline and distributed through 3,900 kilometres of branch lines. The Polock–Biržai–Mažeikiai pipeline, which has been in operation since 1978, transports crude oil purchased in Russia. Part of the crude is channelled to the Mažeikiai refinery for processing and the rest is sent to the Latvian port of Ventspils for transshipment. The annual capacity of this pipeline is 16 million tonnes. In mid-1999, the newly-constructed

Butinge offshore oil terminal in the Baltic Sea began operations. Its annual capacity is 8 million tonnes of oil.

Communications

Communications – the fastest growing sector of the Lithuanian economy – have been attracting an increasing amount of public and private investment, which has translated into new technology and overall modernization. The principal telecommunications firm is Lithuanian Telecom (privatized through an acquisition of 60 per cent of shares by Amber Teleholdings), a Swedish–Finnish consortium (balance of shares privatized through a public share offering in June 2000) with 1,200,000 subscribers as of January 2002.

Mobile phone operator Omnitel brought the region's first satellite-based telecommunications to Lithuania in 1991. Investments by US cell phone pioneer Motorola and Nordic Telecoms have helped Omnitel become the largest wireless provider in the Baltics. Together with the Danish-owned Bite GSM and Sweden's Tele-2, it has kept Lithuania up to date with the most modern mobile technologies. In fact, over the past seven years, the mobile telecommunications market in Lithuania has grown 100 times (from 15,000 mobile phone users in 1996 to nearly 1.5 million at the end of 2002) and service providers say demand is still accelerating. Operating licences have been granted to six mobile communications operators, four paging operators, eight data transmission and satellite communications operators and fifty regional cable television operators.

The postal service, which celebrated its 80th anniversary in 1998, has established EMS, an express mail and package delivery service. It competes with a number of private carriers, including several international companies.

The Lithuanian Radio and Television Centre uses 55 television and 65 radio transmitters. Radio and television programmes are broadcast by 28 radio relay stations and a 1,194 kilometre radio relay line. There are two medium-wave radio networks and three ultra-short FM ones. There are 4 existing national television networks, 10 radio networks and 44 regional television and radio networks broadcasting their programmes in Lithuania. The television colour code system has been changed from SECAM to PAL and is prepared for digital broadcasting through all four national television networks. In the near future the television will allow the broadcasting of 20 to 30 radio and television programmes and the sending of teletext messages, as well as offering paging and other services.

The Government has adopted the National Programme for the Development of Communications and Informatics to 2005.

The new law on telecommunications was adopted on 5 July 2002. The telecommunications sector is expected to be fully compatible with EU legislation in 2004.

1.2

Foreign Investment and International Trade

Lithuanian Development Agency

General economic situation

Lithuania has one of the fastest growing economies in Central and Eastern Europe with the private sector now producing approximately 80 per cent of the country's GDP. Gross domestic product rose by 6.7 per cent in 2002 and is projected to rise an annual 5–6 per cent in the coming years. The *Wall Street Journal* in its 'Index for Economic Freedom', an economic ranking of nations, heralded Lithuania for having 'the most improved economy in the history of the index'.

- Current infrastructure privatization is set to speed up overall economic growth as well as further increase foreign direct investment flows;
- Lithuania's financial infrastructure, including the country's securities sector, banking system, and insurance sector, has developed rapidly since the re-establishment of independence;
- Lithuanian market reforms are coordinated with the International Monetary Fund (IMF) and the World Bank – of which Lithuania is a full member;
- Lithuania offers unrestricted movement of capital and dividends.

Business environment

During recent years, the Government has continued to take effective measures to improve the business climate, reducing bureaucracy and streamlining administrative procedures. According to an annual survey of foreign investors conducted by the Lithuanian Development Agency (LDA) in 2001, 94 per cent of investors are satisfied with their investment, up from 80 per cent in 1997. The Government has set up two commissions for implementing further measures: the 'Sunset Commission' for identifying overlapping and redundant administrative functions, and the 'Sunrise Commission' (with full participation of the business community) for speeding up the implementation of measures to streamline the functions and procedures concerning business and economic matters. Preparations for joining the European Union (EU) bring harmonization of laws and regulations to meet EU standards and practices.

Investment climate

Over the past few years, Lithuania has become a leading location for foreign investors and a competitive centre for product sourcing in the region. The main reasons for this are a high-skilled, low cost alternative to production in the West as well as a stable and strong production springboard to the huge markets to the East. Added to this, impressive economic growth, huge increases in foreign investment, a stable currency and a great investment environment make Lithuania the premier location in the Baltic region.

Lithuania has the largest and most diversified economy of the Baltic States. During the last 50 years intensive industrialization gave birth to enterprises specializing in electronics, chemicals, machine tools, metal processing, wood products, construction materials, food processing and light industry, including the manufacture of textiles, clothing, furniture and household appliances. This industrialization is complemented by strong transportation and service sectors. Since 1990 all of these sectors, along with the banking system, have attracted substantial investments, both 'brown-field' and 'green-field'. The largest cumulative investments are given in Table 1.2.1. Large-scale privatization of many of the larger

Table 1.2.1 Largest cumulative investment by sector as of 1 January 2003

Sector	Total (€ million)	% of total
Manufacturing	1,120	29.3
Financial intermediation	766	20.1
Trade	662	17.3
Communication services	532	13.9
Other	738	19.4

Source: Lithuanian Department of Statistics, 2003

formerly state-owned enterprises and infrastructures create continued investment and modernization.

According to the review of the Bank of Finland's Institute for Economies in Transition (BOFIT), foreign direct investment (FDI) inflows into Lithuania reached 460 million euros in the first half of 2002 – an almost 50 per cent increase compared to the first half of 2001. This made it the leader among the Baltic states in attracting FDI. Siemens, Philips, Motorola, IBM, Marzotto Group, Masterfoods/Mars, Kraft Jacobs Suchard, Lancaster Steel, Partek, Kemira, McDonald's, Telia, Sonera, Philip Morris and Wilhelm Becker are among the multinationals that have chosen to locate production facilities and invest in Lithuania. As of 1 January 2003 cumulative FDI reached 3.8 billion euros.

Foreign investment guarantees

Bilateral agreements on the promotion and protection of investments are already in place with Austria, the Czech Republic, Spain, Italy, Denmark, Greece, Germany, Estonia, Israel, Kazakhstan, China, South Korea, Latvia, Poland, the Netherlands, Norway, France, Romania, Finland, Sweden, Switzerland, Turkey, the UK, Ukraine, Venezuela, Slovenia, Argentina, the USA, Australia, Belarus and the Belgium–Luxembourg Economic Union. The Agreement on Use of Local Currency and the Agreement on Legal Protection for Guaranteed Foreign Investments between the Multilateral Investment Guarantee Agency (MIGA) and Lithuania are in force. Bilateral investment protection agreements with Kuwait, Moldova, Portugal, Russia, Uzbekistan, Hungary and Vietnam have been signed but not entered into force.

Repatriation of profits derived from currency earnings (in both foreign and local currency) is not restricted. There are guaranteed rights to withdraw profits, royalties and interest in convertible currencies.

Property is protected from expropriation – it can only be expropriated in extraordinary circumstances with prompt compensation at market value in convertible currency.

Foreign investment

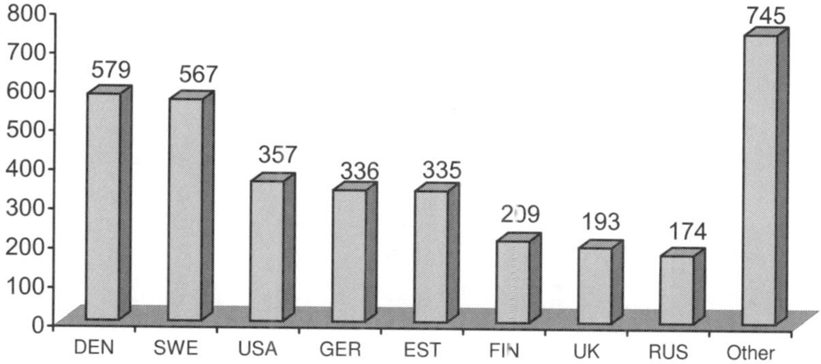

Figure 1.2.1 Major country investors as of 1 January 2003 (€ million)

Source: Lithuanian Department of Statistics, 2003

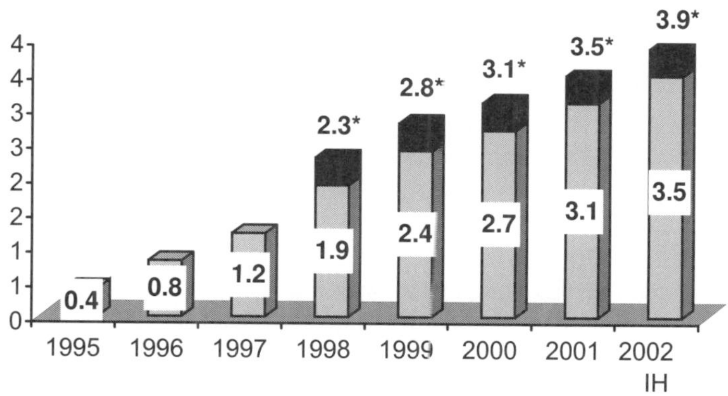

Figure 1.2.2 Cumulative FDI in Lithuania as of 1 January 2003 (€ billion)

Source: Lithuanian Department of Statistics, 2003

Table 1.2.2 Top foreign investors in Lithuania (as of January 2002)

Number	Investor	Origin	JV/Investment	Industry sector	€ million
1	Amber Teleholdings Consortium (Telia/Sonera)	Sweden/Finland comm. 243.3	Lietvos Telekomas	Telecommunications	590.8
2	SEB-Skandinaviska Enskilda Banken AB	Sweden	Vilniaus Bankas	Banking	250
3	Williams International*	USA	Mažeikių Nafta	Oil refinery, pipelines, sea terminal	173.8 comm. 86.9
4	TDC (Tele Danmark A/S)	Denmark	Bite GSM	Telecommunications	150.6
5	Philip Morris International	USA	Philip Morris Lietuva	Tobacco products	84.0
6	Carlsberg Breweries A/S; Baltic Beverages Holding	Sweden/Denmark/ Finland	Švyturys and Utena	Brewery	77.7
7	Den Norske Stats Oljeselskap	Norway	Lietuva Statoil	Petroleum products	60.8
8	Hansapank A/S	Estonia	Hansabankas	Banking	58.9 comm. 43.4
9	Vattenfall A/S	Sweden	Lietuvos Energija	Energy production and supply	57.1
10	DFDS Tor Line A/S	Denmark	Lithuanian Shipping Company	Sea transport	55.1 comm. 69.5
11	Hansapank A/S	Estonia	LTB	Banking	43.4 comm. 43.4
12	Ruhrgas and EON Energie Consortium	Germany	Lietuvos Dujos	Natural gas	43 comm. 20

Table 1.2.2 Top foreign investors in Lithuania (as of January 2002) *(continued)*

Number	Investor	Origin	JV/Investment	Industry sector	€ million
13	Bryggerigruppen (The Danish Brewery Group)	Denmark	Kalnapilis	Brewery	39.2
14	Danisco Sugar A/S	Denmark	Sugar Factories	Sugar production	39.2
15	Amber Mobile Teleholding AB; Motorola; Private Persons	Sweden/Finland/USA	Omnitel	Telecommunications	38.2
16	The Coca-Cola Company	USA	The Coca-Cola Bottlers Lietuva	Soft drinks	36.5
17	Kraft Foods International	USA	Kraft Foods Lietuva	Confectionery and snacks	35.9
18	Tele 2 AB	Sweden	Tele 2	Telecommunications	34.8
19	Mars Inc*	USA	Masterfoods Lietuva	Pet food	31.3
20	Codan Insuracne Ltd A/S*	Denmark	Lietuvos Draudimas	Insurance	31.3
21	AS Hansa Liising	Estonia	Hanza Lizingas	Financial services	29.6
22	Euro Oil Invest SA	Luxembourg	Lukoil Baltija	Petroleum products	29.4
23	Neste OY	Finland	Neste Lietuva	Petroleum products	29.0
24	Siemens Yazaki Wiring Technologies GmbH	Germany/Japan	Baltijos Automobiliu Technika	Electronics	25.0
25	Shell Overseas Holdings Ltd	Great Britain/the Netherlands	Shell Lietuva	Petroleum products	23.3

Number	Investor	Origin	JV/Investment	Industry sector	€ million
26	Partek Insulation; Finnfund; NEFCO	Sweden/Finland	Partek Paroc	Construction materials	22.9
27	Farimex S.A., Profilo Holdings	Switzerland/Turkey	Ekranas	Electronics	21.3
28	Odense Steel Shipyard Ltd	Denmark	Baltijos Laivu Statykla	Shipbuilding	21.0
29	Baltic Fund One LT	USA	Baltic Fund Securities	Financial intermediation	20.9
30	NORD/LB (Norddeutsche Landesbank Girozentrale)	Germany	LŽŪB	Banking	20.6 comm. 18.9
31	Osman Trading AB; Woodison Trading AB; Ferrous Investment Ltd.; Duboil Ltd	Sweden/Ireland/ Great Britain	Klaipedos Nafta	Oil terminal	19.5
32	Tuch Fabrik Wilhelm Becker	Germany	Eurotextil	Textiles	17.4
33	Svenska Petroleum Exploration AB	Sweden	Genciu Nafta	Oil extraction	16.7
34	Cargill Inc*	USA	Lifosa	Fertilizers	16.6
35	AGA AB	Sweden	AGA	Trade in gas	15.3
36	Marzotto spa	Italy	Liteksas	Textiles	12.7
37	Petrol Holding A/S	Norway	Pemco Kuras	Oil lubricants	12.7
38	Danish Brewery Group	Denmark	Vilniaus Tauras	Brewery	11.6

*sold their shares

Source: Lithuanian Development Agency, 2002

Foreign trade

Lithuania pursues a liberal foreign trade policy, and this has stimulated rapid foreign trade growth in the last few years. In 2002, compared to 2001, Lithuanian exports increased by 10.6 per cent and imports by 11 per cent. In 2002, total exports were 5.9 billion euros, imports were 8.2 billion euros and the trade turnover was the biggest in recent years (Figure 1.2.3).

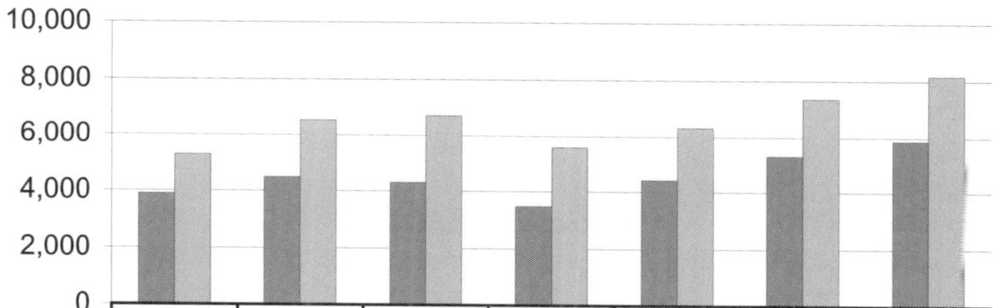

	1996	1997	1998	1999	2000	2001	2002
Exports	3,890	4,476	4,302	3,483	4,417	5,314	5,878
Imports	5,286	6,544	6,717	5,605	6,326	7,366	8,180

Figure 1.2.3 Foreign trade turnover 1996–2002 (€ million)

Source: Lithuanian Department of Statistics, 2003

Foreign trade by countries

The increasing trade volume with the EU is a result of the Free Trade Agreement between Lithuania and the EU which came into force on 1 January 1995. With the exception of textiles and some agricultural products, exported Lithuanian goods are exempt from duties. Bilateral free trade agreements are also in effect with European Free Trade Agreement (EFTA) countries, Poland, the Czech Republic, Slovakia, Slovenia, Turkey, Hungary, Bulgaria, Romania, Ukraine, Estonia and Latvia. The USA, Canada and Australia have granted Lithuania trade preferences under their Generalized System of Preferences (GSP) schemes.

In 1996–2002 the share of Lithuanian exports to the EU increased from 32.9 per cent to 48.4 per cent. Lithuanian exports to the EU in

2001 were 2.842 billion euros. In 2002, compared to 2001, exports to the EU increased by 12 per cent. Lithuania exports largely to the EU (Figure 1.2.4); products include textile articles, machinery and equipment, products of chemical industry, wood and articles of wood, miscellaneous manufactured articles, transport means and mineral products.

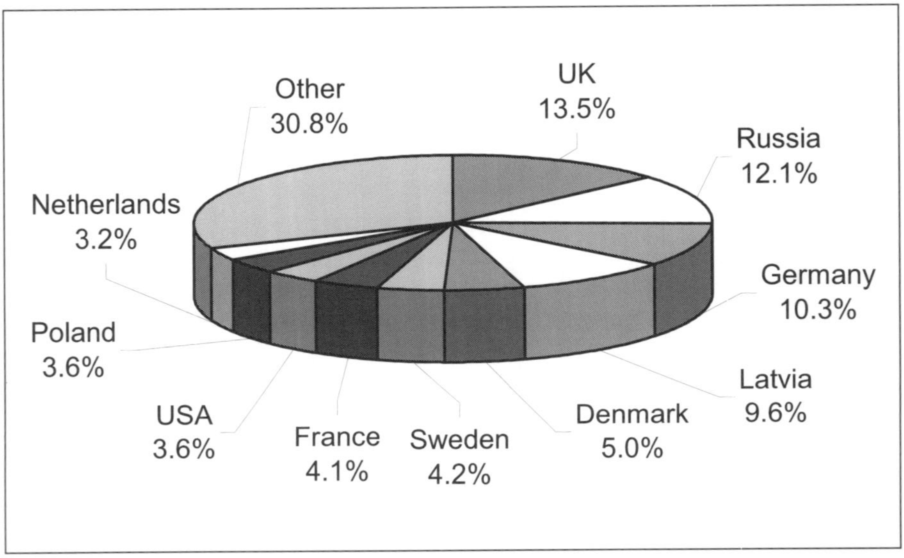

Figure 1.2.4 Exports by country 2002

Countries of the Commonwealth of Independent States (CIS) still remain important markets for Lithuanian exports. In 1996–2002, the share of Lithuanian exports to the CIS decreased from 45.4 per cent to 19.2 per cent. Nevertheless, in 2002 exports to the CIS were 1.128 billion euros and, compared to 2001, increased by 7.7 per cent. In 2002, compared to 2001, imports from the CIS increased by 0.9 per cent and were 2.146 billion euros (Figure 1.2.5). CIS countries are important suppliers of raw materials; from them Lithuania imports energy resources such as oil, gas, timber, ferrous and non-ferrous metals. Key trade partners over the period of 1996–2002 were Latvia, Germany, Denmark, the USA, the United Kingdom, Sweden, Poland, Italy and Russia.

Foreign trade by products

The leaders of Lithuanian exports in 2002 were mineral products with 1.118 billion euros export volume (19 per cent of total exports). In 2002, compared to 2001, exports of mineral products decreased by 10.1 per

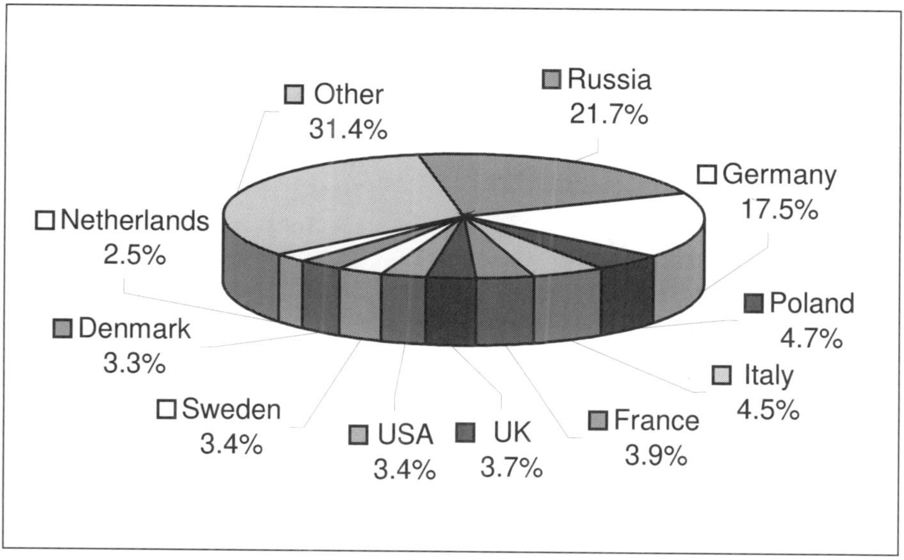

Figure 1.2.5 Imports by country 2002

cent. In second position were transport means with 933.2 million euros export volume in 2002. In 2002, compared to 2001, exports of transport means increased by 90.1 per cent. In the total export structure, textile and textile articles made up 15 per cent. With an active marketing policy this branch of industry is integrating into the western markets more rapidly than the others. State-of-the-art western technologies implemented in textile companies guarantee high quality production output. In the total export structure, machinery and equipment make up 9.9 per cent, products of chemical industry 6.5 per cent, wood and wooden articles 5.4 per cent, base metals and articles thereof 4.7 per cent, prepared foodstuffs, drinks, tobacco 4.5 per cent and animal products 4 per cent. (Figure 1.2.6).

Most of all, Lithuania imports mineral products comprising 17.8 per cent of the total import volume (1.453 billion euros). In 2002, compared to 2001, imports of mineral products increased by 6.9 per cent. Machinery and equipment make up 17.5 per cent of the total import structure (1.429 billion euros). In 2002, compared to 2001, imports of machinery and equipment increased by 16 per cent. In the total import structure transport means comprise 16.4 per cent, products of the chemical industry 8.7 per cent, textiles and textile articles 7.9 per cent, base metals and articles thereof 6.8 per cent, prepared foodstuffs, drinks, tobacco 3.6 per cent, animal products 1.7 per cent and wood and wooden articles 1.4 per cent (Figure 1.2.7).

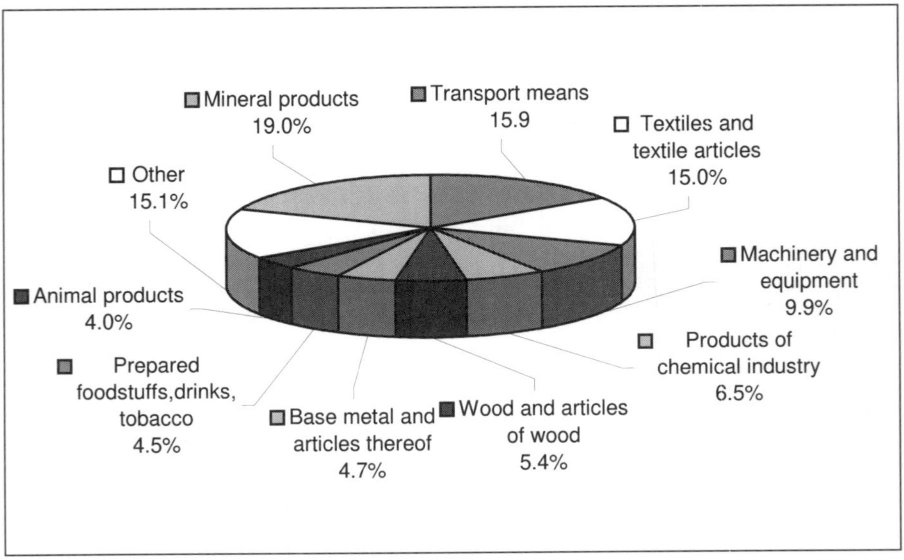

Figure 1.2.6 Exports by product 2002

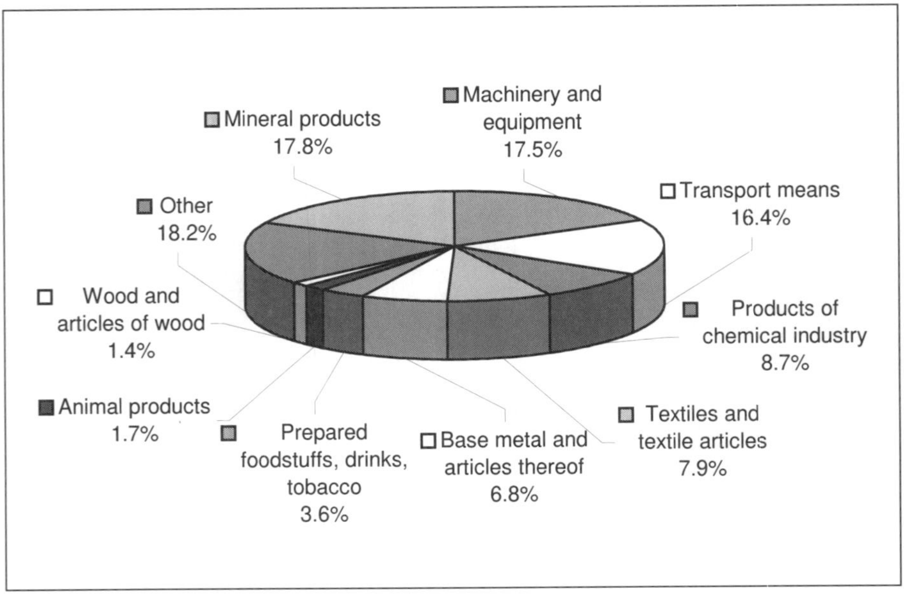

Figure 1.2.7 Imports by product 2002

Free economic zones

Lithuania is continuing to enhance its appeal to foreign investors through the development of a network of Free Economic Zones (FEZs) and industrial parks set up at key transport and industrial centres. Klaipeda, Utena and Kaišiadorys are three cities that were chosen for their superb blend of modern infrastructure, well-developed industrial bases and experienced labour force. At present, Kaunas FEZ is in the process of implementation. Lithuanian and foreign companies, corporations and associations are eligible to participate in the FEZ and industrial parks.

FEZ incentives include:

- For investments over 1 million euros:
  - a corporate tax holiday for the first five years and
  - a 50 per cent tax reduction for the following 10 years
- For investments under 1 million euros:
  - a corporate tax reduction of 80 per cent for the first five years
  - a 50 per cent tax reduction for the following five years
- no customs duties;
- no VAT and excise taxes;
- no road taxes;
- no real estate taxes;
- no foreign exchange restrictions;
- withholding tax exemptions for repatriated profits and dividends;
- streamlined and simplified customs and administrative procedures;
- the same legal guarantees for companies located inside a FEZ as for those outside;
- special write-offs for investments and other expenses on long term assets and new technologies.

Klaipeda FEZ

Size and location

Its 205 hectares (507 acres) are located close to the city's centre and port facilities.

Key activity sectors:

- light manufacturing;
- electronics;
- metal working;
- automotive industry;
- warehousing and transhipment;
- services and other commercial activities.

Advantages

Adjacent to the port of Klaipeda, the FEZ offers transhipment facilities, including a modern road and rail network unparalleled in the eastern Baltic. Increased transit flows and port upgrades continue to improve the investment environment in Klaipeda. Lithuania's port city and the surrounding coastal area has been a magnet for foreign investors – ranking second to only the capital Vilnius – in attracting investment. Klaipeda's seaport itself makes a significant contribution to the growth of the city and is set to develop hand in hand with the FEZ.

Reconstruction of the port is under way in order to meet the increasing demand for freight transhipment. Regular cargo, passenger and Ro-Ro type lines connect Lithuania with Germany, Sweden and Denmark. The construction of a modern cargo terminal was completed in 1999, since when the port has been able to handle all types of cargo. In 2002, 20 million tonnes of cargo were handled in Klaipeda seaport.

Development and management

The mission of the Free Economic Zones Development Centre is to help investors efficiently and effectively establish operations in Klaipeda FEZ by:

- handling matters connected with Government institutions;
- helping investors obtain the best suitable site within the FEZ;
- providing investors with a broad range of services ranging from personnel recruitment to construction management;
- acting as the investor's local resource whenever needed.

1.3

Economic Performance and Market Reforms

Lithuanian Free Market Institute

The growth of the economy

The Lithuanian economy has grown steadily after recovering in 2000 from a recession caused by the Russian crisis. The rate of GDP growth rose from –4.2 per cent in 1999 to 6.5 per cent in 2001 and 6.7 per cent in 2002. A rapidly rising domestic market and growing investments became the deciding factors of economic development in 2002. Export, whose upsurge boosted the economy in 2001 and spurred the domestic market, continues to play an important role, although its growth rate has declined. The economic growth is strengthening the income of individuals as well as corporate investments. The business sector reports a stable financial situation. It is predicted that the Lithuanian economy will maintain similar trends in the medium term. Gross domestic product is forecast to grow by 5 per cent in 2003. Export growth and a rising domestic market will remain the driving forces behind the country's economic development.

In 2002 a slower export growth and rising domestic consumption stimulated an upsurge of domestically oriented sectors of the economy, particularly final consumption and production services. Significant growth was recorded in the following areas: transportation and communication (12.6 per cent), construction (12.8 per cent), financial intermediation (10.6 per cent) and wholesale and retail trade 8.7 per cent. Agriculture rose by 6.1 per cent after a 6.9 per cent decline in 2001. Financial intermediation rose due to a solid performance of banks and insurance companies. Banks achieved the biggest growth over the past decade; the insurance market rose by 67 per cent, mainly due to the introduction of mandatory motor third-party liability insurance and income tax deductions for life insurance valid until 2003. At the same time, the growth of the manufacturing industry slowed down to 5.5 per cent.

A sharp increase in the volume of investments in 2001, preceding the abolition of a zero tax rate on reinvested profits as of 2002, provided a solid basis for ongoing economic growth. Capital investments went up by 38 per cent year-on-year in the last quarter of 2001. Growing investments were one of the key factors of import growth. Import of capital goods rose by 31 per cent in 2001 and by 46 per cent in 2002. These processes will significantly enhance the efficiency and competitiveness of Lithuanian companies as they keep upgrading their production technologies and expanding business activities.

Export grows despite falling markets

Export has been one of the deciding factors behind the country's development. The volume of foreign trade has steadily increased over recent years, reaching its highest level in 2001 when export rose by 20.3 per cent and import went up by 16.4 per cent. Despite a higher rate of export growth, the volume of import exceeded that of export, causing a negative trade balance of 14.2 per cent of GDP. The composition of Lithuania's foreign trade underwent significant changes. Exports to the European Union (EU) rose from 33 per cent of total exports in 1997 to 49 per cent in late 2002. Exports to the Commonwealth of Independent States (CIS) fell from 46 per cent in 1997 to 19.3 per cent in 2002.

The economic decline in the EU diminished the volume of export. In 2001 the volume of trade with the EU grew predominantly because of a sharp increase in the export of oil products – otherwise it was fairly negligible. However, the reduction of export to the EU led to a sharp expansion of Lithuania's trading links with rapidly developing CIS countries, especially Russia. In 2001 Lithuania's exports to the CIS rose by 45.9 per cent, while exports to Russia soared by a striking 86.4 per cent. Admittedly, re-exports, especially of vehicles and foodstuffs, played a decisive role, while Lithuanian commodities constituted a mere third of total exports to CIS countries.

Despite the economic decline in the euro area, Lithuania maintained a fairly high rate of export growth in 2002. Export rose by 10.6 per cent, despite a 10.6 per cent drop in the export of oil products. This confirms that structural export problems are being overcome (an upsurge of electricity export), the economy is being speedily modernized and earlier investments are giving results. In 2002 imports grew 11 per cent.

The litas has a new anchor – the euro

The re-pegging of Lithuania's national currency, the litas, to the euro was an important factor for Lithuanian exporters to the eurozone as it reduced currency risk and put them on a similar footing with their competitors. The euro replaced the US dollar as the anchor currency of the Lithuanian litas on 2 February 2002. The litas was pegged to the euro at a fixed exchange rate of 3.4528 litas to 1 euro. The Bank of Lithuania established this rate according to the euro/US dollar exchange rate announced by the European Central Bank on 1 February 2002. After the re-peg the litas floated against the US dollar in accordance with the euro/US dollar exchange rate on international markets.

All litas in circulation are backed 100 per cent by foreign currency and gold reserves under a currency board system. The currency board, established by the 1994 Law on Litas Credibility, brought transparency and credibility into the Lithuanian monetary system. It put inflation under control, leading to a drop from 45 per cent in 1994 to 0.3 per cent in 1999, and pushed down interest rates.

Lithuania is intent upon preserving a currency board regime until accession to the European Monetary Union (EMU). In January 2003 the Bank of Lithuania proclaimed that Lithuania might seek to join the EMU in 2006 or early 2007 as there were no obstacles to meet the membership criteria. The planned budget deficit for 2003 is 2.4 per cent of GDP, while the EMU requirement is 3 per cent. State debt, which is required not to exceed 60 per cent of GDP, stood at 26.4 per cent at the end of November 2002. At present Lithuania also meets the criteria regarding the level of inflation and interest rates on Government bonds, while a fixed exchange rate with the euro under a currency board system will make it possible to meet the exchange rate requirement.

On 6 November 2002 the euro was legitimated as a legal tender in local transactions along with the litas.

Consumer prices fall

Changes in monopolistic telecommunication and Government-regulated utility prices together with sharp leaps in fuel prices were the main causes of inflation in 2001. Consumer prices went up by 2 per cent, driven mostly by a 21 per cent increase in the prices of communication services and a 6 per cent rise in the prices of foodstuffs. A fall of 11 per cent in transportation prices partly offset these trends. Private consumption grew rather negligibly and had a minimal effect on the general level of prices.

The appreciation of the litas against both the euro and the US dollar resulting from the re-pegging of the litas to the euro was the main reason for a decrease in consumer prices in 2002. From early 2002 until the end of 2002 the litas appreciated by 6 per cent against the euro and by 18 per cent against the US dollar. Prices were also pushed down by increased domestic competition, further strengthened by declining export markets and increased local supply. In 2002 prices edged down by 1 per cent. Unlike the situation in 2001, food prices fell the most, by 5.3 per cent, while transportation prices rose by 9.4 per cent.

Most prices shot up after excise duties on fuel were raised at the beginning of 2002. Excise duties on tobacco went up in October 2002. Prices were also pushed up by rising monopoly telecommunication prices and state-regulated electricity and heating prices. The prices of medicines and medical equipment edged up after a 5 per cent value added tax (VAT) was levied on 1 July 2002.

It is predicted that consumer prices will grow by about 2 per cent in 2003. Growing household consumption and excise duties will be the main factors at work. Lithuania will continue to raise excise duties until they reach the minimum EU norms. In compliance with EU requirements, as of 1 July 2002 Lithuania levies excise duties on three types of commodities: ethyl alcohol and alcoholic beverages, tobacco and fuels. Excise duties on jewellery, perfume articles, electrical energy, coffee, chocolate and other food products were abolished. Yet a turnover tax replaced excise duties on sugar, luxury cars, publications of a violent nature and liquid cosmetic and perfume articles.

The level of prices may be affected by other changes to the VAT, enforced as of 2003. Starting from 2003 newspapers and journals are taxed at a rate of 5 per cent, while newspapers and journals are subject to a regular 18 per cent. A 5 per cent tax is now charged on fresh meat and poultry.

A watershed in the labour market

The labour force in Lithuania has contracted since 1999, mainly due to a sizeable natural decrease since 1994 and a growing number of Lithuanian citizens working abroad. The private sector employs 70 per cent of the working population. In the third quarter of 2002, 20.6 per cent of the working population was engaged in the manufacturing industry, 18.4 per cent in agriculture, forestry and fishery, 15.4 per cent in trade and 9.5 per cent in education. Over past years employment in the agricultural sector has reduced the most – in 2001 it dropped by 18 per cent. Given that the agricultural sector employed approximately one-fifth of the population but contributed only 6.2 per cent of GDP, this decline has been viewed as a positive structural change to the labour market. However, stimulated by the rising domestic market, the agricultural sector revived in 2002 (a 10.4 per cent growth in the first three quarters), showing a sizeable increase in employment.

The year 2002 marked a watershed in the development of Lithuania's labour market. According to the Labour Exchange, the average annual rate of unemployment, affected by a steady economic growth, fell for the first time since 1997 and stood at 11.3 per cent. At the end of 2002, unemployment was 10.9 per cent, down from 12.9 per cent at the close of 2001. Labour force surveys show a higher rate of unemployment – 13 per cent at the end of 2002. The gap between the data of the Labour Exchange and the labour force survey is indicative of a high level of hidden unemployment.

Positive trends on the labour market and expectations of continued economic growth are also reflected in a growing number of permanent new jobs. In 2002 most jobs were created in construction (11 per cent) as well as manufacturing and agriculture (5 per cent). Continued economic growth, rising investments and exports are expected to push down the rate of unemployment to about 9 per cent by the middle of 2003. A falling demand for unqualified labour, a heavy tax burden and strict employment regulations will counteract these trends. In the short term structural reforms, such as restructuring and privatization of the Lithuanian railway and Lithuania Airlines or the privatization of the energy sector, can also impede a faster decline in unemployment.

A growing tax burden on sole proprietors has caused an upsurge in the number of business closures. As of 2002 sole proprietors have been required to pay an additional 15 per cent contribution on their taxable income to supplement the public pension. In addition to that, a new law on personal income tax, effective as of 2003, doubled taxation of sole proprietorship by imposing a 15 per cent income tax in addition to a 15 per cent profit tax.

Employment regulations change

Labour policy has undergone significant changes in the past two years. In March 2001 legislative amendments were adopted, aimed at liberalizing employment regulations. A mandatory form of labour contracts was abolished, layoff benefits were reduced and wage regulations were simplified. A new labour code came into effect starting from 2003; it codified legal provisions regulating the labour market and abolished a number of outmoded regulations, such as listing legitimate causes for terminating labour contracts. Now labour contracts can be ended for reasons related to inadequate employer qualifications or behaviour at work, enterprise restructuring or for economic reasons. New types of labour contracts – temporary, supplementary, household and commission contracts – were legitimated in addition to fixed-term, permanent and seasonal contracts.

Despite these changes, labour relationships are still regulated in an excessively detailed and imperative manner; freedom of contract is limited. Many obsolete regulations, eg mandatory reporting to the labour exchange, remain in place and new restrictions have been adopted.

Employers are prohibited from concluding termed contracts for 'permanent' jobs at the request of employees. The new labour code also expanded the role of collective agreements by spelling out duties for persons who are not party to such agreements. In addition, unpaid leave became the subject of collective agreements. All this will hurt qualified employees in particular by limiting their possibilities to negotiate better terms of employment.

State debt on the rise

In December 2002 Fitch raised Lithuania's rating of long-term loans in foreign currency to BBB and that for loans in domestic currency to A–. In February 2003 Standard & Poor's raised the ratings to BBB+ and A– respectively. Lithuania was thus included in the highest rating group in terms of liabilities in domestic currency, reflecting its favourable macroeconomic climate, strict fiscal policy and continued structural reforms.

Lithuania's stable political and financial situation and falling interest rates on international markets drove down the yield on Government securities. The average interest rates slumped from 9.3 per cent to 6.4 per cent in 2001 and were down to 4.6 per cent in 2002. In 2002 state debt rose by 2 per cent and accounted for 26 per cent of GDP at the end of the year. State debt for Government securities grew by 20 per cent – at the beginning of 2002 the ceiling on Government borrowing was raised to 30 per cent of GDP. The ceiling on foreign debt was set at 25 per cent of GDP, or 70 per cent of total state debt. Also, in March 2002 the Ministry of Finance removed limits on the issues of Government securities offered in auctions 'to help balance the volume of domestic Government borrowing with the amount of free resources'. These changes provide a basis for increasing Government borrowing in light of extensive Government liabilities. In 2001 rouble savings compensation was renewed after a three-year pause and compensation for land recommenced. A housing programme was put into effect. More resources will be required for continued land compensation and pending pension and health-care reforms. If the economy grows at the rate forecast by the Ministry of Finance, Government debt will have grown by more than 40 per cent by 2004. Although the ceiling on Government borrowing set by the Maastricht Treaty is much higher (60 per cent of GDP), a rapid increase in Government borrowing may drive up the costs of borrowing.

In 2000 interest rates on Government securities dropped below the level of interest rates on loans. In 2002 the average interest rate on half-year and one-year Government securities was 3.7 per cent, as compared to almost 6.8 per cent on loans. The average interest rates for one to five years were 5.5 per cent and 7.2 per cent respectively. Despite that, banks' investments in Government securities rose more than their loan portfolio – by 33 per cent and 23 per cent respectively in 2001 and 45 per cent and 40 per cent in 2002.

Privatization continues and monopolies end

The coalition Government of the Social Democrats and the Social Liberals, which took office on 12 July 2001, has maintained the main course of Lithuania's economic policy with integration into the EU and NATO being top priorities. Lithuania has been invited to join the EU in 2004. A referendum on EU accession is scheduled for May 2003. Other priorities on the Government's agenda include improving the business environment and promoting the development of a competitive agricultural sector, reducing unemployment and poverty and promoting the development of education, science and information technology.

The current Government has proceeded with the privatization and restructuring programme. Privatization has been extended to include large infrastructure and strategic items. In March 2002 the last state-owned bank, the Žemės Ūkio Bank, was acquired by the German Norddeutsche Landesbank Girozentrale. In May 2002 a 34 per cent stake in Lithuanian Gas was sold to a strategic western investor – German Ruhrgas and EON Energie. Another 34 per cent will be sold to a gas supplier, in all likelihood the Russian company Gazprom. The current privatization programme also includes energy companies, Lithuanian Airlines, Lithuanian Railway and alcohol production companies (state monopoly of alcohol production was ended at the start of 2003).

The state has a right to retain a 'golden' share granting extra non-property rights if more than half of the public stock in transportation, energy, oil, communications and public utility enterprises is sold. The conducted privatization programme has been criticized for scant use of public sales of shares on the stock exchange and a lack of transparency in direct negotiations. When large items are sold, special requirements pertaining to buyers' qualifications, future investments and job preservation are applied. This has led the Lithuanian Government to assume extensive liabilities towards the investors – the much-criticized sales of the Mažeikiai Nafta oil refinery and Lithuanian Telecom provide the best examples. In 1998 Lithuanian Telecom was granted a monopoly in terrestrial communications until 2003 in return for the investors' pledge to preserve about 10,000 jobs and to invest US $225 million in the company. The buyer of Mažeikiai Nafta, the US-owned Williams International, received from the Lithuanian Government loans and loan guarantees in addition to concessions for the use of the infrastructure and a pledge to compensate the company's losses. In 2002 Williams International withdrew, conceding Mažeikiai Nafta to the Russian company Jukos.

The restructuring of the energy sector was completed. At the end of 2001 electricity production, transmission and distribution activities were separated by splitting the Lithuanian Energy into five companies. The Eastern Distribution Network, the Western Distribution Network and Mažeikiai and Elektrenai electrical power plants were established and began to operate as independent companies starting from 2002. The companies are now being prepared for privatization. Although privatization is expected to enhance the efficiency of the energy sector, a new legislation on electrical energy and natural gas can pose serious constraints – the laws impose licensing on all activities to be conducted on the electricity and natural gas markets. They envisage territorial restrictions on the construction of electrical energy transmission networks and on the use of natural gas transmission systems.

Profound changes have taken place on the telecommunication market after its demonopolization on 1 January 2003 with the enforcement of a new telecommunication law. Being in full compliance with EU norms, the new law abolished licensing of telecommunication activities; however it laid down a number of regulations and restrictions on operators and private agreements. By law the prices of operators having a significant market share will be regulated. Operators will have to ensure, at their own expense, access for their subscribers to the services of other suppliers and preserve subscribers' numbers when they choose another supplier. These and other provisions will undermine competition on the telecommunication market and increase operators' costs.

Overhauling the tax system

The economic environment has changed as almost the entire tax system was overhauled in 2002 and at the beginning of 2003. In addition to new laws on excise duties and VAT, a new law on personal income tax was adopted and profound changes were made to the corporate income tax. On 1 January 2002 the corporate income tax was lowered from 29 to 15 per cent but at the same time a zero tax rate on reinvested profits, effective as of 1997, was abolished. Taxation of reinvested profits is likely to reduce incentives to expand business activities and to upgrade production technologies. By the estimates of market participants, after an increase from 57 per cent in 1998 to 66 per cent in 2001, reinvested profits slumped to 50 per cent in 2002 and are likely to remain at a similar level in 2003.

The new law on personal income tax, effective as of the beginning of 2003, replaced the former eight tax rates with just two: 15 per cent and

33 per cent. Thirty-three per cent is now charged on income from employment, individual business activity and other types of income; 15 per cent is charged on dividends, the incomes of sailors, sportsmen and artists, royalties, proceeds from rent or sale of property as well as pensions and life insurance benefits. According to the new law, education fees, interest on housing loans, contributions to fully-funded pension insurance and life insurance are tax-deductible. The new law is expected to be the main factor to increase the tax burden as the tax rates for certain types of income changed upwards. However, the authorities claim that the state budget will forego some 116 million euros as the tax-exempt minimum income was raised (84 euros) and differentiated by the number of children in a family in an attempt to reduce the tax burden for low-income individuals.

There is more to be done

The country's economic development will depend largely on progress in accelerating today's lacklustre reforms of the pension system and health care. Prolonged political debates on pension reform have seriously halted the development of private pension insurance. A law providing for voluntary fully-funded pension insurance was adopted in late 2002. Insured persons will be allowed to transfer 2.5 per cent of their social security contributions to private pension funds or life insurance companies. The rate of the insurance premium will be increased by one percentage point every year until it reaches 5.5 per cent in 2007. Critics charge that the contributions will be too small to stimulate a proper development of private pension insurance.

Lithuania is living through one of the most successful periods of economic development of the decade. The country should take this advantage and carry out unfinished or delayed reforms. This would not only reverse the current predicament in the fraying social safety net but would also remove one of the remaining drags on growth and prosperity.

1.4

Lithuania and the European Union – a Progress Report on Entry

Lithuanian Free Market Institute

Since the beginning of the 1990s Lithuania's relations with the European Union (EU) have seen significant changes that have radically transformed the nature of its economic and political environment. Currently, Lithuania is one of the 10 countries that completed accession negotiations with the EU in December 2002. The EU is also Lithuania's major trade and investment partner. If the popular referendum and ratification procedures take place as planned, Lithuania is expected to join the EU in May 2004.

Relations between Lithuania and the EU, however, differed markedly in the beginning of the 1990s when the country re-established its independence. The EU recognized Lithuania as an independent state on 27 August 1991 and it is since then that the diplomatic and economic relations between the two parties have been gradually developed. Although for some time the prospects of closer cooperation between Lithuania and the EU have remained vague, the EU demonstrated its different approach to the Baltic States, as compared to the other Soviet Union countries, by extending the PHARE programme (Poland and Hungary: assistance to the restructuring of the economies) to the Baltic States in autumn 1991.

Signed on 11 May 1992, the Trade and Cooperation Agreement between the EU and Lithuania was the first step towards removing barriers to trade between the parties. The agreement came into force on 1 February 1993, removing specific trade barriers that the EU applied to Lithuania as a former state trading economy and introducing the status of the Most Favoured Nation as well as a number of trade preferences and provisions on economic cooperation. The agreement also laid down the possibility of concluding an association agreement some time in the future. However, although the Trade and Cooperation

Agreement was seen as the first important political basis for relations between Lithuania and the EU, its economic significance was limited. It was the Agreement on Free Trade and Trade Related Matters, signed on 18 July 1994, that liberalized trade in industrial products between Lithuania and the EU.

When the Free Trade Agreement came into force in early 1995, the EU lifted customs duties from Lithuanian industrial products (with some exemptions, eg textile products). Lithuania was granted a six-year transition period to remove customs duties applied to imports from the EU. The implementation of the agreement has contributed to the continuous growth of trade between Lithuania and the EU, and by the late 1990s trade with the EU accounted for about half of Lithuania's foreign trade turnover. However the Free Trade Agreement did not liberalize trade in agricultural products and did not prohibit the application of other protectionist measures such as anti-dumping duties. The latter have been applied a number of times by the EU thereby restricting Lithuania's exports to the single market. As barriers to agricultural trade have only been diminished it is most likely that they will be removed only after Lithuania joins the EU.

Lithuania started to be seen by the EU as a potential member in early 1994. Gradual integration and closer political relations followed the well-known Copenhagen Summit in June 1993 when the EU announced the criteria that had to be satisfied by aspiring members (and which were initially aimed at the most likely candidates such as Poland, Hungary and the Czech Republic). In June 1995 Lithuania signed the Association Agreement (also called the Europe Agreement) with the EU that acknowledged Lithuania's prospects to eventually become a member of the EU. The Free Trade Agreement was incorporated into the Association Agreement, which also provided for intense cooperation in a number of economic policy areas, and committed Lithuania to harmonize its laws with EU norms (the so-called *acquis communautaire*). The Association Agreement came into force in February 1998 and continues to be the basis of relations between the EU and Lithuania until the Accession Treaty is signed and comes into effect.

Lithuania applied for EU membership on 8 December 1995. The most important EU-related developments that have been taking place since the mid-1990s include gradual liberalization of trade relations between Lithuania and the EU as well as the transposition and implementation of EU norms in Lithuania regulating the single market.

In 1997, the European Commission announced the Agenda 2000 in which it recommended starting accession negotiations with a group of five applicant countries (Lithuania was not among them at that time). These recommendations were approved by the Luxembourg Summit in December 1997 which also added new instruments to the EU's cooperation with other applicant countries including Lithuania. This has resulted in the EU preparing regular Accession Partnerships for Lithuania since 1998. The Accession Partnerships provided a list of short- and medium-term measures that Lithuania was recommended to undertake in a number of economic policy areas in order to be ready for the accession. The recommendations included privatization of state owned enterprises, reforming energy, transport and other sectors, bankruptcy procedures, and alignment of legal norms regulating economic activities.

In 1998 Lithuania prepared the national programme for the adoption of the *acquis* which was later regularly updated and served as a basis for the harmonization of national legal acts with EU norms. This exercise implies a wide regulatory reform which is expected to result in an economic environment regulated by the same rules as those in force in the EU.

Among the major turning points in Lithuania–EU relations was the annual regular report of the European Commission in 1999, proposing to start accession negotiations with Lithuania (and five other applicant countries). These recommendations were adopted by the Helsinki Summit in December 1999, and in February 2000 accession negotiations were officially opened.

At the outset, the accession negotiations resembled the exchange of information between the EU and Lithuania in which the latter would submit its plans on adopting EU norms in a specific area (the negotiations were conducted on the basis of 31 chapters which in itself shows the extensiveness of EU regulatory norms) while the EU would approve the plans or would ask for some clarifications. The first two to three years of accession negotiations were a process of consultation rather than negotiation. After Lithuania (and some other countries that started negotiating in February 2000) caught up with the 'first group' candidate countries, it became obvious that 10 of these countries were progressing at a somewhat similar speed and the EU's differentiation between them could not be justified on economic, administrative and even more so – geopolitical – grounds. Thus, at the start, the negotiations went through a number of 'easy' chapters including science and research, industrial policy, statistics, education and training, among others. Then followed the chapters where Lithuania had specific issues such as fisheries (because it borders the sea), common external policies (because it had some preferential trade agreements with third countries, eg Ukraine, that would have to be abolished after the accession), justice and home affairs (because it would be the EU's future external border), economic and monetary union and others.

Then there were areas where large investments were required by Lithuania to meet the EU's regulatory standards (product norms, environmental protection norms, security of supply norms, norms regulating the financial standing of enterprises or the way services are provided).

They included free movement of goods, environment, energy and transport. However, the EU was willing to give a number of transition periods for the most expensive norms and therefore the negotiations did not cause much controversy.

Similarly, negotiations over transition periods for politically sensitive issues went rather smoothly. For example, even in 2001 the EU made it clear that it was going to restrict the movement of labour from Lithuania and other Central and Eastern European countries for up to seven years after the accession. Although this provision was adopted by the EU, individual EU member states – Sweden, Denmark, the Netherlands, Ireland and Great Britain – announced that they would remove the restrictions on the movement of labour from Lithuania from the date of its accession. The EU also imposed a transition period of five years for transport companies from Lithuania and other candidate countries to provide services freely inside EU member states (the so-called 'cabotage services'). These two transition periods are likely to slow down the economic integration of Lithuania and other new member states into the single market.

Like other candidate countries, Lithuania's requests for more transition periods were based on the investments needed for the implementation of EU norms (environmental norms, transport and energy regulations) and political sensitivity of certain issues (sales of agricultural land to foreigners). The most important and most difficult chapters were left for the last stage of accession negotiations that took place in 2002 under the Spanish and Danish presidencies. These included mostly redistributive issues such as agricultural support, which are politically sensitive both in the EU and candidate states, and some other issues of symbolic political importance. The latter included the introduction of visas to residents of the Kaliningrad region by Lithuania which had been opposed by the Russian Federation authorities and the EU's financial support for the closure of the Ignalina nuclear power plant in Lithuania.

Agriculture proved to be the most controversial issue in Lithuania and most other candidate countries. Although the EU on the basis of the Commission's Agenda 2000 has been incrementally moving towards reforming the CAP, the accession of 10 new countries some of which like Lithuania (having approximately 16 per cent of its population employed in farming) raised sensitive questions as to how to 'redistribute the pie' without exceeding the limits set for the EU budget spending (at 1.27 per cent of the EU's GDP). The latter point has been particularly stressed by the main net contributors to the EU budget such as the Netherlands and Germany who were concerned about any possible increase of their financial contributions as a result of EU enlargement.

Eventually, the European Commission came up with a proposal (supported by the majority of EU member states) to extend to new members only 25 per cent of direct payments for farmers, one of the most important instruments of agricultural support, from the first year of EU membership in 2004 and then gradually increase this share to reach 100 per cent of that which the current member states receive in 2013. Although the negotiations regarding agriculture covered a wide range of issues including the adoption of veterinary, phytosanitary and animal welfare norms, introduction of administrative and monitoring systems, production quotas and other types of support, the extension of direct income payments proved to cause most controversy. It was only on the night of 13 December 2002 that the final agreement between the EU and candidate countries was reached. Although the EU retained the formula of starting at 25 per cent of direct income support payments, it agreed that candidate countries may extend larger payments from their national budgets to reach the level of 55, 60 and 65 per cent from 2004 to 2006.

The latest days of accession negotiations have focused mainly on financial issues such as agricultural support, budgetary compensations, structural support, the EU's support for closing down the nuclear power plant in Lithuania and for financing the transit infrastructure for the Russian transit through the territory of future member states or border infrastructure. The EU committed to allocate a total of almost 42 billion euros for the period of 2004–2006, while contributions of the new members to the EU budget are estimated at about 15 billion euros.

Lithuania has concluded negotiations with 21 transition periods and two technical derogations agreed in eight chapters. Although initially the European Commission's position was not to allow any transition periods in the area of the internal market, in addition to limiting the free movement of labour and transport services from Lithuania, it also agreed to some transition periods in the areas of free movement of goods, services and capital to be applied by Lithuania. Although some of them are justified by differences in the level of economic development between the EU and Lithuania, the transition period of seven years for removing barriers to sales of agricultural land to foreigners is a result of political pressure rather than economic reasoning. Other transition periods agreed by Lithuania are in the areas of agriculture, environment, transport, energy and taxation. They aim at reducing the pressure to adjust to higher and more expensive EU environmental, product quality, financial standing, security of energy supply norms and higher excise duties on tobacco products.

Notably, Lithuania has negotiated the largest comparative levels of EU budgetary support reaching about 538 euros per capita and one of the lowest levels of contributions to the EU budget (146 euros per capita). A significant share of EU funds (up to 525 million euros until 2006) will be channelled to finance the closure of the Ignalina nuclear power plant (with the first reactor scheduled for the closure by 2005 and the second one by 2010). The EU also committed itself to finance the investments in border infrastructure that are necessary for Lithuania to participate (some time later after the accession) in the Schengen area (around 137 million euros in 2004–2006). Farmers, despite the lower level of direct payments than in the EU member states, will be among the main recipients of EU funds. The EU committed 434 million euros for the rural development for the period of 2004–2006, and about 152 million euros for the direct support.

After the accession, Lithuania will have 13 seats (out of 732) in the European Parliament. It will also have 7 votes (out of 321) in the Council of Ministers, one commissioner in the European Commission and representatives in other EU institutions – the European Court of Justice, the Committee of the Regions, and the European Central Bank. It should be noted that due to the requirement to participate in the Exchange rate mechanism for two years, Lithuania will probably join the eurozone in 2007 at the earliest (although its national currency, the litas, is already pegged to the euro at a fixed rate and the country meets all of the convergence criteria).

With the accession negotiations completed in December 2002, the popular referendum in Lithuania is the next and possibly the last major step before the actual accession into the EU. It has recently been decided that the referendum on EU accession in Lithuania will take place on 10–11 May 2003. Although the ratification of the accession treaty (to be signed in April 2003) will also have to be undertaken in current member states' parliaments and the European Parliament, they are unlikely to pose any major problems.

Unlike in some other acceding countries, opinion polls show that in Lithuania the support for the EU accession increased from around 50 per cent in November 2002 to approximately 67 per cent in January 2003. It is also likely that a large share of people who do not yet have an opinion would vote for joining the EU. However, two potential problems may still arise. The first one is a low turnout in the referendums; this is particularly important in Lithuania where the decision of a referendum is passed if at least 50 per cent of all persons who participated in the ballot vote in support. The other problem is a potential success of some euro-sceptics capitalizing on the outcomes of accession negotiations and a rather low level of information on the EU.

It is very likely that the discriminatory aspect of direct payments to farmers after the accession will be among the main issues raised by the opponents of EU accession (despite the fact that it will be the farmers who stand to gain most financially from EU accession). Other publicly expressed fears might include a potential loss of sovereignty or unfair conditions for competition. Some might also raise criticism for having to reintroduce barriers to foreign trade with non-EU countries, for having a more distorted agricultural policy or for having more regulation of economic activities which to some extent reverse economic reforms undertaken in 1990s.

If the ratification process proceeds smoothly, voters in Lithuania are going to elect their representatives to the European Parliament in 2004 and in May of the same year the actual accession will take place.

Part Two

The Legal Structure and Business Regulation

2.1

Legal Framework for Foreign and Domestic Investment

Lideika, Petrauskas, Valiūnas ir Partneriai

Introduction to Lithuanian legal system

The Lithuanian legal system is principally based on the legal traditions of continental Europe. Naturally, during Soviet occupation the legal system of Lithuania was significantly altered to conform to that of the Soviet Union. Since restoration of Lithuania's independence in 1990 the legal system has been reformed to meet the demands of vast social and economic changes brought about by a return to democracy and a free market economy. In view of Lithuania's goal to accede to the European Union (EU), central priority of these ongoing reforms was the harmonization of Lithuanian law with that of the EU. In view of the expected full EU membership of Lithuania from 1 May 2004, application of EU law will soon bring further changes to Lithuania's legal practice.

In the Lithuanian legal system, the principal body of law is statutory. Main areas of substantive law are codified in codes (eg Civil Code, Criminal Code, Code of Civil Procedure, Code of Criminal Procedure, Labour Code, Customs Code). The system of regulatory acts is hierarchical whereby the Constitution is an act of the supreme power, followed in descending order by constitutional laws, laws (*įstatymai*), resolutions of the *Seimas* (parliament) or the Government (*Vyriausybė*) of the Republic of Lithuania, decrees of the President of the Republic of Lithuania and acts of other Governmental institutions and local municipal authorities. All regulatory acts, including laws, must comply with the Constitution. All international treaties and conventions must be implemented in Lithuania – however, the ones ratified by the *Seimas* prevail over national laws but not the Constitution. The supranational nature of EU law will bring about a change in the hierarchy of Lithuanian law.

The system of general jurisdiction courts consists of the Supreme Court, the Court of Appeals, district courts and local courts that deal with civil and criminal matters. Judges of the Supreme Court are appointed by the *Seimas*, while judges of the Court of Appeals are appointed by the president upon approval of the *Seimas*. Judges of both district and local courts are appointed by the president. In 1999 the system of specialized administrative courts was established to deal with administrative litigation. This system consists of the Highest Administrative Court and district administrative courts.

The doctrine of precedent was not previously acknowledged in Lithuanian law. Nevertheless, the Senate of the Supreme Court has been analysing court practice and adopting recommendations in order to promote uniformity. Now the *stare decisis* is being implemented in practice as the interpretations of law in the published decisions of the Supreme Court must be taken into consideration by lower courts in similar cases.

The Constitutional Court is not a part of the general court system, but is an independent judicial body. It has the authority to determine whether the laws and other legal acts adopted by the *Seimas* are in conformity with the Constitution, and whether the legal acts adopted by the president and the Government conform to the Constitution or laws.

Regulation of foreign investment

Foreign investments in Lithuania are regulated and protected by national legislation as well as numerous international agreements on promotion and protection of investments. Currently, there are approximately 26 bilateral agreements in place with most of the EU member states, the USA, and many Central and Eastern European countries. Such agreements prevail over the provisions of the Lithuanian national laws and usually provide for more favourable treatment of reciprocal investments.

The Law on Investments of 7 July 1999 establishes the following fundamental principles of treatment of foreign investments in Lithuania:

- Principle of Equal Protection – rights and lawful interests of Lithuanian and foreign investors are equally protected by the laws of Lithuania;
- Principle of Equal Treatment – foreign investors enjoy the same rights and obligations relating to commercial activities as Lithuanian domestic investors, including the state and municipalities, and the economic conditions are the same for all investors;
- Principle of Free Access to All Sectors of Economy – foreign investors have free access to all sectors of the economy, except for sectors

relating to the security and defence of the state (with some exceptions) and organizing lotteries.

When a licence or permit is required for a certain type of activity, licensing requirements apply equally to entities owned by foreign and domestic investors. Activities that require prior permission or licence are mostly related to the increased danger to human life, health, environment, and also include activities in certain regulated sectors (such as energy, telecommunications etc).

Forms of investment

Investments may be made by means of monetary funds or other tangible, intangible and financial assets invested for the purposes of generating profit (income), social results (educational, cultural, scientific, health, social security and in other similar areas) or to ensure the implementation of state functions.

The Law on Investments provides for the following forms of investment:

- establishment of an enterprise or acquisition of shares (or other participation rights) in an operating enterprise registered in Lithuania;
- acquisition of securities of any type;
- creation, acquisition or increase of the value of fixed assets;
- lending of funds or other valuables to enterprises in which the investor owns a stake allowing control of such enterprise or considerable influence over it;
- conclusion of concession or leasing agreements.

Foreign entities may also establish branches or representative offices that do not have the status of legal persons. Notably, foreign entities performing economic activities in Lithuania are required in certain cases to register permanent establishment in Lithuania for tax purposes.

Investment protection and guarantees

The Law on Investments emphasizes protection of investments, rights and lawful interests of investors. State institutions or officers have no right to prohibit or restrict the possession, use and disposal of the investment by the investor. Investors can claim compensation of any damage suffered due to unlawful practices of the state or municipal institutions.

Expropriation of an investment may take place only for the public necessity and only in cases and under the procedures established in the laws, and provided the investor is adequately compensated pursuant to the rules established by the Government. Generally, the investor must be compensated at the market value of the assets deprived. The value of the expropriated assets and amount of compensation must be appraised by qualified appraisers according to the legal acts regulating appraisal activity. The compensation must be paid within three months after the day of expropriation in the currency requested by a foreign investor. The compensation must include interest from the moment of publication of the notice of expropriation until the payment of compensation (the interest rate is determined on the basis of the LIBOR rate of the relevant currency). Investors have the right, after having paid all taxes, to transfer abroad their profit (income) without restrictions.

Disputes concerning the rights and lawful interests of a foreign investor are settled according to the agreement between the parties, by the courts of Lithuania, international arbitration or by other institutions. In case of investment disputes, foreign investors also have the right to apply to the International Centre for Settlement of Investment Disputes since Lithuania is a member of the 18 March 1965 Washington Convention on the Settlement of Investment Disputes Between States and Nationals of Other States. The disputes are resolved under the provisions of applicable Lithuanian or foreign law and the relevant international treaties.

Investments related to real estate

Enterprises with foreign capital may own, lease or use real estate in Lithuania. There are no limitations on the ownership or usage of buildings, but some particular requirements may apply if those are buildings with cultural or historical value. Enterprises can lease state-owned land plots for a maximum period of 99 years. Privately owned land may be leased for a maximum period of 100 years.

Foreign citizens and entities engaged in registered commercial activity in Lithuania and complying with certain established criteria are allowed to purchase non-agricultural land plots. Based on the amendments to the Constitution adopted in January 2003, it will also be possible to acquire agricultural land, but subject to a number of restrictions.

Concessions

Currently concessions are regulated by the Law on Concessions of 7 July 1999. The law defines a concession as the right to use the existing or future state-owned or municipal property (such as the continental shelf, the economic zone in the Baltic Sea, the subterranean and natural resources, internal waters, roads, buildings, structures, installations) that can be granted under a concession contract for the performance of certain business activities. Concessions may be granted to enterprises established in Lithuania by domestic or foreign investors. A public tender must be held for the granting of a concession.

The Law on Concessions has, in actual fact, not yet been applied in practice due to its limited scope and other shortcomings. In practice, the state and the municipalities use other legal forms of transactions in order to ensure the provision of public services. In view of these problems, a draft of the new Law on Concessions was prepared and presented, in January 2003, to the *Seimas* for consideration and approval. The drafters of this new law took into account the Organization for Economic Cooperation and Development (OECD) recommendations, relevant principles of EU law and experiences of other European countries. The draft law introduces the concept of concession as a public–private partnership that can take many forms such as design, construction, development, refurbishment, modification, repair, management, operation and/or maintenance of infrastructure objects, provision of public services, and/or the use of state-owned or municipal property (including the exploitation of natural resources).

Incentives

Currently, there are no laws establishing special incentives for foreign investments, although certain tax incentives still continue to apply to some foreign investments that were made during 1993 and 1997. The Law on Investments provides for several forms of incentives, such as compensation of a portion of interest on the loans for investment projects, granting of state (municipal) guarantees, and granting of loans by the state among others. The application of such incentives is, however, subject to the discretion of respective state or municipal institutions.

Some specific incentives may be provided to strategic investors, ie those with whom the Government had executed investment agreements providing for special investment and business conditions. Such investment agreements may be concluded regarding investments that exceed 200 million litas (approximately 57.9 million euros) and comply with certain other criteria. Currently, such investment agreements may not provide for tax incentives. According to the practice of the Constitutional Court, stability clauses can be provided in the investment agreements only to the extent that they do not limit applicability to the foreign investors of any laws implementing the Constitution.

With respect to investments into municipal infrastructure, manufacturing and services, the municipality may enter into investment agreements that meet the criteria established by the Council of the Municipality. Special investment, business and land plot selection conditions may be established in accordance with the competence of the municipality.

Free economic zones

Lithuania is continuing to enhance its appeal to foreign investors through the development of a network of free economic zones (FEZs). Lithuanian and foreign enterprises, corporations and associations are eligible to participate in FEZs. These offer considerable benefits only for the companies registered and operating within their boundaries. These benefits include:

- profit tax incentives: each FEZ enterprise enjoys 80 per cent profit tax reduction for the first five years and 50 per cent reduction for the next five years. If a foreign investor has acquired at least 30 per cent of the shares of an FEZ enterprise and invested more than 1 million US dollars, such enterprise is exempt from profit tax during the first five years and enjoys a 50 per cent tax reduction for the subsequent 10 years;
- no taxes on dividends for foreign investors;
- exemption from customs duties and import taxes for the goods imported from a foreign country into free areas (ie, parts of FEZ territory separated from it and from customs territory of Lithuania which does not belong to FEZ) and exported from the free areas into foreign countries. Those duties and taxes also do not apply to the goods stored, destroyed in or used for functioning of such free areas;
- no value added tax (VAT) and excise tax on goods which are placed in FEZ enterprises operating in the free areas;
- the portion of the income of an FEZ enterprise that is reinvested (ie, used for the acquisition of tangible assets, scientific research and acquisition of new technologies) can be deducted from its taxable income;
- FEZ companies receive the same legal guarantees as those operating outside the FEZ.

It should be admitted that in the light of the EU *acquis communautaire* the above listed incentives (applicable to FEZ companies) are recognized as state aid, which is strictly regulated in EU legislation. Currently the monitoring of the state aid is performed by the Competition Council of Lithuania, but once Lithuania becomes a full member of the EU the monitoring of state aid will be vested in the European Commission.

Currently, one FEZ established in Klaipeda (ice-free port city) is already successfully operating. In 2001 the Competition Council approved the scheme of the state aid, 'Investments into Klaipeda's FEZ'. The Competition Council also established that the volume of state aid granted to Klaipeda's FEZ companies could not exceed 50 per cent and, in certain cases, 65 per cent of investments made into Klaipeda's FEZ (for more information see www.fez.lt).

2.2

Forms of Business Organizations

Lideika, Petrauskas, Valiūnas ir Partneriai

Introduction

Basic regulations regarding the types and procedures of incorporating business organizations and performing business activities in Lithuania are found in different laws and other regulatory acts. At present, the most important of these are:

- the Civil Code of 18 July 2000;
- the Law on Enterprises of 8 May 1990;
- the Law on Companies 13 July 2000;
- the Law on Securities Market of 16 January 1996;
- the Law on Profit Tax of 20 December 2001.

Under Lithuanian law, foreign persons (natural or legal) may establish the following forms of presence in Lithuania:

- a foreign entity may act in Lithuania through its established representative office or branch, or register a permanent establishment;
- a foreign person (natural or legal) may invest capital in Lithuania through incorporation of an enterprise or acquisition of interest in existing Lithuanian enterprises;
- foreign natural persons may also engage in individual business activity without incorporating a separate business unit.

Local presence of foreign companies

A foreign company may operate in Lithuania through its representative office or branch or may register a permanent establishment for tax purposes.

Representative office

A representative office of a foreign enterprise may be established for representational and promotional purposes only and may not engage in commercial activities. The representative office may perform various actions set forth in its statutory documents (eg represent and protect the interests of the foreign parent company (ie the incorporator of the representative office), enter into transactions on behalf of the parent company, perform certain import and export operations).

Lithuanian law could be strictly interpreted as permitting the representative office to enter into transactions on behalf of the foreign parent company only for the purpose of meeting the needs of the representative office. However, practically speaking, the foreign parent enterprise may also conclude transactions not related to the needs of the representative office through its representative in Lithuania (eg manager of the representative office) who may act under the power of attorney of such foreign enterprise. Export and import operations may be performed between the representative office and its foreign parent company or the entities that are related to such foreign parent company. Notably, if the foreign parent company's activities carried out through the representative office amount to permanent commercial activities in Lithuania (ie the foreign company may be deemed to have a permanent establishment in Lithuania), they may become subject to profit tax in Lithuania.

The representative office does not have the capacity of a legal person and is not required to keep a separate balance sheet. The foreign parent company is liable for the obligations of its representative office. The Civil Code established the requirement that at least one of the persons authorized to act on behalf of the representative office must reside in Lithuania.

Branch

A branch of a foreign enterprise is a structural subdivision of a foreign enterprise that has its seat in Lithuania. Different to the representative office, the branch of a foreign enterprise may engage in commercial activities, enter into transactions and assume obligations, however only within the scope of powers provided for in its statutory documents.

The branch does not have the capacity of a legal person. The foreign parent company is liable for the obligations of its branch and the branch is liable with all of its assets for the obligations of the foreign parent company. The activities of the branch are organized and carried out by the manager of the branch who has the right to represent the branch in relations with third parties only upon registration of the branch. At least one of the persons authorized to act on behalf of the branch must reside in Lithuania.

Permanent establishment

Permanent establishment is a notion introduced only by the tax laws. Permanent establishment is not a separate legal entity or subdivision of a foreign enterprise, rather it is just the form of a foreign company's activities in Lithuania which entails tax consequences. The concept of the permanent establishment was only incorporated into Lithuanian tax legislation a few years ago and certain provisions of applicable legal acts remain rather vague. The practice in this sphere has not become routine so far.

The foreign enterprise may be required to register a permanent establishment of its activities in Lithuania to comply with criteria of a permanent establishment. Under the Law on Profit Tax, a foreign enterprise is deemed to have a permanent establishment in Lithuania if it:

(i) permanently carries out commercial or industrial activity in order to receive income or other economic benefit;

(ii) carries out its permanent activity through a dependent representative (agent) in the territory of Lithuania; or

(iii) uses in the territory of Lithuania a construction area, an object of construction, fitting or equipment, or permanently uses equipment or construction for research or extraction of natural resources, including drilling wells or ships used for that purpose.

The criteria of existence of a permanent establishment in Lithuania as well as its taxation are discussed in more detail in Chapter 3.5.

Business entities

Based on the Law on Enterprises, the following types of enterprises may be formed in Lithuania:

- personal enterprise;
- general partnership;
- limited partnership;
- private stock company (*UAB*);
- public stock company (*AB*);
- investment company;[1]

[1] An investment company is a public stock company whose activities principally consist of investing into securities. A special law (the Law on Investment Companies of 5 July 1995) regulates the formation and activities of investment companies.

- state enterprise (owned solely by the state);
- municipal enterprise (owned solely by a municipality);
- agricultural company (*ŽŪB*);
- cooperative company.

A *personal enterprise* may be owned by a single individual or spouses. The owner's liability for the obligations of his/her personal enterprise is unlimited and generally applies to all of his/her personal property. The owner remains liable for the obligations of his/her personal enterprise even after its liquidation.

General partnerships are enterprises with unlimited liability established on the basis of a partnership or joint venture agreement between several individuals and/or legal persons. The general partnership is created through the transfer of property from individual ownership to co-ownership within the partnership, with the purpose of conducting business activities under a common name of the firm. All partners of the general partnership are jointly and severally (solidary) liable for the obligations of the general partnership, including their personal property. The partners remain liable even after the liquidation of the general partnership. The general partnership, however, is not liable for the obligations of its partners if such obligations arise in their activity unrelated to the activities of the general partnership.

A *limited partnership* consists of general and limited partners. The difference between limited and general partnerships lies mainly in the degree of liability of the respective partners. General partners of the limited partnership have unlimited joint and several liability, identical to the unlimited liability of the partners of the general partnership as explained above. In contrast, limited partners are liable only to the extent of their contributions to the partnership under the agreement. The limited partnership must have at least one general and one limited partner.

In general, agricultural and cooperative companies are rarely used by foreign investors for launch of business in Lithuania.

Incorporation of a private or public stock company in Lithuania or acquisition of shares in existing stock companies is the most convenient and common way to invest foreign capital in Lithuania. For this reason key issues related to private and public stock companies are more thoroughly described below.

Private and public stock companies

General

A stock company is an enterprise whose authorized capital is divided into shares. It is a legal person of limited liability and has commercial, financial and organizational independence. The company is liable for its obligations only to the extent of its assets. In general, the shareholders are liable for the company's obligations only indirectly by the amounts paid for the shares subscribed. However, the Civil Code introduced a provision that, in the case of a legal person (including a stock company) being unable to perform its obligations due to unfair actions of its participant (a shareholder in a stock company), the latter may incur subsidiary liability for the obligations of the legal person with its personal property.

The minimum authorized (share) capital for a private stock company is 10,000 litas (approximately 2,896 euros). The minimum number of shareholders in a private stock company is one and the maximum number is 100.

In a public stock company, the minimum authorized (share) capital is 150,000 litas (approximately 43,443 euros). The minimum number of shareholders in a public stock company is one and there are no limitations on the maximum number of shareholders.

The chief executive officer (under the law – the 'head of administration', in practice usually titled the 'general director', 'managing director' or 'general manager') must be employed under an employment contract in both private and public stock companies. Bookkeeping may be carried out by a chief financial officer (usually titled the 'chief financier' or 'chief accountant') who is an employee of the company or by a bookkeeping company under a service agreement. The same person may not hold offices of both the chief executive officer and the chief financial officer. Management structure of stock companies is analysed in more detail in Chapter 2.4.

Shareholders

Shareholders of stock companies may be Lithuanian or foreign natural and legal persons. Each shareholder has such rights in the company that are inherent to the shares owned. The Law on Companies provides for the general 'one share – one vote' principle. It further establishes that the number of votes given by a share must be proportional to its nominal value. Shareholders' rights are divided into:

- property rights (eg to receive dividends if the company generates profit, to receive a portion of the assets of the company in liquidation, to receive shares without additional payment if the authorized capital is increased from the funds of the company);
- non-property rights (eg to attend meetings of shareholders, to receive information on business activities of the company, to challenge in court resolutions of the general meeting or resolutions and actions of the company's other bodies).

The statutory rights of shareholders may not be restricted in any way, except in cases specified by laws or by court order.

Shares

Shares are securities certifying the participation in the stock company's capital and entitling them to certain property and non-property rights. Shares issued by stock companies are divided according to:

- the manner of disposal – registered and bearer shares;
- the rights attached – ordinary and preference shares.

Both private and public stock companies may issue *registered shares*. *Bearer shares* may be issued by public stock companies only. It should be mentioned that Lithuanian stock companies usually choose to issue registered shares. Shares may be material (only in private stock companies) or non-material.

Ordinary shares constitute the main part of the company's shares and may be issued by both private and public stock companies. All ordinary shares must be of equal nominal value.

The total nominal value of *preference shares* may not exceed a third of the authorized capital of the company (either private or public stock company). The fixed amount of the dividend on preference shares as a percentage of the nominal value of the share must be established in the company's articles of association. The established dividend on preference shares may be cumulative or non-cumulative. In case of preference shares with cumulative dividend, if the company's profit is not sufficient for full payment of the dividend on cumulative preference shares, the unpaid sum must be carried over to the next financial year (the unpaid dividend on non-cumulative preference shares may not be carried over to the next financial year). The articles of association may establish that the owners of preference shares have no voting rights.

The Law on Companies also provides for a possibility to issue employees' shares both in private and public stock companies. The employees' shares are registered shares sold on preferential terms or otherwise transferred to the employees of the company.

Public stock companies may also issue bonds convertible into shares. Private stock companies are forbidden to issue bonds. Public trading in shares of private stock companies is not allowed, ie such shares may only be traded privately. In private stock companies the consent of the chief executive officer is required for the transfer of shares to a non-shareholder. Such consent may be refused only if the intended transfer would increase the number of shareholders in excess of the maximum number permitted, ie 100. In addition, the Law on Companies establishes the right of first refusal (under the terms offered by the seller to a third party) for the other shareholders of the private stock company in case the shares are offered to a third person who is not a shareholder of the company.

Public stock companies are prohibited from introducing any restrictions on the shareholders' right to transfer fully paid shares to other persons. Their shares may be traded publicly.

Securities regulations

The Law on Securities Market requires public stock companies to register their shares with the Securities Commission of the Republic of Lithuania prior to their circulation. In addition, certain disclosure requirements are applicable to public stock companies (eg public notification of 'material events', filing of annual audited prospectus reports). Securities issued by public stock companies may be traded either privately (off-exchange) or through the stock exchange. The stock exchange is the only venue for the execution of the secondary purchase-sale of securities included in the official or current trading lists of the stock exchange registered in Lithuania (currently, there is only one stock exchange – the National Stock Exchange).

Insider trading in securities of public stock companies is prohibited. The following additional requirements established in the Law on Securities Market have to be observed when investing into public stock companies:

- if a person, acting independently or in concert with other persons, acquires more than 40 per cent of votes in the general meeting of shareholders of the public stock company, he/she must make within 30 days a mandatory tender offer to buy the remaining securities of the company with voting rights as well as securities granting the right to acquire securities with voting rights. The offered price may not be less than the highest price paid by such person for the securities purchased during the last 12 months. Otherwise, such person must dispose of the securities exceeding the aforementioned limit. Until submission of the mandatory tender offer or disposal of the shares exceeding the aforementioned limit, such person loses all voting rights granted by such shares;

- anyone who, acting independently or in concert with other persons, acquires a block of shares that results in the shareholding to cross, in either direction, the thresholds of one-tenth, one-fifth, one-third, one-half, two-thirds or three-quarters of total votes must within seven days notify the Securities Commission and the company.

Non-profit organizations

Lithuanian laws provide for the possibility of establishing various non-profit organizations. In general (though there are certain exceptions), non-profit organizations are forbidden to engage in commercial activities. In any case, the profit gained by non-profit organizations may not be distributed to its members (participants).

Enterprise groupings

The following types of enterprise groupings are provided in the Lithuanian legislation:

- concerns;
- consortia;
- associations.

A *concern* is an economic structure that unites independent companies related by common interests, agreements on patents and licences, joint scientific research and production technology programmes or other close cooperation. The concern is established through an acquisition of shares in other companies which results in the creation of a pyramid of companies with one company at the top.

A *consortium,* established as a partnership or by a joint-venture agreement, is a temporary and voluntary grouping of enterprises formed for the implementation of large projects or to resolve specific issues. For example, consortia are often used in large privatizations.

An *association* of enterprises is a voluntary group of enterprises with the status of a legal person. The association normally represents the economic interests of its members and coordinates and executes the matters brought to its attention by the membership.

2.3

Practical Procedures for Establishing a Presence

Lideika, Petrauskas, Valiūnas ir Partneriai

Introduction

Having decided to establish a presence in Lithuania, foreign investors usually choose to register one of the following:

- private (or public) stock company;
- representative office;
- permanent establishment.

Since foreign investors mostly form private stock companies rather than public stock companies, which are subject to more complex formation procedures as well as higher capitalization and reporting requirements, the procedures for the formation of the private stock companies are discussed below.

Incorporation of private stock company

There are six major stages in the private stock company's founding process:

- registration of the firm name;
- execution of incorporation documents;
- opening of an accumulating account and payment of initial share capital;
- convening of a founding meeting of the company;
- filing with local municipal authorities for permission to operate;
- filing with the Enterprise Register for the registration of the company.

Though this may seem a multiplex procedure, if handled by professionals, the formation of a private stock company is a rather swift process and may take approximately two weeks.

Registration of firm name

The firm name of a new company must be registered with the Lithuanian State Patent Bureau prior to registration of the company itself. Temporary protection of a registered firm name is given for a period of 12 months from the registration with the State Patent Bureau. The registered name of a registered company is given protection during the active life of the company. The name of a private stock company must contain the words *uždaroji akcinė bendrovė* ('private stock company') or abbreviation *'UAB'*. If the word 'Lithuania' is desired to be used in the company's firm name, it is necessary to obtain permission from the Minister of Justice for which certain criteria must be met.

Incorporation documents

After the firm name is registered, the act of incorporation (or the incorporation agreement in case there are several incorporators) should be signed. The act of incorporation (or the incorporation agreement) prescribes the name of the company, its representation during formation, the authorized capital and shares subscribed by the incorporator (or incorporators) etc.

In certain cases when formation of the company may amount to a market concentration for which permission of the Competition Council is required, such permission should be obtained before subscribing for the shares of the company (for details see Chapter 2.6). Incorporation documents should be signed by individual incorporator(s) and/or individuals having authority to sign on behalf of the incorporating enterprise(s). A company must be registered with the Enterprise Register within four months following the signing of the act of incorporation, otherwise a company will be deemed not incorporated.

Initial share capital

After executing the act of incorporation (or the incorporation agreement), an accumulating account has to be opened in one of the Lithuanian banks. The accumulating account is opened solely for the purpose of collecting initial monetary funds to the share capital of the company, and funds in this account may not be used prior to the registration of the company. After the company is registered, the account is transformed into an ordinary settlement account and funds in the account may be used.

The minimum share capital of the private stock company is 10,000 litas (approximately 2,896 euros). If the minimum share capital is formed, the total amount 10,000 litas will have to be paid in cash. When establishing a company with the share capital above 10,000 litas, if the entire capital is not paid before registration, at least 25 per cent of the issue price of all the company's shares (but not less than the minimum share capital amount, ie 10,000 litas) must be paid in cash before registration. If a company has several incorporators, each of them has to pay at least 25 per cent of the issue price of the subscribed shares. The remaining 75 per cent of the share capital may be paid within 12 months from the signing of the share subscription agreement (which is a part of the act of incorporation or the incorporation agreement). Should a part of the remaining share capital be paid in non-pecuniary (property) contributions, such non-pecuniary contributions have to be appraised by certified experts and their value must be indicated in the act of incorporation. Only assets that may be an object of civil exchange and assessed from an economical point of view (including proprietorship rights) may be non-pecuniary contributions. Works and services are not permitted as non-pecuniary contributions to the company's share capital.

In order to simplify the formation procedure, it is advisable to pay the minimum share capital amount (ie 10,000 litas) in cash at the time of incorporation of the company. The share capital may be increased through additional non-pecuniary or cash contributions at a later date.

Founding meeting

After payment of initial contributions to the share capital and prior to registration of the company, incorporators must convene the founding meeting of incorporators. In cases when the company is formed by a sole incorporator, written decisions of the sole incorporator are equal to resolutions of the founding meeting. The founding meeting approves the articles of association of the company, elects the inspector or audit company and members of management or the board and/or supervisory board (if formed) of the company.

The articles of association of the company may provide that the general meeting of shareholders elects an inspector (internal auditor) of the company to control its financial activities. The auditor or audit company (external auditor) must be elected if the company meets certain criteria established in the Law on Companies.

Permission to operate from municipality

Prior to registration of the company, permission must be obtained from local municipal authorities for the stated activities of the company. The application for permission may be rejected if incorporation documents are inconsistent with the law or if the establishment of the company would result in serious harm to the population or the environment, or in other cases provided for by the law.

Registration with Enterprise Register

Though the Civil Code vests registration of the companies with the Register of Legal Persons, it has not yet been established (it is now expected to start operating by 2004). Therefore, companies continue to be registered with the Enterprise Register administered by several institutions under the Law on Enterprise Register of the Republic of Lithuania of 31 July 1990.

All companies with invested foreign capital are registered with the State Enterprise of Cadastre and Register of Land and Other Real Estate which is currently the chief administrator of the Enterprise Register. In order to register a company, the following documents should be filed:

- application for registration;
- in cases where the incorporator is an enterprise, a copy of the incorporator's registration certificate (extract from trade register) or similar document evidencing incorporator's legal registration;
- in cases where the incorporator is an enterprise, a document specifying the decision of the incorporator (its managing body) to establish the company;
- certificate from the bank in which the accumulative account is opened proving that the initial contributions to the company's share capital are paid;
- firm name registration certificate;
- permission of local municipality to undertake commercial activities;
- permission of the owner of the premises for registration of the company's registered office and operation in these premises accompanied with a copy of the ownership documents;
- proof of payment of the stamp duty for registration;
- act of incorporation;
- articles of association of the company;
- minutes of the founding meeting.

The company will be registered when:

(i) initial contributions to the share capital have been paid;

(ii) the founding meeting has been held and management bodies of the company have been elected;

(iii) incorporation documents have been presented to the Enterprise Register.

All of the above must comply with the requirements of the applicable laws. A decision on registration must be issued within 15 days from the date of filing.

Post-registration steps

After the registration with the Enterprise Register the company should start its activities only after at least some of the following steps (as applicable) are completed:

- transfer of the incorporation documents to the company;
- producing of the corporate seal;
- registration with the Tax Inspectorate;
- registration with the State Social Insurance authorities;
- opening of the settlement account of the company;
- registration as a value added tax payer (if applicable);
- acquisition of special accountancy documents from the State Tax Inspection;
- obtaining of other permissions or licences (if applicable).

Registration of a representative office

Representative offices of foreign enterprises are registered with the Enterprise Register through the State Enterprise of Cadastre and Register of Land and Other Real Estate. After submission of an application and accompanying documents, the State Enterprise of Cadastre and Register of Land and Other Real Estate decides on registration within 15 days. The following documents must be presented:

- application for the registration of a representative office;
- copy of the incorporator's registration certificate (extract from trade register) or similar document evidencing incorporator's legal registration;
- document specifying the decision of the managing body of the foreign enterprise (incorporator) to establish the representative office and to appoint the head of the representative office;

- permission of the owner of the premises for registration of the registered office in these premises accompanied with a copy of the ownership documents;
- proof of payment of the stamp duty for registration;
- firm name registration certificate.

Registration of a permanent establishment

Permanent establishment is not a corporate formation and is registered only as a tax payer with the local State Tax Inspectorate. The following documents should usually be submitted:

- copy of the incorporator's registration certificate (extract from trade register) or similar document evidencing incorporator's legal registration;
- document certifying the powers of a representative (eg power of attorney);
- agreement concluded with Lithuanian business entity on which the activities in Lithuania are based.

All documents in a foreign language must be translated into the Lithuanian language by an authorized translator before submission to the official authorities. Among others, the incorporator's registration certificate or equivalent document should be certified by a notary public and (except where there is a respective bilateral agreement with the incorporator's country) attached with an *apostille* under the 1961 Hague Convention or be legalized under the prescribed procedure.

2.4

Corporate Governance

Lideika, Petrauskas, Valiūnas ir Partneriai

Introduction

Corporate governance is not yet a widespread concept associated with economic reforms or improvement of corporate performance in Lithuania. Today it is more often a topic of MBA courses and seminars attended by the top businessmen of the country. But it is rapidly gaining attention in the biggest and most progressive companies, which generates more widespread interest in this area. Good corporate governance practices are often applied in the Western-owned Lithuanian companies. So far, no voluntary corporate governance code has been proposed or accepted by the corporate community.

For the purposes of this chapter corporate governance will be understood as the relationships among a company's bodies, shareholders and other stakeholders. This chapter will briefly address, from the Lithuanian perspective, the external factors affecting corporate governance and will focus on the internal corporate governance elements.

External factors affecting corporate governance

Companies held by foreign investors constitute about 16 per cent of all the registered companies in Lithuania, but their share in the total capital of companies is far larger. The volume of trade in the Lithuanian capital market where foreign capital is used is growing about seven times faster than that of the local capital. The state and the municipalities still hold approximately a half of companies' capital. However, this number is rapidly decreasing due to the continuing privatization process. At the same time, the role of local investors is increasing.

Ownership concentration is a significant feature of the Lithuanian shareholding structures. In more than a half of companies the controlling stake is held by between three and five shareholders. Institutional investors are not very active and the capital market is not the most commonly used way for raising funds. More often, such alternatives as bank loans or large individual investments are used. Therefore financial investors cannot be expected to play an active role of corporate governance watchdogs. In many Lithuanian companies there is no separation of ownership and control. Often the board and the management are controlled by majority shareholders.

Although in the past occasions of corporate governance misbehaviour, such as sale of assets or products below market value to affiliated companies who would in turn resell these at market price, were more common, lately Lithuania's legislation has been changed. Minority shareholders as well as other stakeholders have become increasingly active in defending their statutory rights in courts. As is often the case, enhanced legal protection of minorities has led to certain abuses of their rights. This sometimes happens in formerly state-owned companies where the majority stakes were privatized to large investors, while a minority of shares (often 5–10 per cent) had earlier been sold to the numerous employees and the public.

In Lithuania there is still a lack of professional (especially independent) board members and executives. This limits the likelihood of efficient management turnover. Often the management implements either the policy of the majority shareholders or is composed of the shareholders themselves. In other cases, particularly in state-owned companies or privatized companies with dispersed ownership, the management has its own strong position, personal goals and is sometimes able to manipulate the shareholders. Finally, the tradition of strong and central leadership is still followed in many companies.

Concentrated ownership structures and the insignificant role of the securities market as a means of raising funds, combined with the position of the management where risk of being easily replaced is low, lead to a very limited market for corporate control. Also, due to certain other external factors (eg heavy investments into growth, maximum prices of public services or minimum employee number undertakings of the owners of privatized companies), management performance is not the single reason for poor performance of the companies.

Internal corporate governance elements

Shareholders

The procedural aspects of company law in Lithuania ensure reasonable protection for shareholders. The company's articles of association define the method of notification (by mail, a notice in the media etc) about the shareholders' meetings. In listed companies, a notice is also given to the Securities Commission and the Stock Exchange (which publishes it on its on-line database). On-line notification on the company's website is not mandatory. The notices are given 30 days in advance and include the date, time, place and agenda items. Draft resolutions must be made available to shareholders on request. Holders of 10 per cent or more of the shares have a right to initiate a meeting, submit proposals for new agenda items, resolutions or candidates to the board. Lithuanian law does not provide for either squeeze-out or sell-out of the minority[1] so the percentage giving the right of initiative is not related to that.[2] The articles of association may provide for shareholders' right to vote in writing. Voting by proxy is permitted in all companies.

In Lithuania, shareholders decide on all matters related to issuance of new shares. There is no difference between the authorized and issued capital, as shareholders decide on issuance of new shares (and they cannot delegate this right to any other body) by the same resolution that authorizes such issuance. The longest payment period for the issued shares is 12 months; at least 25 per cent of the price has to be paid in the first six months. The majority required to outvote the statutory pre-emptive rights of all shareholders is 75 per cent of votes represented at the meeting (quorum is 50 per cent). As a result, the holder of 25 per cent or more of all the shares cannot be diluted against its own will.

Minority shareholders of public stock companies are offered protection through a tender offer which is mandatory at the level of acquisition of 40 per cent of all shares. This protection is not available in private stock companies but there each shareholder has the pre-emption right to purchase, for the same price, the shares offered for sale to non-shareholders. Also, shareholders holding 10 per cent or more of the shares have special investigation rights (through a court-appointed expert in private stock companies and through a shareholder-appointed auditor in all companies). Lithuanian company law provides for many other shareholder rights (such as the right to appeal the resolutions of the company's bodies in court) and establishes certain levels of holding required for their exercise.

Disclosure

The level of disclosure is different for private and public stock companies. The standard of disclosure applicable to listed companies is rather high. The company must make periodic disclosure and make *ad hoc* disclosure of material events in a timely and accurate manner. Changes in ownership structures, financial and operating results, company's

[1] Except in private companies where holder of a third of the shares can request a court order on the squeeze-out of another fraudulent shareholder.

[2] Such relation was proposed by the High Level Group of Company Law Experts in their recent report to the European Commission, which can be found at http://www.europa.eu.int/comm/internal_market/en/company/company/modern/consult/report_en.pdf.

objectives, members of the board, material foreseeable risk factors etc have to be disclosed.

Shareholders' meetings approve the audited annual financial statements and the report of the board (or management, when the board is not formed). However, there is neither mandatory nor voluntary requirement for the annual report to include a statement containing key elements of the company's corporate governance rules and practices.[3] Some elements of such a statement can be found in the board's annual report. However, information on board composition, its members' independence and qualification and the positions they hold in other companies is not mandatory.

Relations (eg contracts) between the company and its major shareholders are only disclosed if it amounts to a material event; however it is not usually easy to verify whether these relations are at arm's length. The conflict of interest between the majority shareholders on the one hand and the company and its minority shareholders on the other hand is not resolved. Unless a minority shareholder has a number of votes sufficient to elect at least one supervisory board or board member (see below) and those bodies approve the relevant transactions, it is not necessarily likely that the minority shareholder would even become aware of such transactions taking place. The impact of such transactions on the company's results may generally come to shareholders' knowledge when the financial statements reflect those transactions.

Boards and management

Board system and independence

Lithuanian company law provides companies with a choice between a one-tier or two-tier board system. When the latter is chosen, shareholders' meetings elect the supervisory board, which in turn elects the board. In the one-tier model only one of the two is elected. Private stock companies may choose not to form any of the two boards and operate through management elected by the shareholders. Usually the boards are not big and they do not form committees.

According to the cumulative system of election of the supervisory board (or the board) at the shareholders' meeting, majority and minority shareholders can elect a number of members proportionate to their shareholding. This ensures the representation of minority shareholders. If supervisory board members were only considered independent when they did not have any other relation with the majority shareholders or the company from which they derive value,[4] in Lithuanian companies

[3] Such a statement on corporate governance was strongly recommended by the High Level Group of Company Law Experts (see footnote 2).

[4] So suggests the High Level Group of Company Law Experts (see footnote 2).

it would be almost impossible to achieve a majority of independent non-executive directors. Where ownership concentration is high, a small group of shareholders elects the majority of directors that are loyal to them.

Nevertheless, certain rules of independence do exist. The candidates to the supervisory board and the board must disclose information on:

- what positions they hold in other companies;
- how their activity is related to that of the company, its controlling or controlled companies;
- holdings of 25 per cent or more of the shares in competing companies or the companies that continue manufacture, market or distribute the company's products.

The law prohibits board members and the chief executive officer (CEO) from acting as supervisory board members. However, former employees, advisors, representatives of controlling shareholders and family members are not prevented from serving on the supervisory board. In addition, board members have an obligation to be honest and reasonable, be loyal and respect commercial secrets of the company. Board members must avoid a conflict of personal and company interests or confuse assets of the company with personal assets. They are prohibited from using the company's assets or information for personal benefit or for the benefit of others. Board members must report any such circumstances together with their transactions with the company. In cases of a breach of any of the above obligations, board members must compensate the damages incurred by the company.

Remuneration

The remuneration of both supervisory board and board members in Lithuania is directly related to the results of the company. Payments from the net profit are the only form of board members' compensation for their membership and those payments have to be approved by the shareholders' meeting.

The only good feature of such a system is that compensation is known to the shareholders. Good corporate governance requires that non-executive members' compensation not be related to the results of the company because this may encourage a manipulation of financial results. Unfortunately, this was not the thinking of Lithuanian legislators who simply thought that board members would work harder to achieve profit if their compensation was related to it. The legislator seems to have overlooked that companies also need competent board members at times when they voluntarily elect to be unprofitable in the short-term in order to invest in growth and gain more profits later. As fixed compensation for the board membership is not allowed there is no motivation for competent people to become non-executive board members.

What happens in practice is that board members are employed in the company in some executive position or become consultants of the company to be able to receive a compensation for their efforts both as such employees or consultants and as board members. Naturally, such payments are not disclosed to shareholders (formally it is a remuneration only for work or consulting) and is not approved at the shareholders' meeting (or the supervisory board). Obviously in those cases board members are not independent. In this way companies put less value on good corporate governance than on hiring competent people.

The above-described system of board members' compensation is one reason (but not the only one) that leads to the concentration of power in the hands of the CEO – the major part of whose remuneration does not depend on the company's results. Fortunately the general principles of the new Civil Code of 18 July 2000 opened the doors for other systems of remuneration to be detailed in company law. The planned legislative amendments are likely to change the system of board members' compensation in the near future.

Responsibilities and liability

In practice, the supervisory board only oversees the activities of the company's board and management once a year by reviewing the annual financial statements. It is supposed to be the shareholders' watchdog, but for many reasons, it does not serve this purpose. One of these reasons is that most supervisory board members are elected with majority shareholders' votes. Then with a simple majority of the votes in the supervisory board all board members are elected from those loyal to majority shareholders. Thus, in most cases shareholders elect to bring shareholder actions directly rather than expect the supervisory board to act.

The board, on the other hand, plays an active role. Broadly speaking the board acts as a trustee of the shareholders, as a supervisor and controller and as a body that directs the company's activities. In implementing this role the board appoints the CEO and other top managers, oversees management's activity, organizes shareholders' meetings, approves the annual financial statements and the board's report and considers and approves major transactions. In many companies the statutory competence of the board is expanded. In recent times the role of the board as a mere collegial body has been modified. It should be noted that since the adoption of the new Civil Code the articles of association may give board members more say in the executive management, including the right to represent the company.

It is often emphasized that in order to ensure good corporate governance, board members need to sign the financial statements and be collectively responsible for their contents. In Lithuania the CEO and chief financial officer (CFO) sign the financial statements even though the board approves them. Furthermore, the board is not required to approve the quarterly results and *ad hoc* disclosure of material events in listed companies, or even to control the company department that has such a responsibility. Therefore, there is no collective responsibility of the board for financial and other results of the company as such.

Board members can, however, be found collectively liable if it is proven that their decisions were adopted in violation of the laws and were harmful to the company or its shareholders. So far there is not much judicial practice in this area – nevertheless, it should be noted that board members can even be subject to criminal liability if their actions *vis-à-vis* the company, its shareholders or others have seriously violated the law.

Audit

After the world-wide audit crisis no substantial changes in audit regulation have occurred in Lithuania. External audit of annual financial statements and the board report is mandatory in all public stock companies as well as medium-sized and large private stock companies that meet the established criteria. Internal audit function is not mandatory.

There are no general requirements that the auditors should not provide non-audit services, or that the audit firms should rotate from time to time. In addition, no rules on who should select the auditor are established, but both the board and the shareholders in their meeting have to approve the selected auditor and its maximum remuneration.

Managing bodies are prohibited from interfering with the auditor's work. The external audit is not required to be supervised by any non-executive committee or body that would monitor non-audit services, meet with the auditor without the presence of executive managers or ensure the auditor's access to information.

Conclusions

The Lithuanian corporate community has reached the point where good corporate governance is understood not only as a progressive way of thinking but also as a means to improve companies' performances. As businesses grow, increasing numbers of investors and managers understand the benefits of sound management and effective control. The latest legislative enactments and the proposed changes that are in the pipeline have opened the door for progressive reforms. As certain current practices leave a lot of room for improvement, those movements are very welcome.

2.5

Agency, Distributorship and Franchising

Lideika, Petrauskas, Valiūnas ir Partneriai

Introduction

For foreign producers and suppliers, agency, distribution and franchising agreements have been quite an efficient alternative to establishing a business in Lithuania. Entering into a contractual relationship with a Lithuanian agent, distributor or franchisee permits avoidance of the costs of establishing and maintaining a business in Lithuania and performing import procedures etc. The benefits of this are such that during recent years a number of Lithuanian wholesale and logistics companies have developed strong distribution networks, particularly in the field of consumer and household products.

Commercial relationships among producers or suppliers of goods and those acting as intermediaries or distributors are now regulated by the new Civil Code of 18 July 2000 (in force from 1 July 2001). Drafters of the Civil Code aimed to embrace the advanced practices regarding the regulation of commercial relationships[1] and to tailor the Civil Code in accordance with European Union (EU) law. This chapter will cover only the basic regulation principles of agency, distribution and franchising relationships in Lithuania. At this point attention should be called to the fact that most of the provisions discussed in this chapter are not mandatory and are applied only if the parties do not agree otherwise. Furthermore, as a number of substantial issues pertaining to agency, distribution and franchising are subject to the provisions of competition law, this chapter will touch upon some practical competition-related matters as well.

[1] For instance, provisions of the 17 February 1983 Geneva (UNIDROIT) Convention on Agency in the International Sale of Goods.

Agency

Concept

The concept of agency under the Civil Code as well as its provisions regulating rights and obligations of principal and agent are to a great extent analogous to the concept and provisions of EC Council Directive 86/653/EEC. The commercial agent is perceived as an independent (self-employed) person (either legal or natural) engaged in continuing business activity to negotiate the transactions on behalf of the principal or to conclude the transactions in his/her (ie the agent's) name or in the name of the principal. In either case this is conducted at the expense and in the interest of the principal.

Form of the agency contract

The terms of an agency contract may be agreed by the parties either in written or in oral form. However, it is advisable to enter into a written contract as a number of conditions have to be agreed in written form in order to be legally binding and enforceable. Examples of these are:

- terms of limitation of liability of the agent and/or principal;
- non-compete obligation;
- grounds of termination of agency contract;
- exclusive rights of the agent;
- dependence of the agent's remuneration on the execution of a transaction by the third party.

Rights and obligations of the parties

Rights and obligations of the parties to the agency contract under Lithuanian law are similar to those specifically provided in Chapter 2 of the Directive. The agent is *inter alia* obliged to:

- act in good faith and dutifully in performing the principal's instructions;
- be loyal and look after the principal's interests;
- communicate information about the concluded transactions as well as other information relevant to the principal's business;
- protect commercial secrets of the principal.

In case of the principal's failure to settle the accounts with the agent, the agent is entitled to exercise a lien on the merchandise of the principal.

The agent is also entitled to demand the audit of the principal if a dispute regarding correctness of calculation of the commission arises. Notably, the non-compete undertaking will be binding on the agent only if such an obligation was stated in the written contract.

Commercial agents are required by law to insure their civil liability. As such, it is advisable to ask the commercial agent to provide a valid insurance policy before, or immediately after, entering into an agency contract. The Civil Code does not provide for a specific amount of insurance, therefore, it is for the principal to assess whether the agent is sufficiently insured depending on the commercial risks involved (eg authorization to negotiate and enter into agreements on behalf of the principal entails a greater commercial risk for the principal than mere authorization to negotiate the agreements).

The principal is *inter alia* obliged to:

- provide the agent with necessary documentation and information pertaining to the marketed goods;
- notify the agent about the acceptance or refusal to execute the transaction procured by the agent;
- provide other information necessary for the performance of agency contract.

Remuneration

The agent is entitled to commission on the concluded transactions as well as transactions concluded by the principal as a result of agent's actions (even if execution of the agreement takes place after the termination of agency contract). For the sake of clarity, it is advisable to agree in the agency contract a reasonable period, commencing after termination of the agency contract, in the course of which the agent stays entitled to the commission.

The agent's remuneration may be subject to the due execution of the transaction by the third party. The agent is also entitled to additional remuneration (*del credere*) if he/she guarantees such due performance of the transaction by the third party. The exact amount of *del credere* is not established by the Civil Code and must be agreed by the parties. The agent's commission does not include the reimbursement of the expenses incurred in relation to the performance of the assignment (eg costs of transportation, packaging or custom duties); such expenses must be reimbursed by the principal separately.

The parties may agree on the moment and procedure of payment of the commission. In any case, however, the commission becomes due upon execution by the third party of its part of the transaction and must be paid at the end of the third month thereafter at the latest. In cases where the payment of the commission is subject to the execution of the transaction by the third party, the agent is entitled to claim an advance payment which may not be less than 40 per cent of the commission.

Termination of agency and compensation

An agency contract concluded for an indefinite period may be terminated by notice of either party. The term of the notice varies from one to four months depending on the length of the agency contract. An agency contract for a fixed period may be terminated prior to expiry of the period only for good cause.

The issue of indemnity and compensation for the damage is somewhat specific under the Civil Code. Article 17 of the Directive (paragraphs 2 and 3) provides two models for compensation of the loss of the agent's benefit upon termination of the contract – indemnity and compensation for damage. The practice of implementation of the Directive in the EU Member States[2] proved that those two models are perceived as alternatives rather than cumulative instruments.[3] In contrast, the Civil Code provides both models of compensation without specifying if they should be considered as alternatives.

According to the Civil Code, the agent is entitled to indemnity if:

(i) the contract has been terminated in the absence of the agent's default;

(ii) the principal continues to derive significant benefit from the business with the customers brought by the agent after termination of the contract;

(iii) the payment of indemnity in a particular situation was equitable.

The maximum amount of the agent's indemnity is equivalent to the average annual remuneration calculated for the period of agency contract. However, if the agency contract goes back more than five years, compensation is equal to the average annual remuneration calculated for the period of the last five years of the agency contract.

According to the Civil Code, the agent is also entitled to compensation for the damage suffered as a result of termination of the contract, particularly if:

(i) such termination deprives the agent of the commission that he would have received in cases of proper performance of the contract

---

[2] Report on Application of Article 17 of the Council Directive on the Coordination of the Laws of the Member States relating to Self-Employed Commercial Agents (86/653/EEC), COM(96)364.

[3] Only relevant enactments of the United Kingdom allow the parties to opt one of the two models of compensation. However, in the absence of the parties' agreement the preference to the model provided in paragraph 3 of Article 17 of the Directive is granted.

while the principal still receives substantial benefits linked to the agent's activities, and/or

(ii) the expenses incurred by the agent in performing the principal's instructions were not amortized on the moment of such termination.

The literal interpretation of those provisions suggests that compensation for damage may be sought in addition to the indemnity. Due to the novelty of the Civil Code, there is no court practice that would deny or support such a conclusion. However, commentators of the Civil Code suggest interpreting the above provisions of the Civil Code in line with the Directive: those two models of compensation should be treated as alternatives and the parties should have discretion to elect one of them. If the agency contract does not specify a particular model of compensation, the agent should have an option to choose one of the alternatives. It remains to see if this interpretation will be followed by the courts.

Distributorship

Concept

A distribution agreement provides for the obligation of one party (the distributor) to acquire, in his/her name and at his/her expense, goods or services provided by the other party (the supplier) and to resell such goods to the customers or other dealers as well as to perform other related activities. Under the distribution agreement the supplier undertakes to sell goods or services to the distributor and to perform other activities related to distribution of goods (services).

Form of the distribution agreement

The distribution agreement must be concluded in written form. Failure to comply with this requirement renders the distribution agreement void.

Types of distribution

The Civil Code makes the following disctinction:

- exclusive distribution – the supplier appoints only one distributor for a specific territory or a specifically allocated group of customers;
- selective distribution – the supplier appoints distributors selected on the basis of specified criteria.

Rights and obligations of the parties

Unless otherwise stated in the agreement, the distributor is under obligation *inter alia* to ensure:

- the effective distribution of goods;
- effective advertising;
- sufficient qualification of the personnel;
- proper warehousing of goods;

and to:

- sell goods under the trade mark of the supplier;
- buy and resell the agreed quantities of goods within the agreed period of time;
- provide warranty repair;
- provide the supplier with information on the market situation;
- protect the commercial secrets of the supplier.

Respectively, the supplier must:

- ensure the quality of the goods;
- train the distributor's employees;
- provide the distributor with advertising material.

The supplier is entitled to control the distributor's warehouses and supervise the distributor's compliance with the terms of distribution agreement.

Product liability

The manufacturer of the goods is liable to compensate consumers for damage caused by deficient goods. However, in instances when deficient goods were imported for the purpose of distribution, the distributor is liable to the same extent as manufacturer.

Termination of distributorship and compensation

A distribution agreement concluded for an indefinite period may be terminated by notice of either party served at least three months prior to the termination. If a distribution agreement for a fixed period is terminated prior to its expiry due to the fault of either party, the defaulting party is liable to compensate damages caused to other party.

Franchising

Concept

A franchise agreement establishes the undertaking of one party (the franchisor) to provide another party (the franchisee) with remuneration and, for a fixed or indefinite period, a package of exclusive rights (eg trade names and trade marks, know-how) to be used for commercial purposes. The franchisee undertakes to pay a franchise fee. A franchise agreement may specifically define a territory or type of commercial activity where those exclusive rights may be exploited by the franchisee.

Form of the franchise agreement and registration

Similar to the distribution agreement, a franchise agreement must be concluded in written form. Failure to comply with this requirement renders the agreement void. A franchise agreement to be invoked against the third party must be registered with the Register of Legal Persons.[4] Issuance of a licence to use certain intellectual property rights under the franchise agreement must be registered with the State Patent Bureau.

Rights and obligations of the parties

The franchisor must *inter alia* provide the franchisee with relevant technical and commercial documentation and grant necessary licences in the manner established by law. Unless otherwise agreed by the parties, the franchisor must:

- ensure due registration of the franchise agreement;
- control the quality of goods/services produced/rendered by the franchisee;
- provide technical support and consulting;
- assist in training the franchisee's employees.

The franchisee is *inter alia* obliged to:

- perform its activities under licensed trade mark;
- ensure the quality of goods/services;
- preserve confidentiality of commercial secrets entrusted by the principal;

[4] In February 2003 operation of the Register of Legal Persons had not yet been launched and the requirement to register franchise agreements unenforced. However, it is advisable to register the franchise agreements once the Register of Legal Persons starts to operate.

- provide clients with services which would have been reasonably expected to be provided had the goods/services been purchased directly from the franchisor;
- disclose that he acts under a franchise agreement.

Assignment of intellectual property rights and change of the trade mark or trade name

Assignment of all or some intellectual property rights (IPRs) licensed under a franchise agreement from the franchisor to a third party does not impede validity of a franchise agreement. However, such a third party must also become a party to the franchise agreement at issue. If the franchisor changes the trade mark or trade name licensed under the franchise agreement, the agreement remains valid with respect to the new trade mark or trade name. However, in such instances, the franchisee is entitled to terminate the agreement and demand damage compensation, or to demand reduction of the franchise fee.

Termination of the franchise and compensation

A franchise agreement concluded for an indefinite period may be terminated by notice of either party issued at least six months prior to the termination. If the franchise agreement is to be concluded for a fixed period it is advisable to specify the detailed grounds and procedure for termination of the agreement. If this is not done a party will be entitled to premature termination of the agreement only if another party fails to carry out all or part of its obligations and provided such a failure amounts to material breach of the agreement.

Pre-emptive rights of the franchisee

Upon expiry of the franchise agreement the franchisee, having duly performed under the agreement, has a pre-emptive right to enter into a new franchise agreement on the same terms and conditions as the previous one. The franchisor may refuse to enter into a new agreement with the franchisee but only if he/she undertakes not to conclude franchise agreements in the same territory with other third parties.

Franchisor's liability

Under the Civil Code, the franchisor is liable, as a subsidiary, for the claims initiated against the franchisee due to deficiency of goods sold under the franchise agreement. This means that if the franchisee refuses to compensate damages or does not respond to the claim within a reasonable period, the third party claimant will be entitled to sue the franchisor.

If the claim against the franchisee was raised on grounds other than deficiency of the goods, the franchisor will be jointly and severally liable with the franchisee. This means that the third party claimant is entitled to sue either the franchisor or franchisee at his/her discretion. Prior addressing of the franchisee with the claim is not required.

Competition-related aspects

The general aspects of competition law are dealt with in Chapter 2.6. This chapter will briefly introduce the main points which should be taken into account when drafting agency, distribution or franchise agreements.

It is assumed that competition law regulates the relationships among independent undertakings. As such, in the case of a genuine agency, provisions of the agency contract do not fall under the scope of competition law. Nevertheless, the Civil Code restricts the validity of the non-compete undertaking of the agent for a maximum of two years.

As a general principle, the agency contract is considered a genuine agency if the agent does not bear any risks, or bears only insignificant risks, in relation to the contracts concluded and/or negotiated on behalf of the principal and in relation to market-specific investments for that field of activity. Since Lithuanian competition law provides no specific guidelines for the assessment of the nature of agency contracts, in practice EC Commission Notice: Guidelines on Vertical Restraints (OJ 2000 C291/1) is followed.

Instances of non-genuine agency as well as distribution and franchise agreements fall under the scope of competition law regulation and must be assessed in light of the Block Exemption for Vertical Agreements of 27 December 1999 (which is to a great extent analogous to EC Commission Regulation EC2790/99 of 22 December 1999). This is unless they are exempted under *de minimis* rule.[5]

The parties may benefit from the Block Exemption if the market share of a supplier in a relevant market does not exceed 30 per cent (in cases of exclusive supply obligation, the market share of the purchaser matters). Furthermore, the Block Exemption is not applicable if the object or effect of a vertical agreement is:

- the restriction of the buyer's ability to determine its sale price (except establishment of maximum or recommended prices);
- the restriction of resale of goods, except:
  (i) the restriction of active sales into the exclusive territory or to an exclusive customer group allocated by the supplier to another

[5] For more details please also see Chapter 2.6.

buyer, provided that analogous restriction is imposed by the supplier with respect to its direct buyers;

(ii) the restriction of sales (active and passive) to unauthorized distributors by the members of a selective distribution system);

- the restriction of active or passive sales to end users by members of a selective distribution system;
- the restriction of cross-supplies between distributors within a selective distribution system;
- the restriction of the sale of the components as spare parts to repairers or other service providers if such a restriction is agreed between a supplier of components and a buyer who incorporates those components and resells (except those instances when a restriction of resale of spare parts has no such effect).

Vertical agreement containing the above restrictions will be null and void unless the parties prove that such agreement does not and may not restrict competition to an appreciable extent.

The Block Exemption is also not applied to some other obligations that may be provided in vertical agreements:

- non-compete obligation, the duration of which is indefinite or exceeds five years (except where the goods are sold by the buyer from premises owned by the supplier, or leased by the supplier from third parties);
- obligation causing the buyer, after termination of the agreement, not to manufacture, purchase, sell or resell goods (except when such obligation:

  (i) relates to goods which compete with the contract goods;

  (ii) is indispensable to protect know-how transferred by the supplier to the buyer;

  (iii) its duration is limited to a period of one year after termination of the agreement.

  However, this limitation is without prejudice to the possibility of imposing a restriction that is unlimited in time on the use and disclosure of know-how that has not entered the public domain);
- obligation causing the members of a selective distribution system not to sell the brands of particular competing suppliers.

Any of the above restrictions is void, unless it does not affect the restricting of competition to an appreciable extent. However, voidance of such a restriction does not affect the validity of the remaining provisions of the vertical agreement.

The parties of vertical agreements falling under the Block Exemption must present brief information on the principal provisions of the agreement to the Lithuanian Competition Council within one month of such an agreement entering into force. Failure to provide such information does not exclude the application of the Block Exemption and does not affect the validity of the agreement.

2.6

Competition Law

Lideika, Petrauskas, Valiūnas ir Partneriai

Introduction

A relatively short history of Lithuanian competition law that started with the adoption of the first Law on Competition on 15 September 1992 has been marked by a gradual adjustment of national competition rules to European Community (EC) competition law standards. Although the 1992 Law on Competition was to a certain extent influenced by the US antitrust law (eg it did not impose restrictions on vertical agreements unless one of the parties was a dominant undertaking), its basic structure and terminology undoubtedly followed the European tradition. Integration into the EU as a political aim was clearly set up in the mid-1990s – that essentially shaped all further developments in the competition law area. The Europe Agreement (establishing an association between European Communities and their Member States and Lithuania, signed on 6 June 1995 and effective from 1 February 1998) provided that the competition system for trade relations between the Community and Lithuania had to be based on the requirements set out in Articles 85, 86 and 92 of the EC Treaty, whereas the Lithuanian rules on competition had to be made compatible with those of the EC. With that in mind, the new Law on Competition was enacted in 1999.

This chapter will cover three main pillars of the Lithuanian competition law:

- the regulation of anti-competitive agreements;
- the prohibition of abusive behaviour by dominant undertakings;
- the merger control.

It will not discuss control over state aid, which is regulated by a special Law on Monitoring of State Aid to Undertakings, and unfair competition rules, which are analysed in Chapter 2.8. The last section will be dedicated to certain aspects of public and private enforcement of competition rules.

Basic concepts

As a starting point, several major concepts used by the Law on Competition have to be defined. Firstly, Lithuanian competition rules are applicable to 'undertakings'. This concept has been taken from EC competition law and includes any public or private persons or individuals that perform, or may perform, economic activities.

Secondly, the Law on Competition establishes the 'extra-territorial' application of national competition rules. In particular, Article 2 expressly states that this law is also applicable to the activities of undertakings registered beyond the territory of Lithuania if such activities restrict competition in the domestic market of Lithuania.

Finally, the definition of a 'relevant market' comprising product and geographical dimensions is of crucial importance in the application of competition rules. The national competition authority – the Competition Council of the Republic of Lithuania – has adopted guidelines as to how it applies this concept in its practice. These guidelines essentially follow the EC Commission Notice on the Definition of Relevant Market for the Purposes of Community Competition Law (OJ 1997 C372/5).

Anti-competitive agreements

Prohibitions

Article 5 of the Law on Competition, reflecting Article 81 of the EC Treaty, states that all agreements which have as their object or effect the restriction of competition, or which may restrict competition, are prohibited and void from the moment of their conclusion. Notably, in this context the term 'agreement' has a broad meaning and includes not only the traditional civil law concept of a 'contract' but also 'concerted practices' and 'decisions by associations of undertakings' as they are known under EC competition law.

Article 5 is applicable to agreements both of a horizontal and vertical nature. As far as horizontal agreements are concerned, the Law on Competition specifically declares that agreements between competitors regarding price fixing, market sharing, restriction of production, sales or technical development and application of discriminatory conditions to other trading partners are always considered as having the object of restricting competition. As a result, justification of such 'hardcore agreements', although not impossible in theory, becomes extremely difficult, with the burden of proof lying with the parties. Vertical agreements are not excluded from the scope of Article 5, but similar to EC competition law, are considered to be pro-competitive unless the parties have a certain degree of market power.

Following the EC competition law model, agreements of both a horizontal and vertical nature can automatically escape regulation of Article 5 of the Law on Competition if they fall within the scope of *de minimis* rule or satisfy the requirements of one of the block exemptions adopted by the Competition Council. Alternatively, an individual exemption could be issued by the Competition Council if the undertakings concerned meet certain prerequisites, as described further in this chapter.

De minimis *rule*

The existing 13 January 2000 Resolution No 13 of the Competition Council on the *de minimis* rule is based on EC Commission Notice on Agreements of Minor Importance (OJ 1997 C372/13). Although the latter has already been replaced by the new notice (published in OJ 2001 C368/13), which *inter alia* raises the *de minimis* thresholds to 10 per cent and 15 per cent of the market share for horizontal and vertical agreements respectively, the Lithuanian *de minimis* rules remain unchanged. Namely, in order for agreements to be considered as producing insignificant effects to the market, the gross annual income of the parties to a specific agreement may not exceed 10 million litas in cases of vertical agreements and 5 million litas in cases of horizontal or mixed (horizontal/vertical) agreements. Even if these turnover limits are exceeded, agreements will also be regarded as having little influence provided that the market share held by each of the parties to a vertical agreement is lower than 10 per cent on any of the relevant markets affected by the agreement, or if the aggregate market share held by the parties to horizontal or mixed agreement is lower than 5 per cent on any of the relevant markets affected by the agreement.

It should be noted that the *de minimis* rule cannot rule out the applicability of Article 5 of the Law on Competition with regard to horizontal agreements (which have as their object the fixing of prices, limiting of production or sales or sharing of markets or sources of supply) and vertical agreements (which have as their object the fixing of resale prices).

Exemptions

Agreements that fall within Article 5 of the Law on Competition are not necessarily void as the law states. On the contrary, a large range of agreements with possible anti-competitive restrictions may nonetheless be permitted because of the beneficial effects they produce. For this purpose the Law on Competition establishes a system of exemptions which may be availed of in two ways:

- by applying to the Competition Council for an individual exemption with respect to a particular agreement;
- by drafting an agreement with terms satisfying one of the block exemptions issued by the Competition Council.

At present there are three block exemptions approved by the Competition Council. As a practical matter, the block exemption for vertical agreements is of greatest importance for daily business (two others are related to the transport and agriculture sectors). This block exemption dated 27 December 1999 was drafted in line with the EC Regulation 2790/99 on the Application of Article 81(3) of the Treaty to Categories of Vertical Agreements and Concerted Practices (OJ 1999 L336/21). The major prerequisite for the parties to be able to benefit from this block exemption is that the market share of a supplier in a relevant market must not exceed the threshold of 30 per cent. All other conditions being essentially the same as those provided in the aforementioned EC regulation, one significant procedural difference still remains: under the Lithuanian rules the parties must, not later than within one month after coming into effect of the agreement concluded according to the conditions of the block exemption, present information on the principal provisions of the agreement to the Competition Council. Failure to present such information does not preclude the application of the block exemption but may result in fines.

Undertakings that cannot benefit either from the *de minimis* rule or from one of the block exemptions may ask for their agreement to be relieved from application of Article 5 on an individual basis prior to its conclusion. Parties applying to the Competition Council for individual exemption have to prove that the agreement in question satisfies certain conditions that are analogous to the ones described in Article 81(3) of the EC Treaty. To qualify for an exemption, the agreement must produce efficiencies that are passed on to consumers and, at the same time, not impose unnecessary restrictions on the contracting parties, nor afford contracting parties the possibility of eliminating competition with respect to a substantial part of the relevant market.

The entire procedure of obtaining an individual exemption may last up to three months and might require quite substantial efforts in producing the necessary documentation to prove the aforementioned benefits. The situation is exacerbated by the fact that national competition rules lack a whole set of the block exemptions that are available under EC competition law (eg exemptions for research and development (R&D), specialization and technology transfer agreements). Trying to address these concerns and provide the business community with more legal certainty, the Competition Council has declared that horizontal cooperation agreements will continue to be exempted on the individual basis. The Competition Council will, however, take into account provisions of the block exemptions approved under:

- EC Commission Regulation 2658/2000 (specialization agreements);
- EC Commission Regulation 2659/2000 (R&D agreements);
- EC Commission Regulation 240/96 (technology transfer agreements);
- EC Commission Guidelines on the Applicability of Article 81 of the EC Treaty to Horizontal Cooperation Agreements.

In other words, parties to R&D, specialization and technology transfer agreements can expect that the Competition Council will apply a 'fast-track' procedure to their applications, provided that the agreements concerned satisfy conditions of block exemptions under EC competition rules. All remaining horizontal cooperation agreements will be assessed in light of the principles set out in the aforementioned EC Commission Guidelines.

Abuse of dominant position

Establishing dominance

Prohibition of abuse of a dominant position is formulated in Article 9 of the Law on Competition, which essentially reflects Article 82 of the EC Treaty. The major difference between the national and EC competition law systems lies in the understanding of the notion of 'dominance'.

The Law on Competition defines a 'dominant position' as the position of one or more undertakings in the relevant market in which the undertaking(s) do not directly face competition or which enables the undertaking(s) to have unilateral decisive influence in the relevant market by effectively restricting competition. Leaving aside certain definitional dissimilarities with the concept of 'dominance' established by Community case law, it is important, for practical reasons, to draw attention to the different understandings of the significance of market shares in the process of establishing a dominant position. Under Lithuanian competition rules, the market share threshold triggering the presumption of dominance is relatively lower; it is set by the Law on Competition at 40 per cent. This has a huge practical significance as such a presumption is hard to deny and the Competition Council is quite keen on applying it.

Another presumption – albeit until now never used in the Competition Council's practice – should also be mentioned: unless proved otherwise, each of a group of three or a smaller number of undertakings with the largest share of the relevant market, which jointly hold 70 per cent or more of the relevant market, is considered to enjoy a dominant position. Apparently such presumption of 'collective dominant position' was designed to tackle oligopolistic markets where no single undertaking could be enjoying a single dominance. Due to the absence of any administrative practice or case law on this matter it still remains to be seen if the Competition Council would dare to use this potentially powerful tool and how strong the presumption of collective dominance would be. As to particular factors used to measure dominance, the Competition Council has adopted guidelines on the definition of dominant position, which were to a large extent influenced by the UK's OFT Guideline No 415 on Assessment of Market Power.

Types of abuse

Maintenance of a dominant position as such is not illegal under the Lithuanian law, only the abuse of a dominant position is prohibited. Article 9 of the Law on Competition contains a prohibition on the abuse of a dominant position within the relevant market through the exercise of any actions that restrict or may restrict competition, limit possibilities of other undertakings to act in the market or violate the interests of consumers. This prohibition, among other things, applies to unfair pricing, restrictions of production, sales or technical development, discriminatory practices, tying. As a practical matter, it should be emphasized that legal provisions prohibiting abuse of dominant position as well as their implementation in Lithuania is generally in line with relevant provisions of EC competition law and practice.

Concentration control

Definition

The definition of concentration includes both mergers and acquisitions of control. The first part of the definition basically covers legal mergers between undertakings, although the formation of an economic unit while remaining legally separate entities is not excluded. The essential feature of the acquisition of control is the ability to exercise a decisive influence over business activities of the controlled undertaking. Creation of a joint venture clearly falls within the second part of the definition and is understood as an acquisition of joint control over an existing or newly established undertaking.

Notification

The Competition Council must be informed of the intended concentration and its prior permission must be obtained when, in the last financial year prior to concentration, the combined aggregate turnover of the undertakings concerned was more than 30 million litas and the aggregate turnover of each of at least two undertakings concerned was more than 5 million litas.

As far as foreign transactions are concerned it should be noted that, in accordance with the principle of extra-territoriality, Lithuanian competition rules are applicable to all concentrations that fall within the turnover criteria mentioned above, irrespective of where the concentration takes place and whether the parties concerned have any subsidiaries in Lithuania. When a party to concentration is an undertaking of a foreign country, its aggregate turnover is calculated as the sum of income received from the sale of its products and services in the Lithuanian market. The notification of concentration must be submitted in the standard form as established by the Competition Council (similar to the C/O form under the EC Merger Regulation).

Suspension

The undertakings participating in concentration have no right to exercise further concentration actions from the date of performance of the first concentration action until the date of the decision of the Competition Council permitting the concentration. Failure to meet this requirement means that any actions performed prior to receiving permission for concentration will have no legal force and effect. At the request of the parties however, the Competition Council may permit individual actions of concentration until the adoption of a final decision.

Timing of notification and issuance of permission

Notification of an intended concentration should be submitted to the Competition Council not later than one week after the 'first legal action of concentration', which may include the following:

- presentation of an offer to conclude an agreement or acquire shares or assets;
- the authorization to conclude an agreement;
- the conclusion of an agreement;
- the acquisition of ownership rights;
- the right to dispose of certain assets.

The Law on Competition establishes two phases of examination of concentration. The initial examination period may not last more than one month. Within one month after receipt of a proper notification of concentration the Competition Council either permits concentration or adopts a decision for further examination of the concentration. Such further examination may last up to three months.

Taking into account the complexity of filing requirements, the short notification deadline and mandatory suspension period, pre-merger discussions and consultations with officials of the Competition Council are strongly recommended. The Competition Council is entitled to limit the scope of the required information if, after preliminary consultations regarding the intended notification, it resolves that such information is not necessary for the examination of concentration. In this case, the scope of the compulsory information to be submitted and the supporting documents might be established in the consultation protocol if so requested by the person submitting the notification. Although formal resolutions of the Competition Council or consultation protocols on this subject appear as an exception, informal oral understandings of a similar nature are common practice. Although such understandings or advisory opinions of the authority are not binding, they have a significant practical effect by helping to reduce the load of documentation to be delivered to the Competition Council.

Substantive test

The substantive test applied by the Competition Council is whether the concentration will establish or strengthen the dominant position and result in substantial restriction of competition in a relevant market. Where the Competition Council finds that the concentration will have such an effect, it may prohibit it altogether or establish terms and conditions that will allow the concentration to proceed without having the prohibited effect.

Given the statutory presumption of a 'collective dominance' (see explanations above), which provides the Competition Council with a tool to control concentrations in oligopolistic markets, it seems unlikely that the existent test of 'dominance' could be replaced by a widely discussed 'significant lessening of competition' standard, unless this standard would be introduced in the EC Merger Regulation. Judging by the latest EU Commission proposal for the EC Merger Regulation reform dated 11 December 2002, such a radical move does not look like a plausible scenario.

Enforcement of competition rules

Public enforcement

The Competition Council is a special institution responsible for public enforcement of the Law on Competition. Usually the Competition Council starts investigations of potential infringements on the basis of complaints received from interested parties or public institutions. It also has the right to start investigations on its own initiative but due to the lack of sufficient resources this is something of an exception.

While performing an investigation, officers of the Competition Council have quite extensive powers, including the power to:

- perform 'dawn raids' on premises used by undertakings;
- examine, copy and seize documents of undertakings under investigation;
- have access to and copy information stored in computers and magnetic disks etc.

Some of the aforementioned actions, such as performing a 'dawn raid' require prior permission of a competent court.

Cases are heard in public sessions of the Competition Council unless a closed hearing is declared in order to protect state or commercial secrets. After completing the hearing of the case, the Competition Council has the right to adopt a resolution to impose sanctions, refuse to apply sanctions if there are insufficient grounds, close the case if there is no breach of law, or reopen the investigation. Resolutions of the Competition Council may be appealed to the Vilnius District Administrative Court. Decisions of the latter may be further reviewed by the Highest Administrative Court of Lithuania.

If a violation of the Law on Competition is found, the Competition Council is entitled to require termination of the illegal activity, restoration of previous situation and/or removal of the consequences of the violation. The Competition Council can also impose fines on undertakings ranging from 1,000 litas to 100,000 litas – or even more but not exceeding 10 per cent of the aggregate annual income in cases of extremely severe infringements.

The Law on Competition establishes a 'lenience programme' which provides that, under certain conditions, undertakings having committed a violation of competition rules can be granted full immunity from or reduction of fines. Notably, this 'lenience programme' is not limited to cartel cases but also extends to anti-competitive vertical agreements and abuses of dominant position.

Private enforcement

Private enforcement of competition rules is still underdeveloped in Lithuania. Apart from the possibility of filing complaints to the Competition Council, there are two other main areas with a potential for private actions. Firstly, a question of invalidity of an anti-competitive agreement could be raised in civil courts; that will require the court to decide a case in accordance with the criteria established by the Law on Competition. Secondly, persons whose interests have been violated by the breach of competition rules may apply to civil courts for compensation of damages. However, so far neither of those possibilities, except in a few cases, has raised any interest of potential litigants.

It might be expected that private enforcement would become more active after Lithuania joins the EU. The preliminary date for this event is scheduled for 1 May 2004, which coincides with the date of the new EC Council Regulation 1/2003 on the implementation of the rules on competition laid down in Articles 81 and 82 of the Treaty entering into force. This could provide a huge impetus for a more vigorous enforcement of competition rules and raise some further questions on the relationship between Articles 81 and 82 of the EC Treaty and national competition laws.

2.7

Employment Law

Lideika, Petrauskas, Valiūnas ir Partneriai

Introduction

Until recently there was no uniform act regulating labour relations in Lithuania. Apart from the old Code of Labour Laws, after re-establishment of independence a number of separate laws were enacted. A new Labour Code was adopted on 4 June 2002 and came into effect as of 1 January 2003. The Labour Code was aimed to meet certain requirements of European Union (EU) law and applicable ILO conventions and codified the bulk of the regulation of labour relations. It also introduced a number of significant changes. Some specific labour matters, such as activities of trade unions, safety and health of employees and support of the unemployed, are regulated by special laws. Formation and status of labour councils will also be regulated by a special law (adoption of this law is pending).

Employment contract

Terms and form

Parties to an employment contract must agree on the employee's place of work (a company, branch) and his/her official duties and/or position. Parties must also agree on remuneration. The employment contract may not establish terms less favourable to the employee than employment conditions stated under the law. An employment contract is deemed concluded when the parties have agreed on the conditions of the employment contract. Employment contracts must be in writing and in accordance with the model form established by the law. The model form for employment contracts contains empty space for additional clauses.

Fixed-term employment

Employment contracts may be concluded for an indefinite period of time or for a fixed period of time if the work is of a temporary nature. It is prohibited to conclude a fixed-term employment contract if work is of a permanent nature, except for the cases when this is provided by laws or collective agreements.

Probation period

Parties may stipulate in the employment contract a probation period that may not exceed three months. Parties may not stipulate a probation period for:

- persons under 18 years of age;
- persons who are transferred from another enterprise upon the agreement of two employers;
- persons employed through competition or elections;
- persons who have passed qualification examinations;
- persons otherwise provided for by the law.

Notification

An employer must register each employee with the local department of the State Social Insurance Board on the same day the employment contract is concluded. Employers must make social insurance contributions and withhold personal income taxes for all employees. An employer should keep in its records a document containing the employee's signature with a statement that the employee accepts and has knowledge of the standard rules and regulations of the company (eg work regulations, job position descriptions). An employer must keep a register of employment contracts in the company and register each employment contract or any amendments thereto.

Foreign personnel

Foreign citizens (except EU citizens) and stateless persons who are not permanent residents of Lithuania may work temporarily in Lithuania under an employment contract provided they have a work permit issued by the National Labour Exchange under the Ministry of Social Protection and Labour. A foreign citizen or stateless person who intends to reside in Lithuania for more than three months per half year (certain longer periods apply for job seekers who are EU citizens) or to work there must obtain a temporary residence permit. Foreigners may apply for such permits to the diplomatic missions or consular offices of Lithuania abroad, or directly to the Ministry of Internal Affairs of Lithuania if he/she has already legally entered the country. The permits are issued to foreigners to work in Lithuania based on quotas for the employment of foreigners as established by the Government.

The law provides for a list of exemptions for persons who do not need work permits. Exempted foreigners are required to obtain only a residence permit, as the case may be. Work permits are not required for persons of various categories, examples of which are:

- citizens of the EU;
- managing directors (their authorized representatives) of foreign enterprises or institutions that have established economic relations with Lithuanian enterprises or institutions;
- managing directors, their authorized representatives or specialists of foreign capital enterprises (ie companies with invested foreign capital).

It should be noted that an employment contract with a foreigner who is not exempted from obtaining a work permit must be concluded in accordance with the standard form of the employment contract for foreigners. It is forbidden for the employee to engage in work other than that specified in the work permit. The employment contract with a foreigner who is not exempted from obtaining a work permit must be registered with the National Labour Exchange within three days from its conclusion.

Termination of employment contract

An employment contract terminates:

- upon the liquidation of an employer without a legal successor;
- upon the death of an employee;
- by agreement between the parties;
- upon expiry of its term;
- upon the notice of an employee;
- on the initiative of an employer with notice;
- on the initiative of an employer without notice;
- as a result of other cases provided for by the law.

Employment termination with notice

The laws do not provide for a detailed list of grounds for termination of employment. An employment contract may be terminated by the employer for good reason, eg due to circumstances related to the employee's qualifications, professional competence or behaviour at work.

An employment contract may also be terminated for economic or technological reasons, due to structural changes at the work place, or for similar important reasons. The Labour Code lists discriminatory reasons that in no case may serve as legal grounds for the termination of an employment contract. These include sex, sexual orientation, nationality, language, social status, religion.

An employer dismissing an employee at the employer's initiative in the absence of fault on the employee's part must give the employee at least two months' written notice. Employees within certain categories qualify for four months' written notice. The law establishes certain requirements for dismissal of groups of employees, priority rights to retain employment for certain categories of employees and limitations on employment termination etc.

Severance pay

Severance payments depend on the employee's length of service with a company. On termination of the employment contract at the employer's initiative (with notice and if the employee is at no fault), the severance payment will be paid as a multiple of the employee's average monthly remuneration and length of service as shown in Table 2.7.1.

Table 2.7.1 Guide to severance pay

Length of service	Severance pay
Up to 12 months	Average monthly wage
12–36 months	Average monthly wage × 2
36–60 months	Average monthly wage × 3
60–120 months	Average monthly wage × 4
120–240 months	Average monthly wage × 5
Over 240 months	Average monthly wage × 6

Employees' rights protection in transfers of business

The change of the owner of an enterprise, or its subordination, founder or name, as well as the merger, splitting or share-out of an enterprise, may not be considered a lawful reason to terminate employment relations. This provision of the Labour Code only partially complies with the 12 March 2001 EC directive relating to the safeguarding of employees' rights in the event of a transfer of undertakings, business or their parts. Under this directive, assignment of business can be understood not only as a formal change of the owner or reorganization of an enterprise, but also as assignment of assets.

However, the case law of the Supreme Court of Lithuania fills this gap in Lithuanian law to a certain extent. The Supreme Court held that the assignment of part of the functions of an enterprise to a new legal entity, together with the property required for fulfilment of the functions of the enterprise, may be considered a change of the owner of that part of the property of the enterprise and equals a reorganization of the enterprise in the meaning of the labour law. Therefore, in such cases it might be required that employees be transferred together with the part of business transferred from one company to the other.

Employment termination without notice

An employment contract may be terminated without notice in the following cases:

- by a respective court decision, or following a criminal judgment whereby the penalty imposed on an employee prevents him/her from continuing to work;
- when an employee is legally deprived of special rights to perform a certain type of work;
- at the request of competent bodies or officials;
- when a medical report concludes that an employee can not occupy a certain position or fulfil certain duties;
- when, in the case of an employee aged between 14 and 16 years, a parent, guardian, doctor or the minor's school requires the termination of an employment contract;
- upon the liquidation of an employer if, according to legal requirements, another person is not obliged to fulfil the employer's labour obligations.

An employer is entitled to terminate the employee's employment contract without notice when there is fault of an employee in the following cases:

- when an employee performs his/her job duties negligently or has otherwise breached discipline, if at least once during the previous 12 months disciplinary sanctions have been imposed on him/her;
- in the event of one-off gross breach of labour discipline (duty) by the employee (there is a sample list of such gross breaches of discipline established in the Labour Code, but this list is not exhaustive).

Employees' representatives

Trade unions and work councils

In labour relations the rights and interests of employees may be represented and protected by trade unions. If an enterprise, agency or organization has no functioning trade union and if the employees' meeting has not transferred the function of employee representation and protection to the trade union of the appropriate sector of economic activity, the employees will be represented by the labour council. Labour councils will be elected by a secret ballot at the general meeting of the employees. Notably, the Labour Code's provisions regarding work councils will come into effect only after adoption of a special law regulating formation and status of work councils.

Formation of trade unions

Trade unions may be established on the basis of professional, office, industrial, territorial or other principles that represent and protect the interests of employees, as determined by the trade unions. A group of trade unions, at their own discretion and initiative, may join together to form a trade union association.

In order to establish a trade union:

- its founding members must account for not less than 20 per cent of all employees in the company, but in any case not less than three employees; or
- it must have at least 30 founding members (then founding members may account for less than 20 per cent of all employees in the company or include other members).

Trade unions have the capacity of a legal person from the moment when their articles of association (by-laws) are registered with the Ministry of Justice, the County Governor or the municipality, depending on the geographic area of their activities.

Collective agreements

Trade unions represent employees when negotiating and making collective agreements at the level of an enterprise, branch of industry, territory or whole country. Work councils will be able to represent employees only in negotiating and making collective agreements at the enterprise level.

Remuneration for work and work hours

Minimum wage

The minimum wage is set periodically by the Government. Since 1 June 1998 the minimum hourly rate has been 2.53 litas (approximately 0.73 euros) and the minimum monthly wage has been 430 litas (approximately 124.54 euros, current as of February 2003).

Payment of wages

Wages must be paid to employees at least twice a month in the national currency (litas). Wages may be paid once per month if an employee presents a respective application in writing asking to pay wages in such a way.

Wage differentials

At least 1.5 times the hourly wage rate, or a proportion of the monthly salary established for the employee, must be paid for overtime and night work (from 10 pm until 6 am). The pay for work on a rest day or a holiday that has not been provided for in the work schedule must be at least at the double rate, or it should be compensated for by granting to the employee another rest day during the month or by adding that day to his/her annual leave. The pay for work on a holiday that has been provided for in the work schedule must be at least double the rate of the hourly or daily pay.

Work hours

The normal work hours for an employee may not exceed 40 hours per week. A daily period of work normally should not exceed eight working hours. A five-day working week is the standard established under the law, but it may be extended to six days. Maximum working time, including overtime, must not exceed 48 hours per seven working days. The duration of working time of specific categories of employees (in health care, care (custody), child care institutions, specialized communications services and specialized accident containment services etc) as well as of watchmen in premises may be up to 24 hours per day. The duration of working time of such employees must not exceed 48 hours per seven-day period, and the rest period between working days must not be shorter than 24 hours.

For employees employed in more than one undertaking or in one undertaking but under two or more employment contracts, the working day (including lunch break) may not be longer than 12 hours. The hours of work and overtime hours worked by employees must be recorded in the register of work hours following the established standard format.

Holiday leave

Annual leave

The minimum annual paid vacation leave is 28 calendar days. The annual paid vacation leave is 35 calendar days for employees under 18 years of age, single parents who raise a child under the age of 14 years or a disabled child under the age of 16 years, and disabled persons.

In general, all employees are entitled to their annual paid vacation leave after they have worked in a company continuously for an initial period of six months. Extended annual leave up to 58 calendar days must be granted to certain categories of employees whose work involves greater nervous, emotional and intellectual strain and professional risk, as well as to those who work in specific working conditions. Additional annual leave may be granted to employees for conditions of work that deviate from normal working conditions, and for a long uninterrupted employment at the same work place or for a special character of work.

At the request of the employee, annual leave may be taken in pieces. One piece of annual leave may not be shorter than 14 calendar days. During annual leave the employee must be guaranteed his/her average wage received at all places of employment.

Special purpose leave

The laws provide for the following special purpose leaves:

- maternity leave (70 calendar days before childbirth and 56 calendar days or, in the event of a complicated childbirth or birth of two or more children, 70 calendar days after it), which is normally paid by the company but covered by social insurance or social aid authorities;
- child-care leave (until the child reaches three years), which is normally paid directly by social insurance or social aid authorities;
- educational leave, which is paid by the company if an employee is sent to study at the company's request (three paid days for each normal examination);
- sabbatical leave;
- leave for performance of official or public duties, which are paid or compensated not less than the average wage by the agency or organization whose obligations are being performed, unless the law provides otherwise;
- unpaid leave.

2.8

Intellectual Property

Lideika, Petrauskas, Valiūnas ir Partneriai

Introduction

During the last decade, Lithuanian legislation on intellectual property protection has been drafted or amended with a view to aligning it with the requirements of the European Union (EU), World Trade Organization (WTO) and WIPO. At present, Lithuania is a party to a number of major international treaties and agreements on intellectual property protection.

The legal acts of Lithuania on intellectual property protection are based on continental Europe's concepts of copyright and industrial property protection. Thus, as a condition for protection in Lithuania, copyright works are not required to be registered while industrial property rights are protected only upon their registration with the State Patent Bureau (SPB) – the authorized state office for registration of industrial property objects (trade marks, patents, industrial designs, firm names, topographies of semiconductor products).

Trade marks

The principal piece of legislation governing protection of trade marks in Lithuania is the Law on Trade Marks of 10 October 2000. Registration of trade marks in Lithuania is performed by the SPB. Trade marks that are allowed to be registered in Lithuania may consist of the following signs:

- words, personal surnames, names, artistic pseudonyms, names of firms, slogans;
- letters, numerals;
- drawings, emblems;
- three-dimensional forms (the shape of goods, their packaging or containers);

- colours or combinations of colours, their compositions;
- any combination of the aforementioned.

The Republic of Lithuania does not recognize the registration of odours as trade marks. The Law on Trade Marks requires that a trade mark may not consist of elements which individually may not be registered as trade marks. However, analysis of the registered trade marks suggests that in practice this provision is not fully followed. Registration of a trade mark may be cancelled, if it is proved that the applicant has unfair intentions regarding such trade mark registration.

A trade mark may be recognized as a well-known one in Lithuania if the results of its use or promotion reveal that it is well-known in the relevant sector of the public. In this case such a trade mark is protected even without registration. A trade mark is recognized as well-known in Lithuania through a judicial procedure and only upon an existing dispute regarding trade mark rights infringement.

The proprietor of the trade mark recognized as well-known in Lithuania has the right to prohibit other persons from using, without having his/her consent, in industrial or commercial activities a sign which is a reproduction, imitation or translation of, and able to create confusion with, such well-known trade mark and is used for identical or similar goods and services. The Law on Trade Marks also introduces protection for the registered trade marks 'having reputation'; criteria to be used in determining the status of such trade marks, however, are not given.

The SPB does not undertake research concerning the novelty of an applied trade mark. There are no requirements of prior use before a trade mark is registered. If a trade mark uses the word 'Lithuania' or similar sign, a prior permission from the Ministry of Justice should be obtained which is issued upon meeting the established conditions. Foreign legal and natural persons must use services of a patent attorney licensed in Lithuania to file applications for registration of trade marks with the SPB.

A trade mark registration is valid for the period of 10 years from the date of submitting the application; registration may be renewed unlimited times.

Industrial design

The principal legal act governing protection of industrial design in Lithuania is the Law on Industrial Design of 7 November 2002. In order to receive protection, an industrial design must be new and have individual characteristics. An industrial design is considered new if, until the date of an application or the priority date (which may be granted under respective international agreement), the design is not identical to another product design disclosed to the public and familiar in Lithuania.

An industrial design is publicly accessible or known if it has been published in the Official Bulletin of the SPB, exhibited at an exhibition, or marketed or demonstrated to the public in another way. The novelty of an industrial design is not disturbed by the dissemination of information about the design if:

- this information has been disseminated within a period of 12 months prior to the filing date of an application or the priority date;
- this information has been disseminated:
  - (i) by the author him/herself or his/her successor in title who had the right to acquire the right to an industrial design;
  - (ii) by another person wishing to harm the author or his/her successor.

An industrial design possesses individual characteristics if an informed user, on the basis of general appearance, is able to differentiate one industrial design from another:

- as introduced to the Lithuanian market; or
- as registered with the SPB and published in its Official Bulletin while the protection of the design is still valid.

Applications for industrial design patents are filed by foreign legal and natural persons with the SPB through a patent attorney licensed in Lithuania. Industrial design protection is valid for five years from the date of application. The term of validity of an industrial design may be extended up to four successive five-year periods (ie a total of 25 years from the date of filing the application).

Notice of the inclusion of an industrial design into the Industrial Design Register of Lithuania is published in the Official Bulletin of the SPB. Interested persons who have paid a fee, on the grounds provided for in the Law on Industrial Design, may file an opposition to the registration of an industrial design within three months of the date of publication.

Natural and legal persons who were legally using, or were making effective, or undertook serious preparations for the use of an industrial design before the date of application or the priority date may continue such use or use the industrial design as envisaged in such preparations irrespective of the will of the owner of the industrial design. The right of prior use may be transferred together with the enterprise or activities, or with that part of the enterprise or activities in which the use of an industrial design or preparations for such use have been made.

The SPB performs a formal examination of an industrial design application, ie experts do not examine the novelty of the design.

Patents

Protection of patents is mainly regulated by the Law on Patents of 18 January 1994. There are three ways for obtaining patent protection in Lithuania:

- filing application directly with the SPB;
- filing application through the Patent Cooperation Treaty (PCT);
- on the basis of the Extension Agreement between the European Patent Organization and the Government of the Republic of Lithuania, which extends the validity of European patent applications and patents into Lithuania ('Euro' and 'Euro-PCT' applications).

The right to a patent belongs to the inventor, its successor in title or an employer in case of a service invention. If the invention is created in an enterprise, institution or organization carrying out scientific research, planning, construction or other contracts for works of a creative nature, and the customer covers the cost of the work, the patent rights to the invention should be established by such contract. If the employer renounces its right to a patent or within four months does not inform the employee of its intention to make use of that right, the right to the patent is transferred to the employee.

Foreign applicants may file their applications only through a patent attorney registered in Lithuania. The filing date of a patent application is the date on which the SPB accepts the documents required for patent registration.

The following objects are not regarded as inventions:

- discoveries, scientific theories and mathematical methods;
- product design;
- schemes, rules and methods of games, intellectual and economic activities, programmes for computers;
- presentations of information.

Patents are not granted for:

- the methods of treatment of people and animals, diagnoses and prevention of disease (except for the equipment and materials utilized);
- varieties of plants and plant-based, as well as biological (except microbiological), methods for protection of people and animals;
- inventions that are deemed contrary to public interest, decency or the principles of humanity.

Where the object of an invention is a process of production, patent protection may also be granted with respect to a product produced by such a process.

A patent application is published no sooner than 18 months from its filing date. Subject to the payment of a fee and subsequent to the filing of a request for publication, it may be published earlier but not sooner than after six months from the filing date of the application.

A registered patent is valid for a term of 20 years from the filing date. Patents are subject to an annual fee. Annual payments are required beginning with the third year from the filing date and are due within the last two months of the current year.

The laws of Lithuania recognize the concept of 'prior use'. Under this concept, an individual or a legal person who in good faith used the invention or made effective or serious preparations for such use before the filing date or, in cases where priority is claimed under respective international agreement, the priority date of a patent application, has the right to continue such use or to use the invention as envisaged in such preparations without consent of the owner of the patent.

If after the expiration of a period of four years from the date of application, or three years from the grant of the patent (whichever is later), the patented invention is not used sufficiently and those willing to utilize it are refused a licence, on the request of any person that proves the ability to utilize the patented invention the court may grant a non-exclusive compulsory licence. The grant of the compulsory licence is subject to payment of equitable remuneration to the owner of the patent in an amount fixed by the court.

After taking into consideration the state or public interests, the Government may adopt a decree, without agreement of the owner of a patent, to allow an enterprise or a person to use a patented invention subject to payment of equitable remuneration to the patent owner.

Copyright

The principal law governing protection of copyright is the Law on Copyright and Neighbouring Rights of 18 May 1999. However, it should be noted that in February 2003 a draft of the new Law on Copyright and Neighbouring Rights was submitted to Parliament for approval.

Copyright exists on original scientific, literary or artistic works that are the result of creative activity, expressed in any objective form (books, brochures, diaries, computer programmes, speeches, lectures, sermons, written and verbal scientific works, dramatic and dramatic–musical works, pantomimes, choreographic works, scenarios, music works, databases, architecture works etc).

Copyright is not applied to:

- ideas, procedures, processes, systems, methods of action, conceptions, principles, inventions and separate data;
- legal acts, official documents of an administrative, judicial or normative nature as well as their official translations;
- official state symbols and signs;
- officially registered drafts of legal acts;
- ordinary informative reports on events;
- works of folk art.

According to the Law on Copyright, only a natural person may be an author. Economic copyright lasts for the life of the author plus 70 years after his/her death or the death of the last co-author in case of a joint work. Protection of collective work lasts for 70 years from the date when the work was made available to the public. The term of protection of pseudonymous or anonymous works expires 70 years from the moment the work was made available to the public. In cases of the identification of a pseudonymous or anonymous author or authors of a collective work, the work is protected for a term of 70 years after death.

Persons that make a previously unpublished work available to the public for the first time obtain all exclusive economic rights of authorship for the following 25 years. If an employee creates the work, the economic copyright is reserved to the employer for five years (if not agreed otherwise) and afterwards passes to the employee. In the case of computer programmes, the economic copyright is vested in the employer for unlimited time, unless the employment contract or other agreement provides otherwise.

In all cases, the term of an economic copyright runs from 1 January of the year following the date of the author's death or from the date that the work is made available to the public. Economic copyrights are inheritable.

The protection of an author's moral rights is of unlimited duration. These rights cannot be inherited or assigned to any person or entity, other than the author.

Recognition of a copyright and its legal protection is not subject to any deposit or registration requirement or any other formality.

Licensing of intellectual property rights

Lithuania has not enacted a special law governing licensing of intellectual property rights. Thus, the general rules of the Civil Code and specific clauses of other laws protecting intellectual property rights are applicable.

Under Lithuanian law, licensing agreements must be concluded in written form. Licensing agreements relating to patents, industrial design, trade marks and topographies of semiconductor products are subject to registration with the SPB. By law, these licensing agreements may be invoked against third persons only upon registration with the SPB. However, non-registration of a licence agreement does not affect the validity of the agreement itself between the parties.

All other types of licensing agreements are automatically effective upon execution by the parties and are free of registration requirements.

Unfair competition

Among unfair competition acts that are prohibited by the Law on Competition of 23 March 1999 are acts based on using intellectual property of other undertakings.

Undertakings are prohibited from performing any acts contrary to fair business practices if such acts may be detrimental to competition interests of another undertaking. This may include unauthorized use of a mark identical or similar to the name, registered, or unregistered well-known trade mark, or other sign having a distinguishing feature of another undertaking in the following cases:

- if this causes or may cause confusion with that undertaking or its activity;
- where it is sought to take undue advantage of the reputation of that undertaking (its mark or sign);
- where this may cause injury to the reputation (its mark or sign) of that undertaking, or reduction of the distinguishing feature of the mark or sign applied by that undertaking.

The Competition Council has competence to hear an unfair competition dispute when it has direct impact on the interests of consumers. In other cases unfair competition disputes should be heard by the courts.

2.9

The Property Regime

Lideika, Petrauskas, Valiūnas ir Partneriai

Introduction

Since restoration of independence in 1990, the reform of the Lithuanian legal system has been based on principles of ownership protection and freedom of contract. The new Civil Code of 18 July 2000 (effective from 1 July 2001) introduced a number of new legal instruments in the sphere of the property law, eg new rights *in rem*, modified regulation of mortgages, established connection between the land and buildings etc. Along with the Civil Code, many supplementary legal acts were adopted or amended, which together resulted in substantial changes in legal regulation of the property regime.

Ownership

Following the Constitution of the Republic of Lithuania, the subterranean resources as well as nationally significant internal waters, forests, parks, roads, historical, archaeological and cultural facilities belong to the Republic of Lithuania under exclusive ownership right. Except these exclusive rights of the state and certain restrictions in respect of the acquisition of land, Lithuanian laws do not provide for any other substantial prohibitions or limitations regarding acquisition into ownership of a property in Lithuania either by national or foreign entities and citizens.

Land

All land in Lithuania is divided into the following types based on the main intended purpose of land usage:

- land of agricultural purpose;
- land of forestry purpose;

- land of conservation purpose (territories of national parks, state reserves etc);
- land of the State Water Fund;
- land of other purpose.

The usage of a particular land plot should comply with its main intended purpose, which is normally indicated in respective registration documents of a land plot at issue. Generally, the land of 'other purpose' may be used for commercial purposes, eg construction and/or operation of buildings and other structures. The main intended purpose of other land must be changed prior to using it for commercial purposes.

A practically unrestricted right to acquire into ownership any land is granted only to Lithuanian citizens. Meanwhile, national and foreign entities as well as foreign citizens (individuals) must comply with certain criteria before they can become owners of land. The land plots to be acquired by foreigners must be of non-agricultural purpose and necessary for either:

- operation of buildings or other structures designated for the direct business activity of the acquirer; or
- construction and operation of new buildings and other structures necessary for the direct business activity of the acquirer.

Notably, foreign entities are not yet entitled to directly acquire land in Lithuania. This may only be done through an enterprise or a branch registered by a foreign entity in Lithuania. The analogous requirements are also applied with respect to foreign citizens. As a precondition for a foreigner to acquire a land plot in Lithuania, he/she should be engaged in registered business activity in Lithuania (eg establish his/her enterprise etc).

Apart from the necessity to engage in registered business activity as noted above, Lithuanian and foreign entities as well as foreign citizens should meet the following conditions in order to be entitled to acquire into ownership land plots in Lithuania:

- the origin requirement, ie foreign entities and citizens engaged in registered business activities in Lithuania and aiming to acquire the land in Lithuania, should be from one of the following states:
  - a member state of the European Union (EU); or
  - a state that is a party to the European Agreement Establishing Association with the EU and its member states; or
  - a state that at the moment of the adoption of the Constitutional Law on Subjects, Procedures, Conditions and Restrictions of

Acquisition into Ownership of Land Plots Provided for in Paragraph 2, Article 47 of the Constitution of the Republic of Lithuania of 20 June 1996 (the 'Constitutional Law'), which enabled acquisition of land by foreign entities and citizens, was a member the Organization for Economic Cooperation and Development (OECD) or a member of the North Atlantic Treaty Organization (NATO);

- the foreign entity must have its main place of business in one of the above listed states for at least five recent years prior to acquisition of the land;
- a permit to acquire a particular land plot into ownership must be obtained. Such permits are issued by a respective County Governor taking into consideration the location of a land plot to be acquired.

When a land plot is required for construction purposes, a person applying for the permit to acquire the land plot should *inter alia* indicate the particular date by which he/she undertakes to finalize construction and commence direct business activities on the land plot.

Land plots belonging to the state may be acquired into ownership with or without holding an auction. The auction must be held for sale of each state-owned land plot whereon no permanent buildings or structures belonging to natural or legal persons are located. Otherwise, if some permanent buildings or structures (including construction in progress) are located on the state-owned land plot, it could be sold to such owners of the buildings or structures without holding an auction. In other words, possession of the buildings or structures on the state-owned land plot helps to avoid a rather complicated auction procedure. Due to this fact even valueless buildings or structures located on state-owned land plots are often sold for considerably higher prices.

Title to the land plot may be held separately from title to the buildings located thereon. However, the sale–purchase agreement of the land plot should discuss the conditions of transfer of the ownership right to the buildings or structures located on it. If this issue is not discussed in the agreement, it is considered that title to the buildings or structures has been transferred to the buyer together with the land plot.

As of March 2003, a draft of the new wording of the Constitutional Law is under consideration in the parliament (*Seimas*) and its adoption is expected in several months. The main change introduced in this draft in comparison with the previously effective Constitutional Law is that both foreign entities and citizens are granted the right to directly acquire land, ie there is no requirement to engage in registered business activities. As a result of the adoption of the new Constitutional Law, any enterprise registered in Lithuania would be entitled to acquire a land plot irrespective of the origin of the capital invested into such enterprise (ie irrespective of the origin of its incorporator). Following the draft new Constitutional Law, the origin's requirements prescribed in the current Constitutional Law would be applied only in respect of foreign entities and citizens intending to directly acquire the land in Lithuania.

Buildings

Acquisition of buildings into ownership is always related to the rights in respect of the land under them. Following the Civil Code, an agreement on sale–purchase of a building or other structure must specify the buyer's rights in respect of the land plot under the building. In case of failure to specify such rights, the agreement on sale–purchase of a building may not be approved by a notary public and, if approved, shall be deemed void.

In case of sale of buildings located on a state-owned land plot, a seller must obtain prior permission of the respective County Governor's Administration to that effect. By such permission it is usually declared that the state-owned land plot under the sold buildings will be sold or leased to the new owner of the buildings. It is common practice that, upon sale of the buildings located on the state-owned land plot, the seller thereof applies to the Administration of the County Governor regarding termination of the agreement on the lease of the state-owned land plot under the sold buildings and the buyer for conclusion of the new lease agreement.

Expropriation

The Constitution of the Republic of Lithuania establishes that property may be taken from the owner (expropriated) only:

(i) for the needs of society;

(ii) according to the procedure established by the laws;

(iii) upon adequate compensation.

Currently valid law allows only the following grounds for expropriation of property:

(i) taking of land for public needs;

(ii) taking of improperly kept cultural valuables; or

(iii) confiscation of property as a sanction for infringement of law (in accordance with the Code of Administrative Law Violations and the Criminal Code).

The procedure of expropriation of investors' property, including calculation and payments of compensation for the expropriated property, is provided in a number of bilateral Agreements on Promotion and Protection of Investments entered into between Lithuania and other states (for more details regarding protection of investments see Chapter 2.1).

Restitution

According to Lithuanian laws, owners and certain qualifying descendants of owners, whose land, buildings or other real estate was nationalized under the laws of the Soviet Union, are still entitled to restore their ownership rights to the existing real estate. It should be noted that currently valid laws provide for two deadlines with respect to restitution of ownership rights – one is for filing the application and the other is for the submission of the documents confirming the ownership rights and relationship with the former owner.

The first deadline for filing the relevant application regarding the restitution of ownership rights was 31 December 2001. Persons who failed to file applications before that date lost the right to restore their ownership rights. Those who successfully filed applications should present documents proving their title to the real estate before the second deadline, 1 July 2003. Failure to present such documents before the said date will result in applicants losing their rights to restore ownership.

It should also be pointed out that ownership rights are not restored *inter alia* to the land plots or other real estate that have been acquired into ownership by third persons in accordance with the applicable laws. Thus, once having become the legal owner of real estate, the investor should not worry about losing it due to restitution of ownership rights. The state shall compensate the descendants of owners of such real estate under procedures prescribed by law.

Lease

The lease of land in Lithuania has always had significant importance because of restrictions established regarding acquisition of the land by foreign entities or citizens. For this reason many foreign investors choose to take the land on lease and make further investments related to the development of real estate or use of the land plot for other needs.

Lithuanian and foreign natural and legal persons are permitted to take on lease private or state-owned land and other property in Lithuania. The lease term of both private and state-owned land plots must be determined by the agreement between the lessor and the lessee; however the lease term of the state-owned land plot may not exceed 99 years and the lease term of private land and any other property may not exceed 100 years. The use of the land for other than agricultural purpose is related to considerable investments and construction of buildings, therefore usually the state-owned land plots are leased for a maximum permitted term, ie 99 years.

A significant part of land and other real estate in Lithuania still belongs to the state and municipalities. The state-owned land plots may be leased with or without holding an auction. Auctions for the lease of state-owned land plots must be held in all cases, except for those in which the state-owned land plots are built over with buildings, structures or facilities owned or leased by respective legal or private persons. In cases of an auction to lease the state-owned land plot, the lease is granted to a person who proposes the highest rent.

When entering into lease agreements with state institutions there is not usually much space for negotiations over the provisions of the lease agreement. The state institutions must follow the standard form of lease agreement and have limited right and willingness to adjust the agreement to the needs of the investor. In addition, the procedure of the auction is generally inflexible.

The land may be leased after it has been formed as a separate land plot and registered as such with the Real Estate Register. In practice, because of the slow process of land reform, in many cases land plots are not legally registered with the Real Estate Register. Similarly, often there are no agreements in respect of state-owned land plots in use; nevertheless such plots are used by entities on a 'historical' basis as land under the buildings owned. From 1 July 2001, under the Civil Code, disposal of the building is only possible when the owner of the building has respective contractual rights to use the land plot under the building.

The buildings and structures are related to the land plot under them, therefore the agreement for lease of a building must specify the lessee's rights in respect of the land plot under the building. There are no other substantial restrictions regarding the lease of the buildings, structures, facilities or movable property in Lithuania either by national or foreign persons.

The Civil Code allows for the possibility to enter into a long-term lease (*emphyteusis*) which is considered a right *in rem*. The term of the long-term lease agreement must be not less than 10 years. Generally, the lessee has the right to use the real estate under the long-term lease to the same extent as the owner of such real estate (with certain exceptions).

The Civil Code establishes new regulations regarding the right of development (*superficies*). The right of development is the right to use the land owned by other persons for construction, acquisition or use of the buildings and structures or to use the natural resources. The provisions concerning the long-term lease and right of development will come into force on 1 July 2003.

Servitudes

Current Lithuanian laws cover only land servitudes (land easements) that represent obligations of the landowner or the user of state-owned land to grant other persons the right to use a part of a land plot.

The land servitudes may be established by a law, a decision of the public authorities on the grounds of public needs or by a mutual written agreement between the owner of the private land plot and other natural or legal persons. On 1 July 2003 the provisions of the Civil Code allowing establishment of servitudes in respect of property other than land will come into effect.

Leasing

Being the leaders among the buyers of personal and commercial vehicles in Lithuania, leasing companies also actively finance acquisitions of real estate and industrial equipment. Due to recent amendments in legal, accountancy and taxation regulations, leasing becomes more popular and its part in financial services grows every year.

The Civil Code as well as the regulations on financial accountancy mainly implement the 1988 UNIDROIT Convention on International Financial Leasing (Ottawa Convention) and International Accountancy Standards. The new laws, however, include important legal clarifications for legal responsibilities of the parties, such as:

- transfer to the lessee the risk of accidental damage and destruction of a property;
- risk and benefit related to a property fall on the lessee;
- lessee's responsibility for maintenance and repair of the property;
- principle of absence of lessor's responsibility for the property's defects (with certain exceptions);
- lessee's ability to raise claims directly against the supplier of the property;
- third party liability for damages done to third parties using the property;
- lessor's right upon termination of the contract to recover the amount of losses, which would return the lessor into the condition in which he/she would have been if the lessee had properly fulfilled the contract.

The Civil Code makes a distinction between leasing and consumer credit and establishes special provisions related to the protection of consumers regarding consumer credit. In addition, the laws prevent land and natural resources from being objects permitted in leasing contracts. Such prohibition is related to the restrictions established in respect of disposal of land in Lithuania.

Mortgage

At present, commercial banks consistently offer residential mortgage products as well as commercial loans for entities based on mortgage security. The market of residential mortgage lending has been recently stimulated by direct state subsidies. In addition, the recently adopted Law on Residents' Income Tax of 2 July 2002 provides for tax benefits in relation to lending for the acquisition of residential real estate; this should also stimulate the increase of the market.

It should also be noted that the secondary bond market is not developed sufficiently to support the exchange of long-term mortgage bonds in Lithuania. However, expected developments in life insurance and pension funds support the need for such long-term investment instruments and the creation of such a market.

A mortgage is defined as an encumbrance over real estate created by the owner of such property (mortgagor) to secure discharge of the existing or future debt obligations against the creditor (mortgagee). The owner of the property retains the ownership rights to it. However, if the debt secured by the mortgage is not repaid when due, the creditor has the right to demand the sale of the mortgaged property through public auction and to use proceeds from that sale to repay the debt.

Mortgage of land does not automatically extend to buildings on it unless the mortgage agreement states otherwise. Mortgage of the building extends to the rights to the use of the land plot (lease). In all cases, any real estate to be mortgaged, with the exception of land, must be insured.

Any mortgage must be executed as a mortgage bond in a standard form approved by the Ministry of Justice and certified at the notary public. The mortgage is valid only after registration with the Hypothecary Register through the Hypothecary Department at a respective local court.

The creditor has the right to receive satisfaction of its claims from proceeds of the sale of the mortgaged property prior to all other creditors. The claims secured by the mortgage include payment of the principal, the interest and the expenses of debt recovery. If proceeds from the sale of the mortgaged assets are insufficient to cover all the debt, the mortgagee's claim for the balance is in line with claims of other ordinary creditors (a certain sequence applies to satisfaction of claims of non-secured creditors).

Upon conveyance of the mortgaged property to another person, the mortgage follows the property. The mortgagee has the right to transfer the mortgage claim or a part thereof, unless the mortgage agreement provides otherwise. Further, the mortgagee is also entitled to pledge the mortgage claim for securing its own obligations to third parties provided that the term of repayment of such a loan does not exceed the term of repayment of the debts stipulated in the mortgage bond.

Registration of real estate and rights to it

Land plots, buildings and other real estate, rights *in rem* to real estate (such as mortgage, servitude etc), long-term lease and restriction of such rights as well as juridical facts (eg attachments, lawsuits, transactions related to real estate or the restriction of rights *in rem* thereto) are registered with the Real Estate Register. The latter is administered by the State Enterprise of Cadastre and Register of Land and Other Real Estate, which consists of central and territorial registrars (branches).

Only legally registered real estate may be sold or otherwise disposed of. Further, the rights *in rem* to real estate as well as restrictions of such rights could be registered with the Real Estate Register provided such real estate has been legally registered.

As a result of the Civil Code that came into effect on 1 July 2001, failure to register the agreements related to real estate (sale–purchase, lease, gratuitous lease etc) does not cause invalidity of the agreement. However, in the cases provided by the Civil Code, failure to register such agreements will preclude parties thereto from invoking them against third persons (eg a lessee of a building could not rely on the lease agreement against a new owner of the building if such agreement was not registered). If the same real estate or rights *in rem* thereto have, for some reason, been acquired by two persons and one of them has registered the agreement and the other has not, it is considered that the real estate or right *in rem* has been acquired by the person who has registered the agreement. Thus, for the purpose of the security of an investor's interests it is always advisable to register the agreements related to real estate or restriction of rights *in rem* thereto with the Real Estate Register without undue delay.

Transactions concerning legally registered immovable cultural valuables must be registered with the Department of Protection of Cultural Valuables under the auspices of the Ministry of Culture within a period of three months from the execution of such transactions.

With certain exceptions, all data contained in the central data bank of the Real Estate Register are publicly accessible. Any person, having paid a set fee, can check information regarding the legal status of any real estate registered with the Real Estate Register.

2.10

Telecommunications

Lideika, Petrauskas, Valiūnas ir Partneriai

Introduction

The extensive development of the Lithuanian telecommunications sector began in the last decade. In 1991, UAB Omnitel was the first in Lithuania to launch public mobile telecommunications services. Two new mobile operators, UAB Bitė GSM and UAB Tele2, entered the mobile telecommunications market in 1995 and 1999 respectively. Provision of the public fixed telephone communications services at the time remained under the exclusive rights of the incumbent operator Lithuanian Telecom (AB Lietuvos telekomas). In the middle of 1998, Lithuanian Telecom was partially privatized by Amber Teleholding A/S, a consortium of Telia (Sweden) and Sonera (Finland), which acquired 60 per cent of shares.

The first Law on Telecommunications of 9 June 1998 provided for the liberalization of the telecommunications market from 31 December 2002 and established Lithuanian Telecom's monopoly rights to operate, until this date, the fixed telephone communications network and provide fixed telephone communications services. Without the aforementioned major telecommunications players, at the end of 2002 there were over 300 private companies engaged in the provision of telecommunications services in Lithuania, mostly related to internet access and data transmission.

The new version of the Law on Telecommunications, adopted on 5 June 2002 and effective from 1 January 2003, has notably changed the regulatory environment for telecommunications. In particular, it revised regulation of telecommunications activities with a view to the demonopolization of the fixed telephone communications market from 1 January 2003. Generally, the new regulatory regime follows the provisions of the European Union's (EU's) telecoms regulatory package of 1998 as well as certain features of the new regulatory framework of 2002. However, the Law on Telecommunications was not intended to, and does not, fully implement the provisions of the 2002 EU telecoms regulatory framework. Therefore, it is planned that a single legislation on electronic communications in line with the new EU directives will have to be introduced in the very near future by a new Law on Electronic Communications. Thus, the present telecommunications regulation will, to a greater or lesser degree, be reversed one more time. It would seem however that this is unlikely to take place before 2004.

This chapter gives an overview of the regulation of the main issues in the telecommunications sector under the Law on Telecommunications and other legal acts accompanying it.

Authorizations

The Law on Telecommunications revokes the previous framework under which an undertaking willing to start providing telecommunications services had to obtain a licence or a permit issued by the state authorities, depending on the nature of services. Under this law, from 1 January 2003 engagement in telecommunications activity is not subject to any prior and explicit authorization or licence. However, there are certain preconditions that should be observed by the new market entrants in respective cases.

Firstly, although the Law on Telecommunications does not require authorizations for telecommunications services, it does establish that where the intended activity involves the use of radio frequencies or telephone numbers, the respective undertaking must obtain a permit to use these resources. The Communications Regulatory Authority (CRA) enjoys the sole authority to issue the permits in accordance with the regulations regarding the national numbering plan and allocation of radio frequencies. Based on the Law on Telecommunications, there are three ways in which the permits may be issued:

- upon the request of the applicant;
- by way of tender;
- by way of auction.

It is also worth pointing out that not every use of radio frequencies is subject to a separate permit. In particular, a separate permit by the CRA is not required when the legal acts providing for general conditions for engagement in telecommunications activity directly grant the right to use certain radio frequencies.

Secondly, in case the intended activity falls within the list of telecommunications activities to be notified to the CRA, the undertaking must notify the CRA 28 days prior to launching such an activity. Although prior authorization from the CRA is not officially required, the CRA may object if the application does not conform to the general conditions for respective activity. Currently, the list of telecommunications activities that must be notified to the CRA includes three types of activities:

- provision of public fixed telephone communications network and/or public fixed telephone communications services;
- provision of public mobile telephone communications network and/ or public mobile telephone communications services;
- provision of leased lines.

Under the Law on Telecommunications, undertakings engaging in telecommunications activity must pay to the CRA the remuneration for the services provided to it by the CRA, particularly for compliance supervision.

Significant market power operators

Until 1 January 2003 the telecommunications market was subject to general competition rules prohibiting abuse of dominant position and providing other measures to ensure competition in the market, besides several specific provisions applicable to dominant operators (particularly, Lithuanian Telecom). Based on the concept from the EU telecoms directives, the Law on Telecommunications introduced the notion of significant market power (SMP) and set forth a number of obligations that may be applied to operators notified as having SMP.

Under the Law on Telecommunications, the CRA is the authority competent to determine, upon performance of market analysis and assessment of shares of the undertakings in the market, that a particular undertaking has SMP in the relevant market. Generally, a share of over 25 per cent by default serves as a guideline that the respective undertaking has SMP. However, the CRA may determine that an undertaking with a share of less than 25 per cent on the relevant market has SMP or, vice versa, that an undertaking with a share of over 25 per cent on the relevant market does not have SMP. In exercising this determination, the CRA shall duly evaluate the undertaking's ability to influence the market, its control over final customers' access to services and certain other factors.

Based on the Law on Telecommunications, the main additional obligations which may be applicable to operators and providers of services having SMP in the relevant market are as follows:

- to meet all reasonable and technically viable requests to interconnect networks;
- to make available to the public information related to access to or interconnection of the networks in line with requirements laid down by the CRA;
- to offer cost-oriented tariffs for interconnection and access to networks;

- to follow the principles of non-discrimination and transparency when providing access to or interconnection of the networks;
- to implement a separate accounting of costs related to interconnection and provision of access to the network;
- to introduce the possibility of carrier preselection on its network (for Lithuanian Telecom as SMP on fixed telephone market, from 1 January 2003; for SMPs on mobile telephone services and network markets, from 1 January 2004);
- to introduce subscriber number portability (from 1 January 2004).

Interconnection

In accordance with the Law on Telecommunications, all telecommunications operators and service providers within categories listed by the CRA have the right and, upon receipt of the request, the obligation to negotiate interconnection of networks. Currently, the following categories of undertakings are included in the list:

- telecommunications operators and service providers that provide public fixed and/or mobile telephone communications networks and/or public telephone communications services and control access to termination points of the network identified by unique telephone numbers;
- telecommunications operators and service providers that provide leased lines services;
- other telecommunications operators and service providers that may be granted the right to interconnect telecommunications networks by legal acts.

The Law on Telecommunications prohibits SMPs in the relevant markets from rejecting requests of other operators to interconnect public telecommunications networks, unless the request is not reasonable or may not be implemented technically. The regulations of the CRA seem to extend the obligation to interconnect to all undertakings within the aforementioned categories.

With an aim to prevent abuse of telecommunications operators that are requested to provide interconnection, it is required that telecommunications networks must be interconnected within three months of the day of receipt of the request. If the parties fail to complete negotiations within this period, any of the parties may refer to the CRA, which exercises its authority to resolve the dispute and must do this within two months.

Interconnection agreements must conform to the general conditions of interconnection of telecommunications networks as approved by the CRA. Importantly, the Law on Telecommunications also requires that interconnection tariffs applied by the telecommunications operator having SMP in the relevant market must be cost-oriented.

Price regulation

The regulation of prices is foreseen with regard to several telecommunications services. Firstly, the Government may establish ceilings on prices of the following universal services:

- public telephone communications services at a fixed location;
- public pay telephones;
- directory services;
- ensuring the possibility to use telecommunications services for persons with physical disabilities or those with special social needs;
- other services which the Government may include in the list of universal services in the future.

Secondly, public fixed telephone telecommunications network operators and service providers having SMP in the market (currently Lithuanian Telecom) are obliged to offer cost-oriented prices, which may include a reasonable return on investments. All telecommunications operators and service providers having SMP in the relevant market are prohibited from cross-subsidizing the services offered on a competitive basis and are required to ensure unbundled and non-discriminatory pricing.

Collocation and facility sharing

A telecommunications operator may request collocation or facility sharing from another operator provided it is impossible to construct new telecommunications lines or install new telecommunications equipment or the costs of exercising such right would be unreasonably high. In the presence of these circumstances, the CRA may refer to any other telecommunications operator and demand that the latter allows joint use of the existing telecommunications infrastructure if this is economically expedient and does not require essential additional work to be performed.

Collocation and facility sharing must be based on a contract between the respective parties. In the aforementioned circumstances, the operator owning the telecommunications infrastructure may not refuse to conclude a contract on joint use of the infrastructure or terminate the contract already concluded, unless the other party is in default.

The CRA has approved the regulations on the joint use of conduits, cable ducts, collectors, towers and poles, which are mandatory for all telecommunications operators performing their activity in Lithuania. In accordance with these rules, the price for the use of the telecommunications infrastructure, irrespective of whether or not its possessor has SMP in the relevant market, must be cost-oriented.

Unbundling of local loop

Along with liberalization of the telecommunications market, the Law on Telecommunications establishes that the notified operator, who has SMP on the fixed telephone network and services market, has the obligation to provide access to a local loop. Such an operator (currently Lithuanian Telecom) must, upon request of the other telecommunications service provider, provide access to a local loop on a non-discriminatory basis. Access to this last segment of the fixed telephone network may be refused only due to objective reasons or the necessity to ensure the integrity of the network.

The current regulatory framework provides that the parties must reach an agreement on access to a local loop within two months of the request. Otherwise, the requesting party may refer to the CRA for resolution of the dispute; in such cases the CRA must adopt the final decision on the matter within three months.

The notified operator is obliged to publish a reference offer on access to a local loop. The CRA enjoys the right to demand amendments to the published offer. Under the Law on Telecommunications, prices for access to a local loop and related services must be cost-oriented, including a reasonable return on investments. The CRA is granted the right to establish the ceilings on prices for access to a local loop and related services.

2.11

Dispute Resolution

Lideika, Petrauskas, Valiūnas ir Partneriai

Court system

The Lithuanian court system consists of courts of general jurisdiction and specialized courts. Courts of general jurisdiction deal with civil and criminal matters and include:

- the Supreme Court;
- the Court of Appeals;
- district courts;
- local courts.

The system of specialized administrative courts was established at the start of 1999 to investigate administrative litigations. This consists of the following courts:

- the Supreme Administrative Court of Lithuania;
- district administrative courts.

Judges of the Supreme Court are appointed by the *Seimas* (Parliament), while judges of the Court of Appeals are appointed by the president upon approval by the *Seimas*. Judges of the district and local courts are appointed by the president.

The doctrine of precedent was not acknowledged earlier in Lithuanian law. Nevertheless, the Senate of the Supreme Court has been analysing court practice and adopting recommendations in order to promote equitable decisions. Now *stare decisis* is in the development process in Lithuania; as of April 1998 interpretations of law in published decisions of plenary sessions or panels of the Supreme Court must be taken into consideration by other courts as well as Governmental and non-Governmental institutions.

The Constitutional Court of the Republic of Lithuania is not a part of the court system but is an independent judicial body. The Constitutional

Court has the authority to determine whether the laws and other legal acts adopted by the *Seimas* conform to the Constitution, and whether the legal acts adopted by the president and the Government conform to the Constitution or laws.

Courts of general jurisdiction: first instance

Civil court procedures are mainly subject to the Code of Civil Procedure of 28 February 2002 (effective from 1 January 2003). Civil cases may be commenced at local or district courts in the first instance. The local court, as the first instance court, investigates all civil cases except those which have to be commenced at the district court (eg cases where the claim exceeds 100,000 litas, claims concerning non-proprietary authors' legal relations, enterprise bankruptcy and restructuring cases, cases where the foreign state is one of the parties in the proceedings etc). Only Vilnius district court, as the court of first instance, hears cases related to the disputes arising out of the Law on Patents, Law on Trade Marks, cases connected with applications of foreigners for adoption of Lithuanian citizens and certain other cases.

Usually the claim should be presented to the local or district court of the area in which the defendant is residing. However, the Code of Civil Procedure allows the claimant in certain cases to select the appropriate court (eg the claim to the defendant who does not have residence in Lithuania may be presented to the appropriate first instance court of the area in which there is defendant's property, or according to the last known residence address of the defendant). Further, certain claims are subject to exclusive jurisdiction, such as those connected with the rights to real estate, abolishment of attachment imposed on real estate etc. The parties are free to agree on the appropriate court as the place of dispute settlement, though exclusive and specific (ie local, district or Vilnius district court) jurisdictions cannot be changed by the agreement of the parties.

The quorum of the first instance court is one professional judge.

Courts of general jurisdiction: appellate jurisdiction

In civil cases three types of appeal may be distinguished:

- appeal;
- complaints;
- cassation.

Appeal

The decision of the first instance court becomes final and enforceable provided no appeal has been presented within 30 days of the date of the decision (or within 40 days for individuals residing or legal persons having their registered address in a foreign country). The appeal must be filed with the court whose decision is being appealed against. The right of appeal is vested upon any party of the case. Claims that were not presented in the first instance court are prohibited in the appeal. No new evidence may be adduced in the appeal unless it was not possible to present it at the first instance court or if the first instance court refused to accept such evidence or such necessity became apparent only at a later stage.

The decisions of the local court may be appealed against to the district court and the decision of the district court may be appealed against to the Court of Appeals. The appeal is not allowed if the claim amount is less than 250 litas (except for requirements to make payments related to employment relations and the like). The decisions and rulings of the appellate instance court become final and enforceable from the date of their adoption.

Complaint

Another type of appeal is known as a complaint which any person involved in a case may raise against rulings of the first instance court. Such complaints are permitted in those cases specifically defined by the Code of Civil Procedure (eg against the rulings for the interlocutory measures as securing of the claim) or when the ruling at issue restrains from further court hearings.

The complaint must be filed through the court having issued the relevant ruling. Having received the complaint, the court of first instance may change its ruling being appealed if it agrees with the arguments of the complaint, or it may refer the complaint to the appellate instance court. The court of appellate instance will usually examine the complaint under written procedure, unless it finds that oral hearings are necessary. Complaints must be filed within seven days of either the date of the ruling or the date of receipt of the ruling when such rulings are passed in the written procedure.

Cassation

The decisions and rulings of the appellate instance court may be further appealed against to the Supreme Court of Lithuania by submitting a cassation appeal. The possibility of presentation of a cassation appeal is restricted; it is not allowed when the claim amount is less than 5,000 litas (except for claims to make payments related to employment relations and the like), or when the decisions and rulings of the first instance court had not been appealed against to the appellate instance court. The Supreme Court hears cassation appeals only on grounds specifically listed by the Code of Civil Procedure: infringement of material or procedural laws that have substantial importance for the application and interpretation of such laws, provided such infringements may lead to the wrong decision or ruling; deviation of the decision or ruling against which the cassation appeal was submitted from the Supreme Court's practice.

The cassation appeal must be filed directly with the Supreme Court within three months of the date when the decision (ruling) came into force. The respondent must present his reply to the Supreme Court within one month of the date when the cassation appeal was entered on the list of cassation appeals. The quorum of the cassation court will normally be three judges, though in certain cases a panel of seven or eleven judges may hear the cassation appeal. The cassation court generally will hear the cassation appeal under the written procedure, unless the panel of judges decides that oral hearings should be held. The Supreme Court may either confirm the decision (ruling) of the lower instance or overturn it wholly or partly and decide whether or not to return it back to the lower instance court.

Procedures

Normally, oral court hearings are open to all persons over the age of 16 years. The proceedings are governed in the Lithuanian language and attending persons have the right to an appropriate translation. The parties have a limited opportunity to request a closed hearing (only to protect the secrecy of personal and family life, as well as in cases when professional, state or commercial secrets could be disclosed during the oral hearings).

Certain issues foreseen by the Code of Civil Procedure, such as appeal and rulings to return the statement of claim with the decision, are investigated through a written process. Further, where certain criteria are met the Code of Civil Procedure foresees simplified procedures, ie requests for court orders and a documental process. Both of these procedures are carried out in writing and may take a shorter period of time in comparison with the oral hearings. Upon the request of the parties or at its own discretion, the court may pass a ruling regarding interlocutory measures to secure the claim (seizure, injunction etc) provided non-application of such measures would make the enforcement of a future court judgment impossible or more difficult.

For the commencement of a civil action in the court of general jurisdiction, the claimant has to submit his statement of claim to an appropriate court of first instance. The claim together with its appendices must be presented in as many copies as there are parties in the case, including a copy for the court. Upon receipt of such a claim, the court examines whether there are any grounds for rejecting the claim (such as the dispute not being within the jurisdiction of the court, an existing court's decision between the same parties over the same dispute etc). Further, the court checks whether all formal requirements are met (payment of an appropriate stamp duty, signing of the claim by an authorized person and the like).

The defendant has the right to counter-claim and is required to send the court his reply. In his own turn, the plaintiff has to send his replication to the defendant's reply and the latter has to send his rejoinder to the plaintiff's replication. In certain cases, the court may require more preliminary documents. After the collection of all preliminary documents, the date of court hearings is fixed. If the court presumes that a possibility of peace settlement exists or if the law specifically requires the court to use its best efforts to achieve peace settlement (eg in divorce cases), the court may appoint preliminary hearings.

Evidence

Each party must prove the particulars on which its case relies and submit the appropriate evidence. If there is not enough evidence, the court may suggest that the parties submit additional evidence. In some cases prescribed by the Code of Civil Procedure, the court may collect evidence at its own discretion. All evidence must be presented before the court hearings; the court may refuse to accept evidence later if it could have been presented earlier and if the acceptance thereof would delay the case investigation.

The following gives examples of the evidence admitted in civil procedures:

- explanations and statements of the parties;
- witness statements;
- written evidence;
- conclusions of experts;
- photos and sound or view records completed in accordance with legal requirements.

Originals or approved copies of evidence are admitted.

Judgments

Four types of judgments can be distinguished:

- final judgments:
- partial judgments;
- preliminary judgments;
- judgments by default.

Usually the final judgment is announced verbally immediately after the court hearings by announcing the introduction and resolution part and short arguments. Full arguments must be detailed not later than within five days of the announcement of the judgment. A written judgment must be sent to all the parties of the case not later than five days from its announcement. In complex cases, the adoption and announcement of the judgment may be postponed for not longer than 14 days.

When only a part of the demands stated in the claim is resolved, a partial decision is passed. Preliminary judgments may state how the case would be solved provided some conditions were met.

In certain cases prescribed by the Code of Civil Procedure – eg if one of the parties that was properly informed about the time and place of proceedings did not appear in the hearings and did not request to hear the case without its participation – a judgment by default may be passed. The party against which such judgment by default is passed has the right to apply for its revision. The court has the right to restart the court hearings provided it establishes that circumstances explaining the absence in the first court hearings are important and if the evidence stated in the application for the revision may have some impact on the validity of the judgment.

Litigation costs and enforcement

In courts of general jurisdiction, litigation costs consist of the stamp duty and costs related to the court hearings (costs related to the discovery of the defendant, service of court documents, amounts paid to experts and the like). Usually the plaintiff has to pay a respective stamp duty on the submission of the claim statement although some exceptions are foreseen by the Code of Civil Procedure. The amount of stamp duty will differ depending on the type of claim. In some cases the paid stamp duty may be returned. The losing party has to pay litigation costs to the winning party.

The enforcement of all judgments, rulings, decisions and orders of general jurisdiction courts is vested in bailiffs. Bailiffs are considered state officers and are appointed by the Minister of Justice, although they do have a certain autonomy. The activity area of the bailiffs is prescribed by the Minister of Justice.

Enforcement documents should be presented for their execution to the bailiff in which activity area such execution should take place. Enforcement costs depend on certain criteria but mainly on a particular type of enforcement action and the amount that was received as a result of the enforcement. The limits of enforcement costs are established by the Minister of Justice.

Administrative courts

Administrative courts hear cases related to the legality of acts adopted and actions taken by state administrative bodies, tax disputes, cases related to the breach of laws on elections and referenda and other cases of an administrative nature.

Arbitration

Although in Lithuania commercial disputes are most commonly adjudicated through the courts, alternative dispute resolution, including arbitration in the first place, is gradually gaining popularity and trust among businessmen, particularly in relation to international business transactions. The principal law governing commercial arbitration is the Law on Commercial Arbitration of 2 April 1996. Lithuania has also been party to the 1958 New York Convention on the Recognition and Enforcement of Foreign Arbitral Awards (the New York Convention) since 1995. It should be noted that the Law on Commercial Arbitration was drafted on the basis of the UNCITRAL Model Law on International Commercial Arbitration, with several modifications.

Institutional and ad hoc arbitration

The Law on Commercial Arbitration recognizes both institutional and ad hoc arbitration. Permanent arbitration institutions may be established by Lithuanian public organizations representing Lithuanian economic entities engaged in industry, business and legal activities (eg chambers of commerce or trade associations). Currently, there are a few main permanent arbitration institutions in Lithuania, among which the Arbitration Court at the Association International Chamber of Commerce – Lithuania (established in 1997) is most well known.

Although arbitration institutions in Lithuania do not yet have a solid operational background, they offer relatively inexpensive and efficient dispute resolution services, including those for international commercial disputes.

Arbitrable disputes

The Law on Commercial Arbitration applies to the resolution of commercial disputes. According to Article 2 of the Law on Commercial Arbitration, a commercial dispute is a controversy between parties arising from contractual or non-contractual legal relations, but does not include disputes that may not be submitted to arbitration. The list of non-arbitrable disputes includes the following:

- disputes arising from constitutional, employment, family or administrative legal relations;
- disputes related to competition law, patents, trade marks and service marks, and bankruptcy;
- disputes arising from consumer contracts.

Disputes involving state or municipal enterprises, institutions or organizations may not be submitted to arbitration without advance consent by the founder of such an entity.

Form of arbitration agreements

An arbitration agreement may be in the form of an arbitration clause in a contract or in the form of a separate agreement concluded by the parties. According to the Law on Commercial Arbitration, the arbitration agreement must be executed in writing. Where an executed contract of the parties refers to a document containing an arbitration clause, such reference will constitute the arbitration agreement provided the contract is in writing and the reference is an inseparable part of the contract.

Appeals against arbitral awards

One of the advantages of arbitration is that arbitral awards may be appealed only on limited grounds. Under the Law on Commercial Arbitration, appeal against an arbitration award may be made to the Court of Appeals on limited procedural grounds (generally similar to those enumerated in the UNCITRAL Model Law). An arbitral award may be set aside by the Lithuanian Court of Appeals if it finds, for example, that the subject matter of the dispute is not arbitrable or that the procedure of arbitration is not in accordance with the agreement or law.

Effect and enforcement of arbitral awards

An arbitral award is effective and binding on the parties from the moment it is made and generally has the same effect as a court judgment. If one party refuses to implement the award, the other party has the right to apply to the district court operating in the same location of the arbitral tribunal for a writ of execution. Arbitral awards are enforced by bailiffs under a procedure similar to the one that applies to the enforcement of court decisions.

Foreign arbitral awards

An arbitral award made in any state that is a party to the New York Convention is recognized and enforced in Lithuania. An award made in a state that is not a party to the New York Convention might be recognized and enforced on the grounds of reciprocity. The party requesting recognition and enforcement of a foreign arbitral award has to supply the Lithuanian Court of Appeals with an original or a certified copy of the award, together with an original or a certified copy of the arbitration agreement (with translations, if applicable).

A request to recognize and enforce a foreign arbitral award is considered in an open sitting of the Court of Appeals. Decisions of the Court of Appeals may be appealed against to the Lithuanian Supreme Court in the three-month period. This court considers appeals without oral hearings.

Recognition or enforcement of an arbitral award made in a country which is a party to the New York Convention may be refused in Lithuania only on the limited grounds contained in Article V of this Convention. Recognized foreign arbitral awards are enforced in Lithuania under a procedure that is similar to the enforcement of local court judgements.

Part Three

Finance, Accountancy and Taxation

3.1

Banking and the Financial Services Sector

Kevin R Smith, AWS Structured Finance Ltd

Introduction

As with any sector in an emerging economy, the financial services sector has undergone massive change in recent years and this change is far from over. All three of the countries in the Baltic States are small; Lithuania is the largest of the three but still only has a population of some 3.7 million. This makes some aspects of change easier but other aspects more difficult.

It remains a common misconception that the Lithuanian currency (litas) is in some form restricted. This is not the case – the litas has been fully convertible for some years.

Banks

At the end of 2002 the Lithuanian banking sector had some 10 banks (including the new VB Mortgage Bank), four foreign bank branches and two bank representative offices. The three largest banks still account for a market share of 74 per cent, despite the fact that this continues to decline slowly due to increased competition. As at 1 January 2003 total assets in the banking system grew 12.2 per cent from the previous year and amounted to 17.2 billion litas, continuing the solid growth in recent years.

As evidenced by the continual growth in banking assets, the number of bank accounts and outstanding loans continues to grow. Loans to individuals increased by 63 per cent to 1.16 billion litas in the first 11 months of 2002; this is expected to grow by a further 40 per cent in 2003.

All of the main Lithuanian banks have now been privatized with the last three, Lietuvos Taupomasis Bankas, the Lithuanian Agricultural

Bank and the Lithuanian Development Bank, being sold in 2002 to Estonian, German and Scandinavian buyers respectively. Partly as a result of the privatizations, registered share capital in the sector continued to grow as did the percentage owned by foreign investors – up from only 16 per cent in 1996 to 88 per cent at the end of 2002. Capital adequacy in the system is good at 14.75 per cent easily exceeding the 10 per cent required by the Central Bank.

As in other countries in this region many of the banks are competing in the same sector and many of the banks initially focused on foreign companies operating in Lithuania and the larger local corporates. Competition has been fierce and has resulted in a number of the banks widening their focus and looking at smaller corporates and the retail sector where competition is also now very fierce.

Given the close proximity of Scandinavia, the Finnish and Swedish banks have had quite a lot of influence on the banking sector although this has not been as pronounced as it has been in Estonia and Latvia. Their influence is obvious and can be seen in the growth and sophistication of electronic banking, back office systems, customer service and other areas.

Overall, the banking sector is both well developed and sophisticated and offers the vast majority of products and services that would be expected in any developed market economy. Telephone and Internet banking is widely available from the majority of banks although at this stage it has not been taken up by many Lithuanians.

The provision of leasing services has become very popular with the market increasing by 56 per cent in 2002 to a total market of 1.7 billion litas. This is on top of growth of some 60 per cent in 2001; the market is forecast to grow by a further 35 per cent in 2003.

One part of the banking sector that until recently has been quite slow to make much progress is the provision of residential mortgages but this market is now growing very quickly. It is undoubted that this market will become very important in the future but due to factors, such as legislation, that make it difficult for the lender to repossess the property in need and the lack of long-term loans it has taken a while to gather momentum. However, all this is beginning to change and most of the bigger commercial banks are now competing aggressively to promote residential mortgages and are experiencing very rapid growth in the size of their mortgage portfolios (albeit from a low starting point). This competition is leading to the availability of longer-term loans and lower interest rates which in turn increases demand still further. Indeed residential mortgages represented more than 85 per cent of all new loans to individuals in 2002.

Another part of the banking sector that has been relatively slow to take off, but is now doing so, is the debit and credit card market. The majority of Visa cards and Mastercards are actually debit cards rather than credit cards as in the UK, but the number of transactions in which these cards have been used is now rapidly increasing.

Financing trade and projects

Approximately 90 per cent of all trade in the European Union (EU) is conducted on an open account basis although many companies have some form of credit insurance. Trade with Lithuania has not as yet reached this level but continues to move towards it.

Over the years there have been many successful projects financed on a non-recourse project finance basis. These have been structured both with and without assistance from the British Export Credit Guarantee Department (ECGD) and other export credit agencies. In recent times the ECGD has changed its policy on financing projects in the region in order to secure more business; this means that projects that were previously unable to obtain cover can now do so. Perhaps the most important change is that the ECGD no longer needs a Government guarantee in certain circumstances but will sometimes consider municipality or large local corporate risk and this practice is spreading to include countries such as Lithuania. In addition, the private insurance market has an increasing appetite for risk in the Baltic States.

The trend towards financing major projects by way of partnerships established between central and/or local Government and private companies has not been ignored in Lithuania although they have not made very much progress on this front and are some way behind many of their neighbours. However, as recognition grows regarding the impact that public–private partnerships (PPPs) can have in developing infrastructure such as roads, rail, water treatment plants and many other large projects, it is expected that momentum will start to build shortly.

In order to make these projects happen, typically laws need to change and attitudes and ideas need to become more flexible. However PPPs offer the most realistic way to finance many of the projects required and, as this becomes more widely understood, the number of PPP projects in the country will increase dramatically. As Britain and British-based firms are world leaders in this type of finance, the development of this sector in Lithuania should be seen as offering many opportunities in the future.

Investment funds

A small number of investment funds and providers of private equity have been active in Lithuania for many years; their role is however continuing to expand as the country's economic growth continues. In an effort to promote the sector the European Bank for Reconstruction and Development (EBRD) has invested in a number of the funds although it is true to say that the majority of equity funds have their roots in either Scandinavia or the USA. In very simple terms the preferred scenario for a fund is to invest between US $1 million and US $5 million in a joint venture company with a local partner and a foreign strategic investor. Clearly this is over-simplified and, for the right project, both smaller and much larger funds can be found. In theory, any commercially sound project can attract funds.

A number of the locally based funds are effectively subsidiaries of the more global funds or linked to banks. As the market continues to mature and stabilize the growing demand for this type of funding is being met by the creation of new funds and the expansion of existing ones. The sector remains difficult given the constraints in which it operates but steady growth is expected to continue.

Insurance

Life insurance, as in all the emerging markets, is very underdeveloped in comparison to Western Europe or the USA, as is the private pensions industry. However the market has now started to grow quite quickly. During the first 11 months of 2002 non-life insurance premiums totalled 675 million litas and life insurance premiums for the same period amounted to 115 million litas – both figures comfortably exceeding the forecasts for the entire year. Newly introduced tax incentives and a flow of new products are expected to ensure that the life insurance market continues to grow strongly during 2003. At the end of 2002 over 10 life insurance companies operated in Lithuania of which Lietuvos Draudimas, ERGO Lietuva, Preventa and IF Draudimas were the largest.

The development of private pensions is also now taking hesitant steps forward. As with every country there is an urgent need to move away from the provision of pure state systems and legislation has been changed to allow the implementation of the second pillar (mandatory contributions to a private pension fund) and the third pillar (voluntary contributions to a private pension fund).

The non-life and general insurance sector is, in general, reasonably well developed but the sector has been hampered by the difficulties in assessing real claims and the low level of payouts made in the past. Third-party motor insurance was made compulsory in April 2002 and this, together with a number of other changes, has stimulated growth in the non-life sector. There are now over 20 general insurance companies present, of which the strongest are Lietuvos gyvybes draudimas, ERGO gyvybes draudimas, VB gyvybes draudimas and Commercial Union Lietuvos gyvybes draudimas (a British company).

Legal system

There is a complete section of this book dedicated to legal issues, but given the impact of legislation on doing business in the financial services sector it is considered appropriate to include a very brief outline here.

The legal sector, or more correctly the law, has perhaps undergone more change than any other sector. A number of international law firms are present and many have been instrumental in adapting old legislation and writing new laws. As the Lithuanian economy moves ever closer to a market driven economy, the need for legislation to change to allow the economy to expand and foreign companies to invest and trade in a safe environment becomes ever greater. The scope and depth of these changes has increased significantly as EU membership beckons.

It is true that many of the laws are not directly comparable with UK or EU legislation but much progress has been made. However, implementing new legislation is only one aspect of changing laws. It is widely recognized that the interpretation of new laws can, on occasion, be questionable and it is also generally recognized that there remains an element of corruption that in some cases can undermine the system as a whole. In addition, the judicial system is lacking in experience although this will of course improve over time.

Accountancy

One of the requirements for any company wishing to raise debt or equity funding, trade finance, or establish any form of partnership with a foreign party has been the need to produce accounts to international accounting standards. Lithuanian accounts are often not very transparent, rather brief and open to interpretation and, as such, not very reliable.

All the large foreign accountancy firms are present and the trend towards international accounts continues to move down towards ever-smaller companies. A separate chapter elsewhere in this book considers these issues in more detail.

Stock exchange

As is common with most of the stock markets in the emerging markets, the stock exchange is not very liquid and only has a limited number of companies listed; this can impact on many other aspects of the financial services sector. For example, the limited market restricts the activities of insurance and pension fund asset managers, does not encourage long-term savings which in turn reduces the possibilities of the provision of long-term loans and is not able to act as a provider of fresh capital to fund growth of local companies.

There is a cooperation agreement in place with the London Stock Exchange, and one Lithuanian company (AB Lietuvos Telekomas) is actually listed in London.

Corporate governance

The way in which business is conducted, the transparency of transactions and relationships, minority shareholder rights and general financial management are some of the main concerns behind corporate governance. As with many aspects of the financial services sector in Lithuania, much has been done but more needs to be done. Much effort is now being put into addressing many aspects of corporate governance, and this is expected to become even more of an issue as Lithuania prepares to join the EU.

Regulation

The banking sector is regulated by the Bank of Lithuania which has received considerable praise recently for the progress made in all aspects of its role. The insurance sector is supervised by the State Insurance Supervisory Authority under the Ministry of Finance and the Stock Exchange and other capital markets are supervised by the Securities Commission.

Regulation and supervision of the various parts of the financial services sector is generally regarded as being relatively good and continues to improve although it is recognized that the lack of experienced professionals is a limiting factor.

Summary

The financial services sector has been totally transformed over the last 10 years and although mistakes have been made and there is still more to be done, the progress made has been remarkable and many of the past mistakes have already been recognized and rectified.

3.2

Privatization Process

Lideika, Petrauskas, Valiūnas ir Partneriai

Introduction

The privatization of state property in Lithuania began in 1991. Since then it has been an integral part of economic reforms in the transition from the plan economy (mostly state ownership) to the market economy (where private ownership dominates). The privatization process can be divided into two phases: voucher privatization (1991–1995) and cash privatization (1995–present day).

The aim of voucher privatization was swift voucher-based (including partial payments in cash) privatization of state-owned property. Vouchers in dematerialized form were distributed to all Lithuanian citizens by depositing them in voucher accounts with local banks. For this purpose, over 2.6 million investment accounts were opened with banks, which accumulated vouchers of the value over 10.2 billion litas.

Lithuanians used the possibility to participate in privatization quite actively. During the first stage of privatization 5,714 entities were privatized and a high level of privatization was achieved in different industries. As an example, 98 per cent of construction and 97 per cent of household service sectors were privatized. A significant part of the mass privatization was completed in the agricultural sector – approximately 1,160 state agricultural companies, formerly known as *kolkhozes*, with the total book value of 183.3 million litas were privatized. As a result, some 97 per cent of the assets in the agricultural sector went into private hands.

After 1995, only privatization for cash was allowed. This stage saw the privatization of big companies controlled by the state, such as Lithuanian Telecom, Klaipėda Stevedoring Company (KLASCO) and Lithuanian Insurance. One of most important changes in Lithuanian economy was the privatization of state-controlled banks, namely the Lithuanian Development Bank, Lithuanian Savings Bank and Lithuanian Agricultural Bank.

Cash privatization (1995–present day)

The second stage of privatization was launched by enactment of the Law on Privatization of State-Owned and Municipal Property of 4 July 1995 (Law on Privatization). The new Law on Privatization was adopted on 4 November 1997 to introduce several substantial procedural changes and a new privatization institution – the State Property Fund – which took over the management and privatization of the state properties included in the privatization list.

During 1996–1997, 324 entities were privatized for 84.2 million litas. In 1998 a total of 344 entities were privatized for the amount of 2.33 billion litas, a major part of which was raised through the privatization of 60 per cent of state-owned shares in Lithuanian Telecom. In 1999, a total of 702 entities were privatized for 489.9 million litas, of which the State Property Fund sold 469 entities for 455.9 million litas. During 2000, the State Property Fund sold a total of 717 stakes and real estate properties for 864.9 million litas.

Under the major privatization transactions concluded from 1998 to 2000, the buyers assumed obligations to invest more than 1.9 billion litas into the acquired companies and to retain or create more than 25,000 jobs. In February 2003, the privatization list, which is updated on a regular basis, comprised the state/municipally-owned stakes in more than 3,000 companies for the total of 1.8 billion litas and 2,154 real estate properties.

Such large enterprises as Lithuanian Gas, Lithuanian Energy, Lithuanian Airlines and Lithuanian Railways are in the process of privatization or are scheduled to be privatized in the future. Privatization of the remaining state-owned medium-sized companies, small blocks of shares and real estate properties is also being continued.

Structure

The assets to be privatized are owned either by the state or local municipalities and are managed respectively by the State Property Fund or property funds of municipalities, or other departments of municipality administration (municipal property funds). Municipalities may also assign privatization of their assets to the State Property Fund.

The bodies responsible for privatization are the State Property Fund, the Privatization Commission and municipal property funds and privatization commissions. The State Property Fund operates as a state enterprise controlled by the Government. It administers the state-owned property and prepares it for privatization, as well as heading the privatization process. Municipal property funds perform the same functions with regard to municipal property and are controlled by the

Municipality Councils. The Privatization Commission is a Governmental institution set up for the purpose of privatization supervision and accountable to the *Seimas* (parliament). Municipalities may also form municipal privatization commissions to supervise the privatization of municipal assets.

The privatization process commences with the inclusion of an object into the list of privatization objects which is approved by the Government on the proposal of the State Property Fund. On the proposal of municipalities, the State Property Fund also includes into the privatization list municipal objects that the municipalities decide to privatize. After the privatization object has been prepared for privatization and evaluated, the privatization programme is approved by a respective authority. The list of privatization objects and the privatization programmes are publicly announced.

The State Property Fund and municipal property funds carry out sale of privatization objects by the methods and under other terms and conditions provided in the privatization programmes.

Privatization methods

Privatization methods include the following:

- public sale of shares;
- public auction;
- public tender;
- direct negotiations;
- transfer of control in an enterprise controlled by the state or municipality;
- lease with the purchase option.

In a public sale of shares, the shares are sold publicly on the National Stock Exchange or in foreign securities markets; the selling price for shares is determined according to the supply and demand ratio. Only shares of public companies can be sold by this method.

In case of a public auction the privatization object is sold in an auction, where the number of potential buyers is unlimited. The privatization agreement is concluded with the highest bidder.

During a public tender the privatization object is sold to the winning bidder, whose written offers regarding the price and investment undertakings, subject to the minimum requirements for preservation of jobs etc, are the best. Negotiations for improvement of the bids may be entered into with one or several potential buyers who have submitted the highest bids not differing from each other by more than 15 per cent.

Privatization through direct negotiations results in the sale of the privatization object to the winner of direct negotiations whose written offers have been found to be the best regarding the price and investment, subject to the requirements for preservation of jobs and other conditions stipulated in the privatization conditions. Direct negotiations are usually conducted with strategic investors while privatizing objects of strategic importance.

Transfer of control in the enterprise controlled by the state (municipality) is carried out by the issuance of convertible debentures or new shares for additional contributions. This results, or may result, in the reduction of the state's or municipality's share in the authorized capital falling below the level of two-thirds, one half or one third of all voting shares. This privatization method may only be used if the attempt to sell the shares in the enterprise has failed or when not less than half of the shares owned by the state or municipality in this enterprise have already been privatized in other manner.

Lease with an option to purchase is a public method of privatization when a potential buyer acquires the right to possess and use long-term tangible assets. The potential buyer acquires the title to the privatization object only after having fully paid for the object and meeting other terms set forth in the privatization agreement. Lease with an option to purchase may be applicable to the privatization of long-term tangible assets, the privatization of which has failed by public auction.

Practice

The most common methods of privatization are the public tender and public auction. In cases of public tender, potential investors are usually given the possibility to get acquainted with the privatization object and, in some cases, conduct a due diligence.

Initial price expectancies or price minimum are not always indicated. However, privatization programmes usually contain the requirements for the future investor to maintain a certain percentage of working places and to invest certain amounts of funds into the activities of the privatized company.

After the winner of privatization is chosen, some negotiations with the State Property Fund or municipal property funds are possible, although it is not usually possible to deviate from the conditions of the privatization programme.

Guarantees and indemnities in respect of the enterprises to be privatized are not wilfully issued. The concerns about specific problems discovered during due diligence are usually expected to be taken into account when offering the price. However, in case the tender party is in a strong position (eg it is the only bidder and the privatization of the enterprise is desired), the investor may succeed in including certain guarantees and indemnities into the privatization agreement.

Concerns

The acquisition of more than 40 per cent of shares in a public company (*AB*) may result in the buyer's obligation to submit a mandatory public offer to purchase the remaining shares in that company. It should also be mentioned that if the new owner of the privatized enterprise does not fulfil the undertakings under the privatization agreement, various sanctions may be implied – even an annulment of the privatization.

3.3

Regulation of the Financial Market

Sigitas Zutautas, Lithuanian Financial Analyst Association

Significant progress in the regulation of financial services in Lithuania has been made over the last decade. The development of national financial regulation was begun in the early 1990s after declaration of the country's independence. At the outset, the system was mainly promoted by a number of active individuals; gradually a certain structure and profile of financial regulation and supervisory institutions was established and this has continued for a number of years.

Legal basis

There are laws that regulate the activities of financial institutions. The Law on Companies defines the general principles for establishing and developing an incorporated business. In addition to that, there are a number of laws specific to the national financial industry.

The Law on Commercial Banks defines the specific requirements and principles for banking, which historically makes up the largest portion of the financial market. Activities of credit unions (which did not gain a significant share of the financial market) are defined in the Law on Credit Unions. Similarly, the Law on Insurance regulates the fast growing insurance industry. The Law on the Securities Market, among other things, regulates the operations of the brokerage companies and other financial intermediaries.

A Law on Financial Institutions, which was passed in 2002 and effective from 1 July 2003, is aimed at providing top-level regulation of entities engaged in the provision of various financial services. Among others things, this law defines a financial institution and a financial group as well as establishing the structure of supervision in terms of which supervisory authority is responsible for the financial group that is engaged in providing several supervised activities.

There are a number of other laws and underlying acts, such as decrees of the Government and supervisory institutions, that should also be considered in order to gain a full picture of industry's regulation. Supervisory authorities have also issued several recommendations for particular business activities of the financial institutions. Although not mentioned specifically in many cases, such recommendations are seen as 'best practice' and referred to during inspections by these authorities. The contents of the laws and the compulsory regulations passed by the supervisory authorities may be seen as rather detailed in a number of cases.

As part of the country's process of accession to the European Union (EU), laws and other legal acts have been reviewed a number of times in recent years to bring them in line with relevant EU legislation. Officials claim that a significant convergence has been achieved.

Supervisory authorities

Several authorities are in charge of supervising the players in the financial market. Although the voices that support the idea of a unified financial supervisory authority are getting more powerful with time, such an authority has not yet been created. At present there are three key supervisory institutions:

- the Bank of Lithuania – this acts as a supervisor of commercial banks;
- the Insurance Supervisory Authority – this performs the supervision of insurance companies;
- the Securities Commission – this is a primary supervisor for brokerage companies and other financial intermediaries.

As a general rule, the financial institutions are visited by the supervisor for an on-site inspection on an annual basis. The scope and depth of the inspections vary.

The framework of a consolidated supervision is being developed as financial institutions diversify their activities and the number of financial groups increase. Groups of companies such as a parent bank investing in subsidiaries that provide leasing, factoring, life and/or non-life insurance services and even real estate development are relatively commonplace in Lithuania. The new Law on Financial Institutions (as referred to above) defines that supervision of an entire group of financial institutions will be primarily performed by the authority that supervises the parent company in this group. In such instances however, an insurance subsidiary of the bank will still be obliged to follow the requirements of the Insurance Supervisory Authority in addition to the Bank of Lithuania's requirements for the group as a whole. Certain financial services remain without specific regulation, eg leasing and factoring services are regulated only to the extent that the parent group is regulated.

The supervision process is changing in order to reflect changing business and the internationalization of the financial markets, which is strongly noticeable in Lithuania. The three largest banks in the country – Vilniaus Bankas (a member of SEB Group), Hansa Bankas (a member of Swedbank Group) and Lietuvos Zemes Ukio Bankas (a member of Nord/LB Group) – who jointly account for more than 70 per cent of the Lithuanian banking market in terms of assets, loans and deposits, have expressed their intentions to review many of their risk management policies in order to make them as close to the corresponding policies applied by the parent groups as possible. Such an approach may require a certain amount of flexibility by the regulating authority while judging the level of compliance of these policies with national regulations.

Accounting and reporting

A Law on Companies requires that annual general meetings of all incorporated businesses are held within four months after the end of the financial year (which corresponds to the calendar year in the vast majority of cases). The Law on Commercial Banks brings the deadline for banks forward by one month.

Companies are required to apply national accounting principles, which attempt to comply with the International Financial Reporting Standards (IFRS) in most cases. In addition to that, listed companies are required to file the annual financial statements prepared in accordance with IFRS with the Securities Commission.

Specific requirements apply with regard to accounting and reporting in financial institutions. Banks are required to prepare the annual financial statements in accordance with IFRS and also in accordance with the statutory requirements. Insurance companies have to prepare the annual reporting in accordance with national statutory requirements. Banks and insurance companies then have to publish their summarized financial statements by 31 March of the following year; later deadlines are set for the publication of their full annual reports. In addition, banks are required to publish key risk management indicators on a quarterly basis.

It is general practice that banks appoint a 'Big 4' firm as auditor, while insurance companies and financial intermediaries use both international and local auditors.

Capital market

The Lithuanian capital market is still on a low level. Shares of 10 issuers are listed in the Official List of the National Stock Exchange of Lithuania (NSEL). The secondary listing, called the Current List, is far more extensive; however shares of barely more than 50 companies are traded actively. In addition, only a few corporates have issued debt securities. According to the information of the NSEL, less than 10 per cent of transactions are made in the central market – the remaining ones being over-the-counter transactions.

The market is primarily supervised by the Securities Commission and Central Securities Depository. One of the key objectives of the regulators is to ensure that fair information is delivered to all market members.

Strong initiatives are being formulated by the financial market in order to create an environment that will encourage the development of more derivative financial instruments and the market as a whole. Currently, a number of financial institutions, together with the Lithuanian Free Market Institute, Lithuanian Industrial Confederation and Financial Analyst Association, are contributing to the development of the general principles for mortgage-backed securities.

It is often claimed that the regulation of financial institutions is broadly similar across all three Baltic States. However, each country still has different laws and supervisory authorities that may differ on specific matters.

Summary

The regulatory environment of the financial market is fast developing together with the political and economical situation. A change that occurred in the last can hardly remain unnoticed.

Convergence with EU legislation will undoubtedly have an effect on the national financial environment. Lithuania has to use the remaining years before gaining full EU membership to ensure that joining the EU will be of utmost benefit to its financial market.

3.4

Accountancy and Audit

Deloitte & Touche

Accounting standards

The development of a market economy in Lithuania has triggered changes in its generally accepted accounting principles and practices. The tendency is to synchronize with International Financial Reporting Standards (IFRS) and relevant European Union (EU) regulations. The rate of change varies according to industry depending on the level of regulation. The current legal framework establishes the core basic principles. Generally accepted accounting principles differ depending on the industry. For example, in the highly regulated banking sector banks' statutory financial statements do not differ from those prepared in accordance with IFRS requirements. In contrast, there are differences between the statutory and IFRS financial statements of limited liability companies operating in non-financial industries due to current accounting regulations or an absence of regulations in the areas of accounting treatment and disclosure.

Accounting regulatory framework

The current regulatory framework, developed as an integral part of recent change towards synchronization with IFRS and applicable EU regulations, establishes the core of future developments in accounting standards and is made up of:

- The Accounting Law (6 November 2001, Law No IX-574);
- The Company Law (13 July 2000, Law No VIII-1835);
- The Financial Statements Law (6 November 2001, Law No IX-575);
- The Consolidated Financial Statements Law (6 November 2001, Law No IX-575);
- Various regulations issued by the Ministry of Finance.

The Law on Accounting establishes core financial accounting principles that are binding for limited and unlimited liability legal entities, foreign enterprises' permanent establishments and representative offices, farmers, notaries, attorneys and proprietary businesses. Farmers, notaries, attorneys, proprietary businesses, foreign enterprises' permanent establishments and representative offices, industry specific accounting requirements of the banks and other financial institutions, brokerage companies and pension funds may be regulated by other legal acts with regard to specific accounting requirements.

The Accounting Law requires limited liability business entities to comply with the Business Accounting Standards established by the Accounting Institute of the Republic of Lithuania. These standards are currently in the development stage and will come into force from 1 January 2004. Until that date various regulations issued by the Ministry of Finance partially substitute these absent standards. State and municipal institutions must comply with the requirements of the Accounting Standards of Budget-Funded Institutions approved by the Ministry of Finance. From 1 January 2004 publicly listed companies have to comply with IFRS.

Lithuanian accounting principles in comparison with IFRS

In one key area the absence of Lithuanian rules may lead to important differences with IFRS requirements, namely that relating to accounting for business combinations, subsidiaries, joint ventures and associates. International Accounting Standards (IAS) 22, IAS 27, IAS 31 and IAS 28 (currently relevant regulation for the preparation of the consolidated statements) is in place; however the enforcement date was delayed until 1 January 2004.

Lithuanian accounting may differ from that required by IAS because of the absence of specific Lithuanian rules on recognition and measurement in the following areas:

- impairment of assets (IAS 36);
- treatment of research costs (IAS 38.42);
- treatment of lease incentives (SIC 15);
- construction contracts (IAS 11);
- provisions (IAS 37);
- employee benefit obligations (IAS 19);
- deferred tax (IAS 12);

- accounting for an issuer's financial instruments (IAS 32.18/23);
- non-recognition of financial assets (IAS 39.35);
- hedge accounting for derivatives (IAS 39.142);
- accounting for events after the balance sheet date;
- proposed dividends (IAS 10).

Furthermore, there are no specific rules requiring the disclosure of:

- the fair values of financial assets and liabilities (IAS 32.77);
- the fair values of investment properties (IAS 40.69);
- related party transactions (IAS 24);
- discontinuing operations (IAS 35);
- segment reporting (IAS 14);
- earnings per share (IAS 33).

There are inconsistencies between Lithuanian and IAS rules that could lead to differences for many enterprises in certain areas. Under Lithuanian rules:

- start-up, reorganization and certain other intangible items can be capitalized (IAS 38.57);
- revaluations of tangible fixed assets do not need to be kept up to date (IAS 16.29);
- trading, available-for-sale and derivative financial assets are not recognized at fair value (IAS 39.69);
- trading and derivative liabilities are not recognized at fair value (IAS 39.93);
- operating lease payments are recognized when payable even if this departs from a straight-line basis (IAS 17.25);
- contingent liabilities are not always disclosed (IAS 37.86);
- gains or losses from the sale of an enterprise's own shares are recognized as income (SIC 16);
- extraordinary items are defined more widely (IAS 8.6).

Conclusion

While accounting reform is ongoing and business accounting standards are not yet in force, the statutory financial statements of different companies can be incompatible. Some companies will generally follow IFRS where statutory regulations are absent, others will simply ignore the issues related to impairment, and in certain cases revenue and expenses matching principles, or other general rules. Therefore in order for an outside investor to be able to properly evaluate the financial position and results of the operations of an enterprise, credible financial statements prepared under IFRS (or another internationally accepted method, eg US GAAP) should be obtained.

Auditing

The auditing profession in Lithuania has a relatively short history. As with other professions that are part of an economic infrastructure in a market-oriented society, it simply did not exist as such before independence was restored in 1991. Previously, in a state-planned and managed economy where the owner of the resources and the user of the resources was the state itself, the only relatively similar profession that existed was that of the state controllers who worked for varying Governmental ministries.

The creation of the profession started in the early 1990s when the largest international accounting and auditing firms ('The Big Six' – Arthur Andersen, Deloitte & Touche, Ernst & Young, KPMG, PricewaterhouseCoopers) began entering the market and the newly obtained economic freedom of entities created the need and demand for consulting and accounting services. At this time the auditing profession was not governed by any specific legislation and so several professional unions and associations were created. The first certification procedures were put in place by the most prominent professionals and the local authorities.

At present appropriate auditing legislation is in place; the Lithuanian Chamber of Auditors unites close to 400 certified Lithuanian statutory auditors and National Auditing Standards (NAS) are in force. Further development is taking place in order to ensure quality, consistency and improvement within the audit profession.

Auditing regulatory framework

Audit requirements

The Company Law requires that the annual financial statements of all public companies be audited and that the audit be completed prior to the shareholders' annual general meeting. An audit of the annual financial statements of private companies is obligatory only if at least two of the criteria listed below are met or exceeded:

- annual revenue – 5 million litas (1,448,100 euros);
- average number of pay-roll employees – 50;
- total assets – 2.5 million litas (724,050 euros).

The Law provides for obligatory audits of commercial banks, insurance companies, investment companies and state and municipal enterprises.

As provided by the Company Law, any shareholder of a company or group of shareholders has the right to enter into a contract with an audit company in order to determine whether there are any indications of insolvency, fraudulent activities, misappropriation of assets, loss-yielding contracts or violations of the shareholders' rights.

Auditors

Under the Audit Law, only individuals that have passed the auditor's qualification examination, taken an oath, obtained an auditor's certificate, joined the Auditors' Chamber and become an owner, general partner or an employee of an audit enterprise are authorized to sign statutory audit opinions. An auditor is not allowed to work or hold any other paid position in other companies, except the Auditors' Chamber, auditors' professional associations or academic and scientific fields. Under the Audit Law the minimum entry requirements needed for Lithuanian citizens to take the qualification examination are as follows:

- a university degree;
- three years' professional experience in an audit company;
- an irreproachable reputation.

Non-resident foreigners are eligible for the examination if they have the highest auditor's qualification granted by an authorized institution of a state included in the list of states recognized by the Government of the Republic of Lithuania. The auditor's certification is recognized in the Republic of Lithuania after the individual passes, in Lithuanian, the qualification examination regarding Lithuanian law and taxes.

Audit companies

An audit company is an enterprise incorporated in accordance with Lithuanian laws and included in the list of audit companies. The legal form of the audit company should be one of the following:

- personal enterprise;
- general and limited partnership;
- private limited liability company.

According to the Audit Law:

- only the auditor can be the owner of a personal audit enterprise;
- at least three-quarters of interest in a general and limited partnership must be held by auditors;
- the following shareholders of the private limited liability companies must hold at least three-quarters of the voting rights: auditors, audit companies, audit companies incorporated in the foreign states that are on the list of states approved by the Government.

A company must have valid professional liability insurance for the minimum limit of 50,000 litas (14,113 euros) per year. The maximum fee concentration provision under the Audit Law states that the total fees from one client should not exceed 20 per cent of the total two-year revenues of the audit company.

The audit enterprise may be engaged in the following services only:

- audits;
- other attest services;
- assets appraisal services (only if the appropriate licence is obtained);
- bookkeeping services;
- consulting in accounting, taxes and other business consulting services;
- expertise services in accounting (upon the request of the court);
- enterprise bankruptcy administration procedure services (only if the appropriate licence is obtained).

Chamber of Auditors

The Lithuanian Chamber of Auditors (LCA) is a self-governing non-profit organization unifying all licensed auditors. The LCA's main objectives are:

- coordination of auditors' professional activities;
- organization of audit training and establishment of minimum professional training requirements;
- protection and representation of auditors' interests with the state institutions;
- initiation of the establishment, amendment and development processes of audit and accounting related laws and regulations;

- data collection related to auditors and audit companies;
- public relations.

The LCA undertakes the following activities:

- development, approval and interpretation of the NAS;
- development, approval and interpretation of the auditors' professional ethics code;
- development, approval and interpretation of the Auditors' Court of Honour regulations;
- organization and coordination of auditors' professional and qualification improvement.

The governing body of the LCA is the general meeting of auditors, presidium and administration. The membership of a certified auditor is obligatory. Members are bound to:

- follow the Code of Ethics;
- conduct attest services in accordance with NAS;
- pay the membership fee;
- improve their qualifications;
- follow the resolutions of general meetings or authorized bodies.

National Auditing Standards (NAS)

Statutory audits must be performed in accordance with Lithuanian NAS. Since 2000 the following NAS are in force:

- Objectives and General Principles Governing an Audit of Financial Statements;
- Terms of Audit Engagement;
- Planning;
- Using the Work of Another Auditor;
- Risk Assessments and Internal Control;
- Quality Control for Audit Work;
- Audit Evidence;
- Documentation;

- Using the Work of an Internal Auditor;
- Fraud and Error;
- Analytical Procedures;
- The Auditor's Report;
- Other Information in Documents Containing Audited Financial Statements;
- Auditing in a Computer Information Systems Environment;
- Audit Considerations Related to Entities Using Service Organizations;
- Related Parties;
- Using the Work of an Expert;
- Audit Sampling;
- Audit Evidence, Additional Considerations for Specific Items;
- Subsequent Events;
- Management Representations;
- Going Concern;
- Audit Materiality;
- Audit of Accounting Estimates;
- The Examination of Prospective Financial Information;
- Initial Engagements, Opening Balances;
- Knowledge of the Business;
- Consideration of Laws and Regulations in an Audit of Financial Statements.

The NAS follow the same principles and are, in general, in line with the International Auditing Standards issued by the International Federation of Accountants.

Conclusion

In the present Lithuanian audit environment, an audit infrastructure is required to ensure a high quality statutory audit function and the issuance of correct and credible financial statements by all that practice in the profession. This would include:

- control over the quality of audit services using the principles established by the respective International Auditing Standard;
- rules on auditors and audit firms and mutual recognition;
- a united auditing association;
- national professional standards on auditing based on International Auditing Standards;
- ethical rules and independence based on the IFAC's ethics code;
- disciplinary procedures and a sanctions infrastructure.

Given that the audit profession is relatively young in Lithuania and that most of the regulations were established and developed during the last three–five years, a consistent quality of the statutory auditors' work is not yet in place. Of the 200 audit companies in Lithuania some perform high quality audits while others do not; additionally, some focus mainly on tax-related issues. The step needed to ensure the quality consistency and improvement within the profession will come in the form of the Audit Quality Committee's statutory auditors' work reviews that should commence in 2003.

3.5

Business Taxation

Deloitte & Touche

Introduction

Due to the transition from a centrally planned to a market economy the Republic of Lithuania had to restructure its economic and legislative framework. The Tax Law was no exception – bearing in mind that the previous tax system was totally oriented towards central planning and therefore did not respond to changes in the status of the country and its economy, it was necessary to adopt legislation that could 'fill in the gap'.

Taking into account the circumstances in which the need for the national tax law arose, it is no surprise that the tax law was actually adopted more on an *ad hoc* basis than following any general concept on what the tax system should look like. Later, the practical application of the law very explicitly indicated the need to look at the tax system as a whole. Particular attention needed to be paid to the interaction of separate taxes bearing in mind that the lack of a conceptual approach to the tax system leads to cases of double taxation and/or tax avoidance.

In 2002 Lithuania faced a major reform of the tax system. New laws on value added tax (VAT) and excise tax were harmonized with European Union (EU) *acquis* and requirements of other international organizations. The new laws on corporate income tax and personal income tax were adopted and came into effect.

Structure

The main pieces of legislation such as the Law on Income Tax, Law on Personal Income Tax, and the Law on Value Added Tax were adopted in 2001–2002. Public, private, state and municipal companies are considered separate legal entities; other forms of companies are not. For tax purposes, partnerships and most sole proprietorships are not treated as separate legal entities subject to profits tax; instead, profits are taxed in the hands of the partners or owners.

Currently the tax system of Lithuania consist of the following taxes:

- corporate income tax;
- personal income tax;
- value added tax;
- excise duties;
- real estate tax and land tax;
- environmental taxes (tax on pollution, tax on natural resources);
- inheritance tax;
- fees and charges for services performed by public bodies;
- turnover tax – contributions to State Road Foundation.

Corporate taxation

Taxation

A company is considered resident if it is registered in Lithuania. Permanent establishments of non-resident companies are also required to register as taxpayers in Lithuania. Such non-resident companies are therefore effectively subject to the same rates of taxation as residents.

The Lithuanian tax year generally corresponds to the calendar year. However companies may seek permission to use a tax year that does not correspond to the calendar year. Companies are required to file annual financial statements and tax returns by 1 October of the next tax year. Companies must also file quarterly advance returns on income tax, provided that taxable revenues exceed 100,000 litas.

Residents (corporate entities, partnerships and private (individual) enterprises) and permanent establishments are subject to profit tax on their worldwide income at a standard rate of 15 per cent. The special rate of 13 per cent applies to small companies (with less than 10 employees and an annual turnover below 500,000 litas (approximately 145,000 euros)).

Tax losses may generally be carried forward for a five-year period. Capital losses arising from the sale of securities may be carried forward for a three-year period and may only be offset against gains on sale of securities.

Dividends

Dividends paid or received from abroad are taxed at a rate of 15 per cent and double taxation treaties are applied. Lithuanian legislation also allows the application of tax credit. For Lithuanian entities exempt dividends are included in income. Dividends received from Lithuanian entities are non-taxable. Dividends received pursuant to the participation exemption principle are included in income.

Withholding tax

A withholding tax of 10 per cent is levied on royalties derived from trade marks, licences or business names, and paid to non-resident companies. A withholding tax of 10 per cent is also levied on payments for copyrights and auxiliary rights, patent rights, industrial design, company name and franchise, if this income is paid to non-resident legal entities.

A withholding tax of 15 per cent is imposed on interest to non-resident legal entities as well as payments to non-residents upon the sale or lease of immovable property. A withholding tax of 15 per cent is also levied on dividends paid to residents and non-residents. A participation exemption applies whereby dividends paid are not subject to withholding tax provided that the shareholding is greater than 10 per cent and the holding period of shares is at least 12 months. Withholding taxes on payments to non-residents may be subject to a lower rate, or entirely exempt, if the recipient is located in a country with which Lithuania has entered into a double tax treaty.

Controlled foreign corporation regime

A controlled foreign corporation regime was also presented by the new law on income tax. The highlights of the regulation include the 'positive income' of Controlled Foreign Corporations (CFCs) at least 50 per cent owned by a Lithuanian resident subject to tax in Lithuania ('positive income' will be defined in follow-up legislation) and the *de minimis* rule whereby CFC income is not subject to Lithuanian tax if revenues of the CFC comprise less than 5 per cent of the controlling Lithuanian enterprise's revenues.

Income tax incentives

The incentive applied to reinvested profits has been abolished. Incentives available to credit unions and foreign capital investments will, however, continue to be available until the end of 2003. Subject to pending legislative acts, tax incentives still apply to the following:

- companies producing agricultural products;
- companies established in Free Economic Zones;
- enterprises that employ handicapped employees.

Transfer pricing

Transfer pricing was introduced by the new income law, effective as of 1 January 2002. As of 2003 state revenue authority is granted the right to adjust the value of transactions between related parties, where the transactional value does not reflect the true market price. True market value is deemed to be the amount that can be realized upon an exchange of assets between unrelated parties entering into a direct transaction. State revenue authority will apply transfer pricing methodologies which are to be set by enabling legislation. It is expected that the final transfer pricing regulations will be based on Organization for Economic Cooperation and Development (OECD) guidelines.

Thin capitalization

Lithuania has no thin capitalization rules in place. Interest incurred pursuant to a written agreement is generally deductible.

Specifics for loans from shareholders
Interest arising on a loan from a shareholder may be recognized only to the extent that the rate of interest on the obligation does not exceed the average rate of interest on Government securities offered by the Republic of Lithuania for the previous quarter. Interest in excess of this set rate incurred on shareholder loans may not be deducted for tax purposes.

Capital gains tax

Capital gains are included in taxable income and are subject to tax at the regular tax rate.

Value added tax

A new law on VAT came into effect on 1 July 2002. This law is harmonized with the provisions of the EU 6th VAT Directive. The law provides for a clear definition of taxable supply: the supply of goods for consideration within the territory of Lithuania by a taxable person. Precise regulation of goods for private use is also provided and special taxation conditions for agreements on property contributions are defined. The time of supply is no longer tied to the issuance of a VAT invoice, but to the moment goods and services are transferred or a consideration received.

A major change from current law is the taxation of non-resident entities. Goods sold and services rendered from abroad will be taxable without any exceptions. For non-residents there is an obligation to appoint a fiscal agent and compute VAT. For those non-residents who did not register as VAT payers, a reverse charge will be applied. Goods sold and services rendered by non-residents will be subject to VAT.

Other highlights include the fact that transport services will include pipelines and electricity transmission lines and the annual VAT declarations. Lease of fixed assets will be levied with VAT only if related to commercial activities. Input VAT on vehicles purchased will no longer be recoverable. In some cases VAT will be due upon receipt of advance payments.

Taxable supply

The new law provided for a clear definition of that which is subject to VAT, namely if the supply of goods and services is:

- for consideration;
- within territory;
- performed by a taxable person;
- for import.

Goods are considered to be tangible goods (movable and not), as well as electricity, heat, gas, etc together with rights *in rem* (long-term lease, collateral rights, usufruct), per Book IV of Civil Code.

Pursuant to the law provisions, services are deemed to be activities and their results, the transfer of property rights, the transfer of securities and construction, rent and leasing.

Rates

Except for a number of exempt items, all goods and services are subject to VAT at a standard rate of 18 per cent. A special rate of 5 per cent applies to public transport services provided on certain routes, medicines, books, publications; a 9 per cent rate applies to the supply of heating energy. There also exists a rate of 6 per cent for certain agricultural products and services. Exports are zero-rated. A reverse charge applies to services rendered by non-residents.

Social, education, medical services, radio and television, sport activities, as well as postal, insurance and finance services are VAT exempt.

Personal income tax

Residence

Pursuant to the law on personal income tax a person is deemed to be permanent residence if he/she:

- is domiciled in Lithuania;
- has the centre of his/her vital interests in Lithuania more than abroad;
- stays in Lithuania more than 183 days during the taxable period;
- stays in Lithuania for more than 280 days during the sequent taxable periods, if in one period the person stays in Lithuania no less than 90 days.

Taxable income

Taxable income may differ depending on the residency of the individual. Permanent residents pay income tax on worldwide income. Residents mentioned in the last two points above pay income tax on Lithuanian-sourced income: interest, dividends, income from immovable assets, situated in Lithuania, labour-related income, income from sport and performing activities, royalties and income from registered movable assets sold. Non-residents pay tax on income from individual activity through PE and on Lithuanian-sourced income.

Income tax rates

Income tax rates are as follows:

- 15 per cent – dividends and interest, income from real estate situated in Lithuania, income from property sold, income from individual activity, income of sportsmen and performers, royalties and life insurance payments.
- 33 per cent – all other income.

Non-taxable income

The law provides for a finalized list where concrete income is stated. It includes allowances, compensations, insurance payments, interest and other income received under strictly prescribed conditions.

Credit for taxes paid abroad on foreign source income

Tax is included to the extent of the tax amount computed in Lithuania.

Tax treaties

Currently, Lithuania has effective conventions for the avoidance of double taxation and prevention of fiscal evasion with respect to taxes on income and capital with Belarus, Canada, China, Croatia, Czech Republic, Denmark, Estonia, Finland, France, Germany, Iceland, Ireland, Italy, Kazakhstan, Latvia, Moldova, the Netherlands, Norway, Poland, Slovenia, Sweden, Turkey, Ukraine and the USA.

Property tax

Legal entities and non-residents that possess or hold Lithuanian buildings, constructions and land pay property tax. Technological equipment is not taxable. The property tax rate is 1 per cent, depending on the total appraised value of taxable property.

Stamp duties

Stamp duties are paid for actions performed or documents issued by state institutions. The Lithuanian Government confirms the stamp duty rates.

Land lease tax

Corporate and personal enterprises are obliged to pay tax on land lease. Taxes on lease of state land are:

- 1.5 per cent on agricultural land;
- 3 per cent on urban land.

Road tax

Road tax is paid from a turnover. Depending on the type of company's activity, rates from 0.3 to 0.48 may be applied.

Other

Both employers and employees must make social security contributions. Employees make a contribution equal to 1 per cent of their wages. Employers make a contribution equal to 31 per cent of total wages.

Tax is charged on gifts and inheritances consisting of real estate, shares and securities, precious metals and cash. The rates are 5 per cent on inheritances with a taxable value of up to 500,000 litas and 10 per cent on inheritances with a taxable value in excess of that amount. Gifts from spouses, parents and children are non-taxable, gifts from other persons are only taxable if the value exceed 6,960 litas.

Excise duties are levied on the sales price or customs value of certain goods, including tobacco products, alcohol, gasoline, and certain luxury goods. Rates vary, depending on the goods.

Other taxes include levies on the use of natural resources and on the pollution of the environment.

3.6

Mergers and Acquisitions: Market Overview

Rytis Jakaitis, Arunas Raščius, Prime Investment

Introduction

Having lagged behind its central and eastern European neighbours – and to some extent even its smaller Baltic neighbours, Latvia and Estonia – in both overall mergers and acquisitions (M&A) activity and the size of individual transactions, Lithuania has, since 2002, been one of the most dynamic M&A markets in Central and Eastern Europe. It is also likely that it will continue to draw the attention of M&A practitioners in the next couple of years.

The entry of Jukos into Mažeikių Nafta (the national oil company in which it replaced Williams International as a strategic investor) and privatization of Lietuvos dujos (the gas distribution monopoly) to EON and Gazprom, which captured the spotlight in 2002, seem to be just a prelude to a flurry of privatization announcements. The Government has put the national airline, two energy distribution companies, two shipping companies and four alcohol producers up for sale. At the same time impressive economic growth combined with availability of cheap financing is likely to facilitate domestic consolidation activity while growing consumption and strong high-tech and manufacturing potential provides a strong investment incentive to foreign strategic investors looking to expand their markets or seeking a cost-efficient production base.

Market development to date

Despite its currently accelerating development, the Lithuanian M&A market is still in its early years of evolution. It made its first steps with the start of the mass privatization programme in 1991, shortly after the restoration of independence. The sale of the Klaipeda tobacco factory to Phillip Morris and Kaunas Confectionery to Kraft Jacobs Suchard in 1993 were the first international M&A deals in the country. Large-scale privatization began in 1998 following the adoption of the Law on Privatization of State and Municipal Property and the foundation of State Property Fund (SPF) whose mandate was to manage the state assets singled out for privatization and to handle their sales.

Since the establishment of the SPF, it has sold 1.25 billion euros worth of state companies and other assets to local and international investors (Table 3.6.1). Although some large-scale privatization tenders were protracted and often surrounded with political controversy, the privatization of most strategic sectors, including financial services, telecommunications and petrochemicals was almost fully completed by the end of 2002. However, the partial sale of Lietuvos dujos (Lithuanian Gas) to Gazprom has not been completed yet and privatization of the electricity sector is only starting with two power distribution companies scheduled to be tendered out in the second half of 2003.

Table 3.6.1 Privatization volumes during 1998–2002 (million euros)

Year	Total privatization volume		SPF privatization volume	
	Entities privatized	**Income (million euro)**	**Entities privatized**	**Income (million euro)**
1998	344	675	137	666
1999	702	142	469	132
2000	947	263	717	250
2001	842	136	620	126
2002 (Q1–Q3)	686	85	386	74

Source: Ministry of Economy, 2002

Compared to privatization-related M&A transaction volumes, M&A activity in the private sector has been developing at a somewhat slower pace and the size of transactions in the sector has tended to be considerably lower. This is primarily due to the fact that very few of the larger industrial enterprises in the country acquired by local entrepreneurs in a voucher privatization were subsequently sold in cross-border or domestic transactions. Most international buyers have bought into companies established after 1990 that commanded lower valuations compared to long-established former state companies with a considerable under-utilized asset base and numerous inefficiencies. In general, private enterprises in retail, media and telecommunications services have attracted the biggest interest of strategic investors.

Cross-border activity

Most of the largest transactions involving foreign buyers originated from privatization tenders, although a number of successfully closed deals in recent years did not involve state companies. In 1998 Telia and Sonera acquired Omnitel, the largest GSM operator, from its founder Dr Joseph P Kazickas, a prominent American-Lithuanian entrepreneur. In1999 Carlsberg bought Švyturys and SEB bought Vilniaus Bankas in public-to-private transactions. Danish brewery Bryggerigruppen bought Kalnapilis in 2001, the third largest brewery in Lithuania as it was disposed by Baltic Beverage Holding following the consolidation of its holdings in Lithuania with Carlsberg. Ica Ahold acquired Ekonomija, the second largest food retail chain in a trade sale transaction from its Lithuanian founders in 1999. The most recent private sector acquisitions in Lithuania involving western buyers are Faser's acquisition of the Gardesis bakery from its founder and the sale to Navision Denmark of Navision Software Baltic, an ERP licence distributor by Alna, the leading Lithuanian IT group.

A relatively new tendency in cross-border M&A is the involvement of Russian companies in Lithuanian acquisitions. Jukos, Russia's largest company in terms of market capitalization, became the first Russian corporation to buy into a major Lithuanian company after it acquired Mažeikių Nafta from Williams International. Jukos was followed by Gazprom, which placed a bid to acquire a thermo power plan in Kaunas from the city municipality and which is currently negotiating with the Lithuanian Government the terms of acquiring a minority stake in Lietuvos dujos. It is likely that Russian businesses will be scouting the Lithuanian market with increasing intensity, not only in a search for their downstream capacity extension (Jukos) or control of their product distribution (Gazprom) but also in an attempt to establish a manufacturing and distribution base within an EU member country. The cumulative foreign direct investment in Lithuania is displayed in Table 3.6.2.

Domestic activity

Domestic M&A transactions in the 1990s were still a rather rare phenomenon as local companies preferred to focus on organic growth, mainly due to a lack of funds and a shortage of experience in the

Table 3.6.2 Cumulative foreign direct investment in Lithuania, (billion euros)

	1996	1997	1998	1999	2000	2001	2002
Foreign direct investment	0.8	1.2	2.3	2.9	3.1	3.5	4.2

Source: Lithuanian Development Agency, 2003

management of the M&A process. However, as the availability of cheaper financing and management resources increased in 2000–2001, the level of domestic M&A started to pick up and growth through acquisitions became recognized by many Lithuanian corporations as a viable strategic development option.

The domestic M&A marketplace today is dominated by the largest and most aggressive players in IT and food processing who have adopted M&A as their growth strategy as well as a number of diversified conglomerates continually expanding their holdings. Alna and Sonex, the two leading IT companies completed several domestic acquisitions in 2001–2002 and have declared their intention to look for targets outside of Lithuania, particularly in Latvia and Estonia. Achema Group, the largest industrial conglomerate, Vilniaus Prekyba, the largest retail and investment group, and MG Baltic, a diversified holding with interest in distribution, logistics and real estate, are currently some of the most active participants in the M&A game.

Financial investors either exiting their investments or attempting to buy into promising companies have also triggered a number of domestic transactions. However, limited investment resources of local investment funds and restrictive investment policies of foreign private equity players have so far limited financial investors from taking part in larger-scale transactions. The most notable private equity transaction to date is a secondary buy-in by Hermis Fondu Valdymas (HFV) into Snaige, a rapidly growing producer of home refrigerators – the 21.13 per cent stake of which HFV acquired from the Baltic Investment Fund. The level of M&A activity driven by financial sponsors is likely to increase in the coming years as greater availability of bank financing and investment resources will add to their purchasing power and original early stage investors begin to actively seek exit opportunities.

M&A activity by industry

M&A activity by sector in Lithuania followed the pattern typical of most Central and Eastern European countries with banking and finance, technology, media and telecommunications (TMT), food and beverages and retail attracting the largest amount of foreign direct investment. Privatization in the oil and gas sectors have drawn a lot of public attention, more due to their political controversy than the size of transactions. Having said this, the partial sales of Mažeikių Nafta and Lietuvos dujos are likely to be on the high end of the deals completed in Lithuania to date. The sale of public utilities – first of all power distribution companies – to strategic investors are expected to be headline deals in 2003–2004.

Banking and finance

Lithuanian financial services are today dominated by foreign capital institutions as the former state insurance company and all major banks were acquired by foreign strategic investors in the period from 1999 to 2001. Vilniaus Bankas, the largest private bank was acquired by SEB in 1998 for 64 million euros. Vilniaus subsequently bought Hermis Bank, its largest private competitor for 66 million euros. In 2001 the Government sold Lithuanian Savings Bank to Hansa Bank, the largest banking group in the Baltics owned by Swedbank for 43 million euros. In 2001 NordLB, a German state bank acquired Žemės Ūkio Bankas in a privatization tender agreeing to pay 21 million euros for a stake of 76 per cent. In the insurance sector the largest transaction was the acquisition of former state insurance company Lietuvos Draudimas by Codan of Denmark for 30.4 million euros, completed in 1999.

Technology, media and telecommunications

Privatization of Lithuanian Telecom, a monopoly fixed line carrier, is likely to be the largest transaction in dollar value ever completed in the country. The Government collected 590 million euros for a 60 per cent stake sold to Amber Teleholding, a joint venture controlled by Telia and Sonera. Telia and Sonera are also believed to have paid top dollars for a 55 per cent stake in Omnitel, a privately owned GSM operator, although the value of this transaction was never publicly disclosed. Media enterprises, in particular television companies, have also attracted foreign investors. Three privately owned national television companies – LNK, TV 3 and Baltic TV (currently TV4) – were acquired by Bonnier Media Group, MTG and Polsat respectively. At the same time cable television networks remain largely independent and fragmented and may be bound to consolidate as competition in the market increases and growing demand for value added telecommunications services makes large investments into network upgrading inevitable.

Food and beverages

The food processing and beverage sector was the first in Lithuania to attract sizeable foreign investment. Phillip Morris and its food processing arm, Kraft Jacob Suchard, bought the Klaipeda tobacco factory and Kaunas Confectionery respectively in 1993. The sector remained one of the most active M&A arenas as dairies consolidated around Rokiskio Suris supported by the European Bank for Research and Development's (EBRD's) equity investment, and Pieno Zvaigzdes – which received investment from Swedfund International AB and SwedenAgri Invest, the companies representing Sweden's largest agriculture cooperative. All of Lithuania's largest breweries have been taken over by Scandinavians with Carlsberg controlling the two largest through Baltic Beverage Holding. A further two are owned by Danish Bryggerigruppen and Olvi of Finland controls the fifth.

Oil and gas

Following the Jukos investment into Mažeikių Nafta and EON's and Gazprom's (yet to be completed) investment into the national gas distributor, the only remaining oil-related company still predominantly controlled by the Government is Klaipedos Nafta, an oil product terminal on the Baltic sea. Its privatization may be expected sometime in 2004, after the company pays down the bulk of its debt guaranteed by the Government which was used to construct a modern refined product handling facility.

Energy and utilities

The restructuring of the Lithuanian energy sector has been ongoing since 1995 with the establishment of Lietuvos energija, a vertically integrated energy company; it was further accelerated with the adoption of the National Energy Strategy in 1999. Since 2002 five new companies, including two electricity distribution companies serving about half of the country each, were spun off in preparation for their privatization in 2003. In February 2003 the Government initiated the process for selecting privatization advisors and it expects to launch the privatization tender in the third quarter. This privatization has attracted considerable attention of both potential advisors and strategic investors. Currently RWE, EON and EDF are considered the most realistic contenders, with Fortum, Tractebel and several other European players also expected to join in the bidding.

M&A activity in the sector is also expected to accelerate as several regional thermo power plants are prepared for privatization and several municipalities are preparing to tender out their water and district heating companies. Over the last two years Dalkia has been the most active participant in municipal tenders winning several guaranteed-result contracts to supply services for heating networks, including a 15-year 141 million US dollar deal with Vilnius municipality to lease and modernize the Vilnius heating company.

Transaction values and structures

Deal pricing

The transparency relating to transaction valuations in Lithuania has traditionally been a sensitive issue, especially with regards to private sector transactions. Although the SPF is required to disclose the value of all major completed transactions, private entities – local and foreign alike – prefer to keep the valuations of their deals to themselves, unless they are required to make them public as part of their statutory reporting. However, most Lithuanian companies involved in cross-border or domestic transactions are either closed stock companies or stock companies that are not included in the current trading list and are therefore not required to disclose the terms of their deals.

Deal structuring

For simplicity reasons share acquisition is preferable to asset acquisition in the majority of M&A transactions in Lithuania. Practically all larger privatizations are shares-for-cash transactions and most other M&A deals are also completed as share purchases. Asset acquisition structures are typically used in cases when target companies or their shareholders are only willing to dispose part of their business and/or assets and also when the buyer prefers not to assume all the liabilities of the target company. This structure, although often more complex from a tax and accounting perspective due to the need to allocate the total purchase consideration to various classes of assets, is also used by Lithuanian acquirers in order to benefit from tax deductible goodwill amortization. According to Lithuanian law on corporate profit tax, all goodwill resulting from an asset acquisition is deductible for tax purposes. Amortization of goodwill from share acquisition, however, can only be used to offset taxable gains from other share transactions and does not reduce earnings from ordinary business activities while calculating annual profit tax.

M&A advisory services

Although still relatively new and until recently known only to a limited audience of corporate leaders and Government officials, specialist M&A advice has already been generally accepted as an independent service offering. The market for M&A services can be divided into privatization advisory services and those offered to private companies.

Privatization advisory, particularly where it relates to large-scale Government privatization mandates, has been dominated by large European investment banks. However, due to a limited number of such

Table 3.6.3 Largest disclosed privatization deals

Investor	Target	Stake in the company (%)	Million euros
Amber Teleholdings (Telia/Sonera)	Lietuvos telekomas	60	591
Williams International	Mažeikių Nafta	33 (new issue)	87
Vialogas	KLASCO	80	58
DFDS Tor Line A/S	LISCO	76	55
Hansapank A/S	Lietuvos taupomasis bankas (Savings Bank)	91	43
Ruhrgas AG, EON Energie AG	Lietuvos dujos	34	34
Codan	Lietuvos draudimas	70	30
Norddeutsche Landesbank Girozentrale	Žemės ūkio bankas	76	21
Lithuanian Western Industry Corporation	Geonafta	81	15

Source: Prime Investment, 2003

Table 3.6.4 Largest private sector deals with known valuations

Investor	Target	Stake in the company (%)	Million euros
Carlsberg	Švyturys	100	57
Vilniaus bankas	Hermis	100	66
Bryggerigruppen	Kalnapilis	87	39
Jukos	Mažeikių Nafta	26	87
Hermis fondu valdymas	Snaigė	21	13
Olvi	Ragutis	50	7

Source: Prime Investment, 2003

larger transactions and a relatively small market for financial advisory services, large international institutions do not have permanent representation in Lithuania. Smaller scale privatizations typically attract smaller regional investment banking firms, corporate finance departments of commercial banks and major international accounting companies and local corporate finance boutiques. Local enterprises are traditionally using services of Lithuanian firms and a few regional players. Due to their good knowledge of local business specifics and the legal environment, as well as high professional know-how, Lithuanian or pan-Baltic investment banking firms are playing an increasingly important role in advisory consortiums formed by major international banks seeking large privatization mandates.

M&A activity in 2003 and beyond

The level of M&A activity in Lithuania to date has largely been a function of the Government privatization programme and is likely to be even more so in 2003. Privatization of Lithuanian Shipping Company and Klaipeda Transport Fleet, the two shipping companies still in state hands, are planned to close in the first half of 2003.

Fifteen international investment banks are parading at the SPF in their quest for an advisory mandate to sell two power distribution companies expected to fetch in the range of 200–250 million euros by the end of 2003. The sale of four alcohol producers is also drawing considerable attention and two of them – AB Stumbras, the largest liquor producer, and AB Alyta, a sparkling wine maker – are likely to be some of the most contested privatization tenders as a large number of both local and foreign buyers are lining up for the prize. Lithuanian Airlines, the national carrier, has attracted only one bidder and will be the most difficult case for the SPF to handle, particularly given the global industry-related difficulties faced by the international airlines industry.

Subject to the successful completion of the privatization programme outlined for 2003, Lithuania will have effectively completed the sell-out of former state companies. The only exceptions will be Lithuanian Railways, Klaipedos Nafta, a refined oil product terminal and several regional power plants and municipal infrastructure companies.

Although the M&A marketplace in 2003 will be dominated by what will be practically the last major privatization initiative, private sector M&A is also likely to continue picking up. The following factors would indicate that the intensity of both cross-border and domestic M&A activity in the private sector is likely to increase:

- High level of gross domestic product (GDP) growth and other solid macroeconomic fundamentals coupled with NATO and EU accession suggest that the comfort of foreign companies eyeing Lithuania for their investments will be increasing;

- Lithuania is increasingly recognized as an extension of domestic sales markets for Scandinavian companies particularly in retail and wholesale distribution, financial services and food and drinks sectors;
- Most industrial and service sectors are fragmented and therefore bound for consolidation;
- An increasing number of Lithuanian companies realize the need to expand across the Baltic States in order to service their current clients on a pan-Baltic scale, suggesting that the level of cross-border M&A in the Baltic States will increase in the next couple of years;
- Increased availability of financing and management talent enables Lithuanian companies to access resources critical for adopting M&A as the primary growth strategy;
- Improved transparency and access to corporate information, which has inhibited the target screening and prospecting by more acquisitive companies and their advisors;
- Change in owner–manager philosophy as many founding shareholders are surrendering their management powers to hired professionals and are more willingly considering the sale of their companies.

Implications for M&A advisors

The nature of M&A activity in Lithuania is likely to change considerably in the next few years as the country completes the privatization of its assets. In addition the focus of corporate finance advisors will increasingly shift to servicing local companies, private equity players and foreign strategic investors. As large international banks will have too few large enough deals to justify their presence in Lithuania, the market will be divided among regional investment banks, local M&A boutiques and corporate finance departments of commercial banks.

The service offering will grow more complex to include strategic development advice in addition to conventional transaction support. As the number of acquisitive local companies driving the market will not be particularly large, advisors who are most consistently investing in building corporate relationships with those companies are likely to end up dominating the M&A market in the next few years.

3.7

Mergers and Acquisitions: Legal Aspects

Lideika, Petrauskas, Valiūnas ir Partneriai

Introduction

Lithuanian legislation applicable to mergers and acquisitions (M&A) has evolved gradually and is still in the process of formation. The driving forces for this development are the overall modernization of the legal system, business needs of foreign and local investors, the emergence of certain standard practices and practical problems that arise in the process of applying existing rules. Certain rules are adopted while implementing European Union (EU) law or following the guidelines proposed by EU institutions.

A great number of acquisitions occur in the privatization process of state and municipal assets. Private M&A transactions became increasingly important in the past few years, driven primarily by the growth of the Lithuanian economy and local businesses, which became attractive targets for acquisition. As the ownership concentration is high in most of the larger companies, public takeovers happen very seldom.

Entities involved in M&A transactions

All types of enterprises may be involved in M&A activities. This chapter focuses on the legal aspects of transactions that involve public or private stock companies. Public stock companies are more heavily regulated than private stock companies. Additional requirements apply to the public stock companies that are listed on the official or current lists of the National Stock Exchange of Lithuania (NSE). Acquisitions of private stock companies and certain public stock companies often involve agreements with the controlling shareholders who, in most cases, also run the business. Thus, it is important to consider the issue of the post-acquisition future of the management team when that team holds shares or is closely linked to the shareholders.

Preparation for M&A transaction

Acquiring control

When preparing an offer it is important to investigate what rights the percentage of shares offered would grant to the buyer. For example, 33.4 per cent is a blocking minority for all major decisions at the general shareholders meeting, 50 per cent plus one vote is a simple majority that grants the majority of seats on the board and 75 per cent plus one vote is the majority that gives control of all general shareholders meeting resolutions. The supervisory council (or the board, when a supervisory council is not formed) is elected through cumulative voting at the general shareholders' meeting. For having all seats in the supervisory council, the percentage to be acquired has to be equal to $n/(n+1) \times 100$ per cent (where 'n' is the number of seats).

Negotiations

The whole M&A process usually begins with informal contacts between prospective buyers and sellers. When investment banks (consultants) are involved, they often prepare an information memorandum about the target company. Letters of intent are frequently used when the negotiations have reached a certain stage. These are enforceable to a certain extent through damages that may be claimed from the party that unreasonably refuses or avoids executing a binding agreement. Letters of intent are often complemented by a confidentiality agreement (if not signed earlier in the negotiations) which is valid under Lithuanian law. Breaches of confidentiality may result in fines and damages.

When preparing an offer, the buyers try to gather as much information as possible on the target company. Public records can provide certain data, including financial statements of public companies and company's articles of association. Financial and legal due diligence investigations are very common in Lithuania. These are usually carried out by auditors and lawyers, except for environmental and other technical audits.

Employment issues

Investors are strongly advised to analyse labour relations in the target company. Procedures for dismissing employees, collective agreement benefits, compensations for labour accidents and other financial liabilities of the target company towards employees may increase the expected business costs. Investors should consider retaining key employees in order to restrict their competing activities in further employment.

In cases of acquisition of the target company's shares, as well as in cases of merger, division, realignment or change of the company type, the employer remains unchanged (ie employment relationships between employees and the company continue). A takeover does not in itself constitute grounds for dismissal of employees unless subsequent changes in the work organization of the company necessitate a reduction in the number of employees. As long as the change of shareholders is not expected to change the position of employees, Lithuanian law does not require the employer to consult with employees on transfer of shares (unless this is required by the collective agreement).

Lithuanian law also offers some protection to employees in case of an asset deal. Employees remain employed by the employer who sells the assets, but in most cases should be offered a transfer to the buying company on the same conditions. Employees should agree to the transfer, otherwise they remain with the seller who in turn may dismiss them with due notice and compensation. In asset deals, unlike in cases of shares acquisition, consultation with employees is practically always necessary.

Privatization transactions of big Lithuanian companies often include additional employment guarantees; for example investors may be required to retain a certain number of jobs in a privatized company for a certain period of time.

Merger control

Generally, the mandatory merger notification process applies only to concentrations that meet these thresholds:

- combined aggregate turnover of the undertakings concerned is more than 30 million litas (approximately 8.7 million euros) in the last financial year prior to concentration;
- aggregate turnover of each of at least two undertakings concerned is more than 5 million litas (approximately 1.5 million euros) in the last financial year prior to concentration.

For more information on concentration control please see Chapter 2.6.

Conduct of M&A transactions

There are several common legal structures of M&A transactions used in Lithuania. A number of acquisitions are privatizations carried out according to standardized privatization procedures described in Chapter 3.2. Other legal methods are described in this chapter.

Shares and assets acquisition agreements

While choosing between a shares acquisition and an assets acquisition, such issues as taxation, special permits or licences held by the target company and other aspects are important. Asset transactions may seem to be difficult to carry out from a technical standpoint, but they are less burdensome procedurally than the reorganization, for example, and they offer some flexibility if only part of the business is acquired.

Many of the major M&A transactions in Lithuania are either governed by, or their content is strongly influenced by, foreign law. This is because Lithuanian companies are often targeted for acquisition by foreign companies that seek to have the contracts to be governed by law familiar to them. In certain cases agreements for acquisitions by foreign companies are governed by Lithuanian law (eg in nearly all cases of privatization).

Application of Lithuanian law to a share or asset purchase agreement is not mandatory. Use of the Lithuanian language, however, is mandatory in cases where one of the parties is a Lithuanian entity. Use of foreign language in addition is allowed and such foreign language may prevail.

The agreements commonly used by local entities acquiring shares in Lithuanian companies are governed by Lithuanian law and are usually fairly short. As Lithuania is a civil law tradition country, when drafting the agreements lawyers often rely on the regulation by law and the statutory protection granted to parties. However, because many legal provisions are rather new, it is advisable to define clearly the parties' rights and obligations.

Lithuanian legislation does not specifically address the sale of shares, except for several formal requirements. General rules on the sale of goods contracts, which are applicable to the shares and assets purchase agreements, provide for the following basic protections:

- the goods subject to sale must be delivered by the seller to the buyer, including transfer of the documents evidencing ownership right to the goods;
- the seller must warrant peaceful possession (ie no claims by third parties relating to the shares, the shares are sold free of charges and encumbrances);
- the seller must provide the buyer with a guarantee against hidden defects of the goods.

Lithuanian law does not require notarization of a share purchase agreement. However, it is required in assets deals where real estate is transferred.

Acquisition of enterprise as a going concern

Based on the Civil Code, a company may be purchased through an 'acquisition of an enterprise'. This transaction involves the purchase of an enterprise as a complex of assets, rights and liabilities with all their ancillary elements. The procedure is new and very seldom applied in practice. However, it is rather risky to avoid using it in cases when assets are acquired separately from the liabilities of the company. If an asset transaction is entered into with the purpose of avoiding the transfer of a company's liabilities, it is likely that the target's creditors would successfully prove in court that the transaction had to take the form of an 'acquisition of an enterprise'. In such a case the creditors would be granted the extensive protection they would have had in such an acquisition transaction.

Mergers and split-ups

Mergers may involve several companies that are dissolved into one new company, or one or several companies that are dissolved into another company that continues its operations. Split-ups can be the splitting of one company into several new companies, or the dissolution of one company into several existing companies.

Merger and split-up procedures are rather lengthy and complex. The most important procedural element is the publicity and protection of the rights of all creditors and shareholders. Any failure to comply strictly with the procedural rules may lead to the validity of such reorganization being challenged in court.

Joint ventures

It is quite common for two or more parties to join forces to gain control over a company or combine the required experience and finances necessary to qualify as potential buyers. Joint ventures (incorporated as separate companies) are often used as a vehicle not only to acquire but also to operate a joint business. Lithuanian law provides for rather favourable legal treatment for joint ventures, as shareholders' (voting) agreements are allowed and enforceable. Stand-still clauses and other restrictions on transfers of shares are also allowed between the shareholders that are parties to the agreements.

Voluntary public offer

Any person that has decided to launch a public offer for the acquisition of shares of a listed public stock company must notify the NSE and apply to the Securities Commission for the registration of the public offer documents. The offer may relate to all or part of the securities of the target company. It is possible to make the offer conditional upon acquiring a minimum number of acceptances. The offeror may pay for the shares acquired through the public offer in cash, in liquid securities of other issuers or with a combination of cash and securities.

The board of the target company must prepare and publish a statement regarding the public offer. When formulating its statement, the board must take into account the interests of the target company and its shareholders, and must not reflect the personal interests of the target company's management.

Defensive measures against hostile takeovers are not often used in practice. However, in certain instances defensive measures have been used with the aim of achieving a higher share price. The legislation applicable to public offers restricts the use of certain defensive measures.

Financial assistance

Some acquisitions of companies are structured as leveraged deals in which a portion of the purchase price is obtained through loan financing. In such a transaction, the buyer may use the shares of the acquired company to secure the loan, but the target company (both private and public) is prohibited from granting financial assistance for the acquisition of its shares, ie advancing or lending funds or providing security with its assets. It is quite difficult to structure a leveraged deal under Lithuanian law where the buyer cannot offer anything other than the assets of the target company to secure its obligations. A statutory merger between the purchased company and the purchasing company could be used as a method of avoiding the financial assistance prohibition, but it is a rather burdensome procedure.

The concept of group companies having common interests is not legally recognized in Lithuania. Thus, the giving of a guarantee by a company to secure the debts of its affiliated company may be seen as not being in the company's best interests. On the other hand, the interest on the loan by a shareholder is capped. In addition, the company cannot pledge its assets to secure a shareholder loan.

Post-transaction obligations

Disclosure of blocks

Shareholdings that grant one-tenth, one-fifth, one-third, one-half, two-thirds or three-quarters of all votes in the public stock company's general shareholders meeting must be disclosed to the Securities Commission and the target company. Both the seller and the buyer must make a disclosure as notice is made upon reaching the respective threshold in the case of an increase or decrease in the holding. The aggregate shareholding of several related persons is considered as one block.

A person that has failed to notify is deprived for two years of all newly acquired votes. Before the notice is made, the acquiring person should not attempt to replace the managers of the target company or adopt decisions which could violate the rights of other shareholders.

Mandatory offer

Where one or several related buyers acquire more than 40 per cent of the shares of the target public stock company, they must offer to purchase all the remaining shares at the largest price per share which they paid for the shares of the company during the last 12 months. From the moment of acquisition of the 40 per cent stake until the date when the buyer registers a mandatory public offer, it is deprived of the votes granted by its shares at the general shareholders meeting.

Compulsory acquisitions of minorities

Compulsory squeeze-outs or sell-outs of minority shareholders are not allowed in public stock companies. In private stock companies, a holder of more than a third of all shares is able to request a court order to force the sale of the shares of the shareholders who act contrary to the company's objectives.

Part Four

Key Sectors of Trade and Investment

4.1

The Electronics Sector

Lithuanian Development Agency

In the former Soviet Union, Lithuania was a leader in the electronics industry, particularly regarding the production and development of television sets, television equipment, computers, semiconductors and radio measurement equipment. Lithuanian companies were also among the major suppliers of electronic products to the Soviet military industry and space programmes.

During the transition period, the electronics industry in Lithuania experienced restructuring, attracted investments and installed modern technologies. Now it is successfully competing in western markets; in 2002 the Lithuanian electronics sector covered 162 companies in the electronics industry and employed more than 14,500 workers. Of the 162 companies operating in the sector, 24 attracted foreign capital in 2001. The production of the electronics industry is distributed among these branches:

- electric equipment and appliances;
- radio, television and communications equipment and appliances;
- medical, precision and optical equipment.

The fastest growing branch of the electronic industry in Lithuania is medical, precision and optical instruments. The total sales of this branch have more than doubled within the last four years and amounted to 93 million euros in 2001. Main leaders in this sub-sector are companies producing medical hardware and developing and manufacturing precision measuring means.

An intensive growth during the period from 1997 to 2002 was also observed in the branch of radio, television and communications equipment and appliances. This branch has survived thanks to its exclusive feature to preserve existing potential and to re-orient itself towards the production of television technologies. In 2000 the total sales in this branch increased by 34 per cent and in 2001 by 10 per cent compared with the previous year (Table 4.1.1). The estimated growth of this branch in 2002 was 20 per cent.

Table 4.1.1 Total industry sales by branches (million euros)

Industry branch	1997	1998	1999	2000	2001	2002*
Electrical equipment and appliances	126.2	116.1	119.0	122.4	133.3	130.7
Radio, television and communications equipment and appliances	136.3	139.2	158.5	213.0	233.3	279.3
Medical, precision and optical instruments	37.3	58.6	56.3	57.8	93.0	95.5
Total	299.8	314.2	333.9	393.2	459.7	505.5

*preliminary estimation

Source: EKT Group, 2002

Products from the three largest companies, sold in appropriate markets, account for over 80 per cent of the total electronic sector production level. The leaders in this group are producers of:

- standard colour picture tubes and 21-inch true flat colour picture tubes;
- deflection yokes and transformers;
- television sets.

There are several smaller-size enterprises operating with the aforementioned companies on a subcontracting basis. From a development point of view, this is the area with the most prospects in the Lithuanian machine-building and instrument-making sector.

Products of the Lithuanian electronics industry are very specialized and most are exported. In 2002 30 per cent of the electronics industry's production manufactured in Lithuania was sold in the domestic market and 70 per cent was exported. Of that exported, 44 per cent went to European Union (EU) countries and 26 per cent to the Commonwealth of Independent States (CIS) countries, Latvia, and Estonia. In 2001 the export of electronic products amounted for 4 per cent of Lithuania's total exports.

Industry leaders

Production of large-scale electronics products

The production volume of television sets and parts had been steadily growing in Lithuania between 1997 and 2000. In 2000, 14 per cent more colour television sets were produced in Lithuania compared with 1999. Screen tube production increased by 52 per cent during the same period. The market leaders in this area are AB Vilniaus Vingis, AB Ekranas and AB Siauliu tauro televizoriai.

AB Vilniaus Vingis

AB Vilniaus Vingis is the largest producer of deflection yokes for mono and colour picture tubes in the Baltic and CIS region with more than 40 years of experience in manufacturing. Moreover, the company's products include low-strength transformers of various purposes for television, radio and household electronics devices. The company has accumulated many years' experience in manufacturing specialized technological equipment and equipment for the above-mentioned electronics products.

In 2001 Vilniaus Vingis' sales exceeded 36.7 million euros – a 14 per cent growth compared to 2000. In 2001, the company exported 68 per cent of its products: 38 per cent of exports went to Germany, 10 per cent to Spain, 9 per cent to Great Britain, 5 per cent to the CIS, 5 per cent to Poland and 1 per cent to other countries. The major buyers of the company's products abroad are Samsung SDI (Germany and Hungary – 38 per cent of all sold products), LG Philips Displays (Great Britain and Spain – 19 per cent) and Thompson Multimedia (Poland). In 2002 Vilniaus Vingis became the largest supplier of deflection yokes to the EU.

AB Erkranas

For the last 40 years AB Ekranas has been manufacturing glass components (panels and funnels) and colour television tubes. The company specializes in small and medium-sized colour picture tubes (14-inch, 20-inch, 21-inch and 21-inch FST), which account for 94 per cent of its total sales. The company's production capacity amounts to more than 3.5 million CPT per year.

AB Ekranas is an export-oriented company, selling approximately 90 per cent of its products in foreign markets. Sales to western markets account for 87 per cent (of which 60 per cent go to Turkey) and are managed by the company's shareholder, Farimex SA. AB Ekranas also markets its products in Lithuania (12 per cent) and the CIS (1 per cent). The main customers include Profilo-Telra, Vestel and Beko (Turkey), Tecnimagen and Sanyo (Spain), Sanyo (UK), Great Wall and Continental

(France), Daewoo (Poland), Mivar and Formenti (Italy), Siauliu tauro televizoriai (Lithuania).

With a production output of 2.85 million television tubes, AB Ekranas held a 12.2 per cent market share and was one of the leaders in the small and medium size tube segment in Europe. The company enjoys very strong positions in the 14-inch tube market segment, where its share increased from 8.2 per cent in 1998 to 15.7 per cent in 2001. With regard to the segment of 20–21-inch CTP, a market share of 10 per cent was achieved in 2001 – up by 3.1 per cent from 1998.

AB Siauliu tauro televizoriai

AB Siauliu tauro televizoriai produces television sets, equipment for television studios, and special technological and testing equipment. In 2001, the company's turnover amounted to 24.9 million euros and exports amounted to 60 per cent of its total output. Investments into the company in 2001 were 0.87 million euros and during the first quarter of 2002 the company generated sales of 8.34 million euros – 64 per cent more than in the corresponding period of 2001. The company enlarged its sales in the Lithuania market almost by 60 per cent during the first quarter of 2002. Since the spring of 2002, the company has cooperated with Samsung electronics (South Korea).

Microelectronics

The microelectronics industry is oriented to high quality production. This industry distinguishes its innovation policy as the concentration of strong scientific potential, accomplishment of scientific researches and the implementation of new products and new materials. Microelectronics products manufactured in Lithuania are in high demand in foreign markets because of their comparatively low price and high quality.

AB Telga

AB Telga manufactures printed circuits. The turnover of the company amounted to 1.04 million euros in 2001; target turnover for 2002 was 1.04 million euros. Telga is an export-oriented manufacturing company. Of its total production 99 per cent goes to CIS countries. Presently recovering CIS markets influence the growing sales of this company. During 2001, investments into equipment and technological lines comprised 43,400 euros.

UAB Hibridas

UAB Hibridas is a microelectronics thick-layer hybrid schemes producer. This company orients its products towards exporting to the EU as the domestic market for such products is quite small. The company is rather active in scientific research activities; strong scientific potential enables the company to generate new products and to sell licences for foreign enterprises. The company employs highly qualified staff and its main investments are directed towards improving employees' skills.

UAB Vilniaus ventos puslaidininkiai
UAB Vilniaus ventos puslaidininkiai produces semiconductors. In 2001 the company employed 300 people. The biggest part of production goes to foreign markets; more than half of the exported products goes to Italy, Spain, Great Britain and Sweden. The company's sales should grow because of the growing world semiconductors market.

Production of laser devices

In 2001 there were approximately 10 companies occupied with laser devices production activities, which employed more than 200 people (more than 30 of them scientists) with a total turnover of 14.5 million euros. More than 90 per cent of such production is exported to EU markets, Switzerland, Japan, the USA and other countries. The list of countries exported to totals almost 100.

Lithuania's laser technology companies have established themselves in export markets as producers of lasers for scientific research work. The share of multi-colour lasers in the world market that are produced in Lithuania amount to 60 per cent. According to data at the end of 2001, there are more than 400 multi-colour and picosecond (short impulse) lasers in use in the world that were made in Lithuania. For the most part, these lasers were exported to European countries and Japan (Figure 4.1.1).

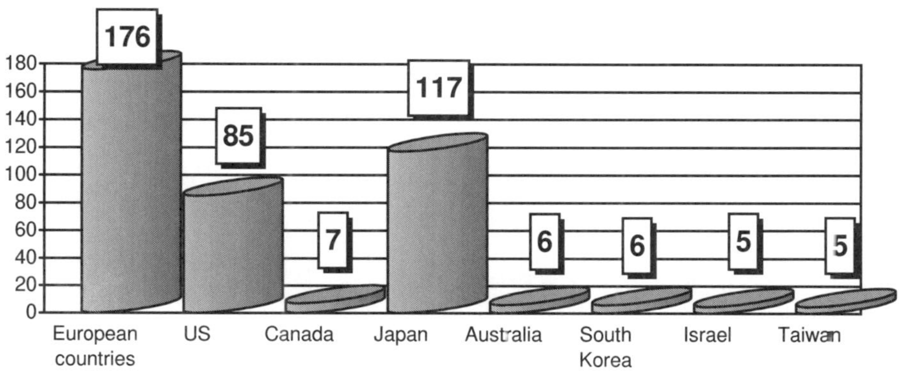

Figure 4.1.1 Lithuanian multi-colour and picosecond lasers in the world

Source: EKT Group, 2002

UAM Eksma

UAM Eksma produces laser machines for industry, medical measuring devices and optical components as well as providing various services related to laser technologies. It has also patented several devices of laser technologies. Eksma, well known in the international market was, in 1987, the first company to export a laser made in Lithuania to the western market. Currently it has a network of its commercial branches in Western Europe, Japan and the USA. Eksma has established joint ventures with German and Austrian companies for the production of medical preparations, and those with Russian growers of non-linear crystals. The company's employees work with such scientific research institutions as the National Institute of Materials and Chemical Research (Japan), the Tokyo Institute of Technology (Japan), Lawrence Livermore National Laboratory (USA), the Defence Research Agency (Great Britain), Nuclear Research Centre SOREQ (Israel), SAAB Dynamics AB (Sweden), and many others.

UAM Eksma's annual turnover in 2001 was 5.7 million euros and the workforce consisted of 92 employees.

UAB Ekspla

UAB Ekspla produces lasers and laser systems for scientific research, industrial use and various detectors of light. It provides various services related to laser technologies. It started its activity with the production of lasers and separate laser components in 1992 and now has reached a new qualitative stage of production creating and producing particularly intricate laser measuring complexes, ie laboratories that cost more than a few hundred thousand US dollars.

Such works are not only patented but also presented at major scientific conferences and published in scientific magazines. This is achieved by closely cooperating with scientific institutions of physics as well as with the main users of lasers, ie institutes of chemistry and biochemistry. Ekspla picoseconds lasers have been covering approximately 50 per cent of the international market for several years already.UAB Ekspla's annual turnover in 2001 was 1.9 million euros and the workforce consisted of 35 employees.

UAB Sviesos konversija

UAB Sviesos konversija was established in 1994 and is closely cooperating with the Centre of Laser Research of Vilnius University. The company produces and sells parametrical generators of ultra-short impulses of widely tuned length waves, solid-body lasers and optic corealators as well as optic coherent gauges of distance, surface profile and thickness of transparent layers. The company is successfully competing in the western market: the sales of parametric generators cover 60 per cent of the world market. The company's products are exported to many countries of the world. The largest proportion of the production output is exported to Germany and the USA. More than 180 parametric light generators TOPAS have been produced and sold during recent years. The annual turnover in 2001 was 1.6 million euros and the workforce consisted of 27 employees.

Conclusion

The main scientific research work in the laser technology field is performed at the Laser Research Centre of the Quantum Electronics Department of Vilnius University. Experimental research is carried out with unique laser set ups, which are also used in performing international projects in the fields of laser physics and laser medicine.

Lithuanian electronics companies certify their production according to ISO, GOST (Russia), BSI (Great Britain), VDE (Germany) and UL (USA). The tendency of a close cooperation existing between scientific research and manufacturers is, and will continue to be, one of the critical success factors. The present growth in the Lithuanian electronics industry illustrates the benefits of such cooperation. The application of available knowledge and experience could be employed in different projects between scientific institutions and enterprises. International projects could facilitate the implementation of research and development activities in production. Lithuanian electronics sector exporters have business cooperation with worldwide enterprises such as Siemens, Philips, Toshiba, Samsung, Kitron, Gemplus and Unicom Consulting to name but a few.

4.2

Knowledge Economy

Lithuanian Development Agency

Lithuania's science and technology traditions have made a successful transition to a modern market economy. Once known as the Soviet Silicon Valley, the country now has world-class specialists in biotechnology, lasers, telecommunications and information technologies bringing leading-edge products and services to global markets.

The National Agreement for Economic and Social Progress was signed on the 3 December 2002 and states the paramount importance of knowledge economy. All major political parties signed the document, as did the country's Industrialists' Confederation, university rectors, student and youth organizations, the Foreign Investors Forum and associations that link business and science, such as Infobalt and the Knowledge Economy Forum.

The present situation within the knowledge economy could be described as taking four major components of the knowledge economy into consideration:

- the economic, institutional and regulatory environment;
- educated, creative and skilled people;
- dynamic information infrastructure;
- effective national innovation systems.

Presently, four Governmental institutions are acting within the field of information society development. The Parliament of the Republic of Lithuania has presented the strategy for developing an information society. Knowledge economy is one of the priority issues in the country's long-term development strategy. A number of public organizations are also supporting the knowledge economy development initiatives.

Strong human capital has been accumulated in Lithuania. The number of people in education grew by 34 per cent in 2001, compared to 1991 figures. The number of students in further education grew almost twice between 1995 and 2001. Of high school graduates, 74 per cent were seeking higher education in 2001. More than 10,000 specialists were annually prepared in the main studies and 6,000 specialists in second-level studies during the years 2000 and 2001. The Lithuanian higher education population has grown and amounted to 126 per 1000 inhabitants (12.6 per cent of the population) during the last 20 years. The growth of recent years is shown in Figure 4.2.1.

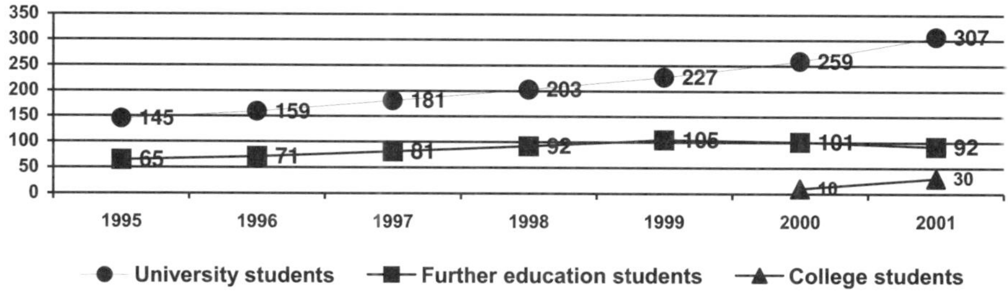

Figure 4.2.1 Number of students (10,000 inhabitants)

Source: Ministry of Education of the Lithuanian Republic

The use of various information technology (IT) means in Lithuania is lower than the average in European Union (EU) countries, but according to the research data the intentions to obtain and to use IT devices is exceeding EU averages. Almost a third of the population is computer-wise, with one-fifth using the Internet. The usage of IT means is rapidly growing among both private and business users; the average share of the population using the Internet is three times bigger than the share of world Internet users. Among the Baltic States, Lithuania is in second place after Estonia in this respect (Figure 4.2.2). Of the Lithuanian population 12.9 per cent have personal computers, 2.1 per cent own a fax and 5.8 per cent have an Internet connection at home.

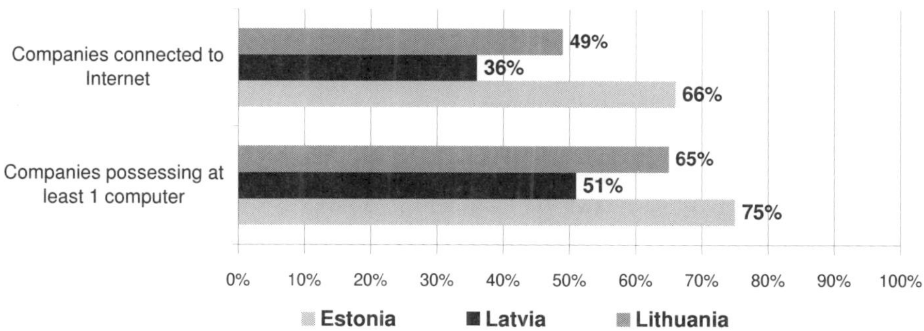

Figure 4.2.2 Use of IT means in Estonian, Latvian and Lithuanian companies

Source: SIC Market Research: IT and Internet Market

The innovation environment is favourable for the development of the knowledge economy in Lithuania. Institutions operate in Lithuania to provide support for innovations, stimulate scientific potential and innovative business, inform about innovation in commerce and to create dialogue between the science and business sectors.

It is possible to distinguish four rapidly developing directions in the knowledge economy:

- biotechnology;
- laser technology industry;
- information technologies and telecommunications;
- research and development (R&D) system.

Biotechnology sector

The cultivation of the biotechnology industry has proved its competitiveness in world production and the science market. In 2001 the turnover of this industry was more than 15 million euros. The following certain activity tendencies have been formed in the biotechnological sector:

- the manufacturing of biotechnological products designed for fundamental research;
- biopharmaceutical product manufacturing;
- the manufacturing of biotechnological products designed for environmental protection;
- the manufacturing of biotechnological products designed for animal feed.

Raw materials are bought mostly in European countries (58 per cent) although 34.2 per cent are purchased in Lithuania. The raw materials used to produce biotechnological products for the production of animal feed are purchased mostly from Lithuanian manufacturers (92.5 per cent).

Approximately 75 per cent of the total production was exported to 42 countries around the world. Based on separate trends in the biotechnological field, the main countries to which the products are exported are as follows:

- The products designed for fundamental research, ie 99% of manufactured products, are exported to Western and Eastern European countries, North and South America, Japan, Australia, China, India and 45 other foreign countries;

- The biopharmaceutical products, ie 50% of the manufactured products, are exported to Pakistan, Mexico, South Korea, Russia, Belarus, the Ukraine, Algeria and others;
- The biotechnological products designed for the production of animal feed (95% of exported products) are realized in Russia; the rest is realized in the neighbouring countries, Latvia, Estonia and also in Italy and Holland.

The main companies in the biotechnology sector are AB Fermentas, UAB Sicor Biotech, AB Biosinteze and UAB Biocentras. AB Fermentas develops biochemical and chemical agents for genetic engineering, molecular biology and varied biotechnology uses. It has a large international distribution network and branches in the USA, Canada and Germany.

UAB Sicor Biotech is the only genetic engineering pharmaceutical maker in this part of the world. Its medicines have already established a name in Eastern Europe and the Far East and are now entering Western markets thanks to a new production facility built by the company's Dutch strategic investor in compliance with EU and US standards.

AB Biosinteze is a producer of biotechnological products designed for the production of animal feed. The company successfully trades with Western and Eastern European countries and has a subdivision in the Russian Federation (Moscow). Exports are 32 per cent of production output.

UAB Biocentras develops and applies biotechnology methods to remove chemical pollutants.

The potential of biotechnologies was created after the establishment of the Biotechnological Institute and starting production of modern biotechnologies. At the end of 2001 there were 16 laboratories and institutes associated with the production of classical biotechnological products and four laboratories associated with modern biotechnology. The total number of people working in the field of biotechnology is around 2,000. There are 400 members of scientific staff (including R&D). For this reason, the biotechnology sector and R&D have accumulated the basis for their specific production and the numerous scientific staff.

By 2006 the estimated investment into the biotechnological industry will amount to 23–46 million euros. As a result of this, new job places could amount to 100–200, annual turnover could reach 29–58 million euros (at present 15 million euros). In 10 years the annual turnover could reach 145–290 million euros.

Laser technology industry

Lasers as sources of powerful coherent light have greatly influenced the progress of science and technology. The unique qualities of laser beams were promptly adapted to create devices on new principles, measuring methods and technologies. The influence of lasers is especially noticeable in the development of the science of materials, biomedicine and information technologies. It is forecast that in the next decade the comparative weight of laser technologies will increase in optic informatics (eg the creation of optic computers, the editing of optic information and the means of optic communication, the remote probe of atmosphere, hydrosphere and the Earth), the creation of new materials (nano- and femtotechnologies), medical diagnostics and therapy methods and equipment. Lasers are also important in the search of alternative energy sources such as directional transferring of solar energy from space, artificial photosynthesis and laser-controlled thermonuclear energetic systems. A wide range laser use in military devices and systems must be mentioned, from laser target identification and pointing to the warning and rocket disorientation and elimination.

It should be noted that during the last decade a cluster structure for the production of laser technologies formed in Lithuania. In 2001 there were approximately 10 companies of various size that were involved in the business related to light technologies, having more than 200 employees and a total turnover reaching 14.5 million euros. According to the prognosis of market analysts, the maintaining of the current positions in the scientific market would guarantee a 10 per cent annual growth to Lithuanian laser companies. Meanwhile, a successful integration into the industrial market would increase the annual growth by up to 25 per cent. More than 90 per cent of this sector's production is exported to the countries of the EU, Switzerland, Japan and the USA – to 100 countries overall.

The leaders of this sector are Eksma, Ekspla and Sviesos Konversija. Eksma is the largest manufacturer of laser components and appliances, whose major export markets include EU countries and the USA. Eksma anticipates a 10 per cent revenue growth this year.

Ekspla, the second-largest laser manufacturer expects to increase its revenues by about 1.5-fold this year, largely due to a new market in South Korea, development of new products and more active operations in the US, European and Japanese markets. The company's annual sales are projected to reach 2.9 million euros. Ekspla has more than 50 per cent of the global pico-second laser market.

Sviesos Konversija, Lithuania's third-biggest laser company also anticipates growth this year. Sviesos Konversija sells about 50 per cent of its products to the US market. Its main customers are universities and it has a 60 per cent share of the global multicolour laser market.

The strongest scientific centres of laser physics, laser technologies and laser optic electronics are functioning in Vilnius University and the Institute of Physics and Semiconductors. Some potential is also concentrating in Kaunas Technological University.

Currently there are four centres of scientific research:

- Laser Research Centre of Vilnius University (LTC);
- Institute of Research of Materials and Engineering Sciences of Vilnius University (MTMI);
- Laboratory of non-linear optics and stretoscopy of the Institute of Physics (NOSL);
- Laboratory of optic electronics of the Institute of Semiconductor Physics.

Research centres employ and train a wide spectrum of laser physics specialists, working with local companies and international institutions, including the EU and NATO.

Apart from scientific centres, funded mostly from the budget, the engineering scientific research and the works of technological development are also successfully carried out in private companies.

Information technologies and telecommunications

The sector of information technologies and telecommunications (ITT) is among those that are developing most rapidly. The Lithuanian ITT market grew by approximately 28 per cent in 2001, this way revealing a strong market development potential for the coming two or three years. The growth was influenced by several factors. The first one of these is the mobile user boom – in 2001, mobile penetration doubled from 13 per cent to 27 per cent. This enabled the mobile market to increase by approximately 45 per cent. Secondly, Lithuanian GDP growth in 2001 exceeded all forecasts and reached 5.7 per cent. This, in turn, resulted in increased investment in IT, both in the business–customer segment and the fast developing household consumption market. Hardware and software sales surged by 30 per cent and helped Lithuania exceed the growth rates in Latvia and Estonia. Despite unfavourable export conditions, the leading IT companies managed to significantly improve their sales both in Western and Eastern markets.

The sales of ITT in 2001 amounted to 1,518.4 million euros. Growth within this sector is illustrated in Figure 4.2.3. The share of IT in GDP amounted to 6 per cent in 2002 and is expected to generate 25 per cent of GDP in 2015.

Until now, over 10,000 qualified specialists and more than 350 companies were working in the ITT sector. Several leading Lithuanian software companies were awarded the title of Microsoft Gold Certified Partner. The leaders of this sector are Lietuvos telekomas, Omnitel, Alna, Sonex Group and Penki kontinentai.

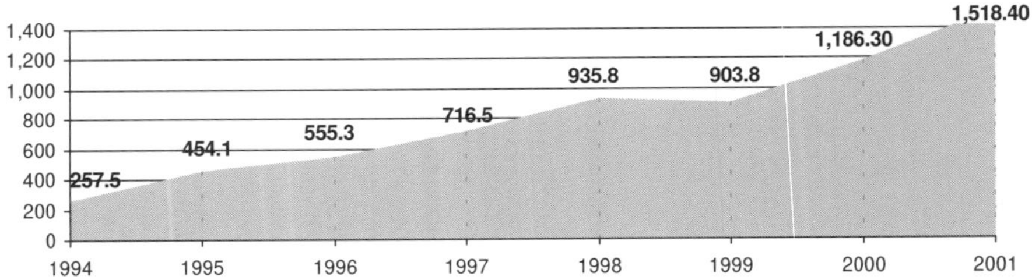

Source: Infobalt

Figure 4.2.3 The development of the Lithuanian ITT sector (million euros)

Lietuvos telekomas is the only company in Lithuania providing fixed line services, having had the monopoly until 31 December 2002. It is the largest telecommunications company in Lithuania. Currently the company has more than one million fixed line clients. Almost 0.5 billion euros was invested in modern technologies and the digitalizing of the network.

Omnitel is a high profile telecommunications company, providing mobile (GSM 900/1800 MHz) lines, Internet and other data transfer services. The company distinguishes itself by providing services combining telephone and computer possibilities. UAB Omnitel represents FaxSav in Lithuania. In 2001 Omnitel invested 47.8 million euros – 37.5 per cent more than in 2000 (34.8 million euros). Approximately 90 per cent of the investment was used for the development of the network with the remaining 10 per cent used for IT administration.

Alna offers innovative IT solutions and services, provided by highly competent, professional and customer-oriented staff. Well known foreign companies and institutions such as Bentley Systems, Ericsson, British Telecom, London Metro, BMW, the Danish Ministry of Finance and many others are permanent clients of the company.

Sonex Group is one of the biggest IT companies not only in Lithuania but in all the Baltic States. The strategy of Sonex Group is to dominate the IT market in the Baltic States on the basis of innovation, professionalism and a strong trade mark.

Penki kontinentai, established in 1992, stands among the largest and oldest Lithuanian IT and is experienced in the creation of intellectual software. The company is cooperating with the most outstanding providers of banking, computer and network equipment, eg Microsoft, Wincor Nixdorf, Cisco Systems, Zyxel, Bull, Unisys and Umax.

The need for informatics specialists is going to increase rapidly. Such tendencies are indicated in the EU forecast (that by 2005 the need for informatics specialists will increase to above 1 million) and the USA forecast (that the increase will be on a larger scale). Thus the training of informatics specialists is being developed and the enrolment of students to major in informatics-related studies is being increased in the whole country. There is a strong study and research infrastructure with 22 higher education institutions (the proportion of graduates is one of the highest in Central and Eastern Europe with 3.3 university graduates per year per 1000 inhabitants).

R&D system

Currently the R&D system is based on the Law of Higher Education (VIII–1586) which was issued by the Parliament of the Republic of Lithuania on 21 March 2000 and took effect from 1 September 2000. The research policy is formed and implemented by the Department of Science and Higher Education under the Ministry of Education of the Lithuanian Republic and the Lithuanian Scientific Council. The Lithuanian Scientific Council mediates when parliament and the Government are making decisions concerning the sponsorship and organization of research and higher education. The formation and activities of the Scientific Council are regulated by parliament's resolutions.

The Lithuanian Academy of Science is an autonomous institution, subsidized by the state. The Academy organizes scientific activities of Lithuanian and foreign scientists, whose scientific activity is related to Lithuania.

The main priorities of R&D are:

- international acknowledgement of research in various fields;
- inclusion of research in international research programmes;
- development of applied sciences research (its importance to Lithuanian society and the development of economy is highlighted);
- organization of the main applied sciences and engineering research in the fields of Lithuanian language, culture and history.

More than 170 scientific institutions were operating in 2001 (Figure 4.2.4), employing 15,000 people. Of these employees, more than 5,000 had PhD degrees. The R&D expenditure during 2001 amounted to 0.68 per cent of the GDP. The main R&D system potential is concentrated in higher education and Government sectors:

- higher education:

  10 universities;

  5 academies;

  5 state research institutions;

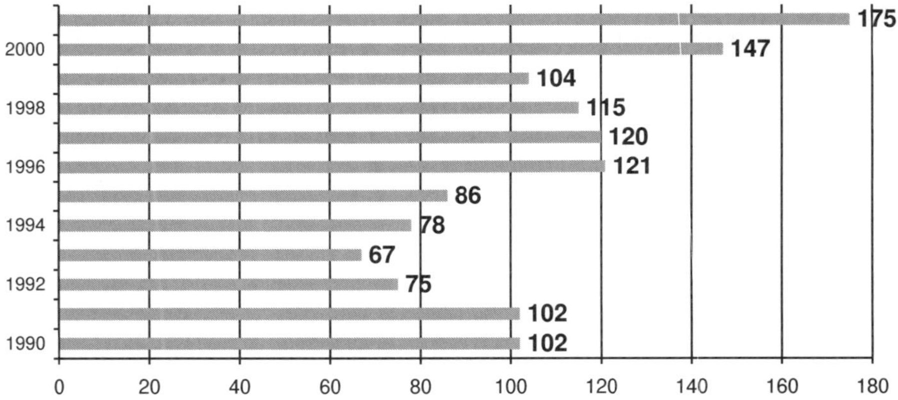

Figure 4.2.4 The number of Lithuanian research and development institutions

Source: EKT Group, 2002

- state sector:

  29 state research institutes;

  15 state research institutions;

  15 other subjects;

- business/private–non profit sector:

  more than 25 subjects.

The scientists of Lithuanian R&D institutions have a lot of experience working with foreign firms and institutions. As an example, Lithuanian scientists have cooperated with such well known foreign firms and institutions as Saab, Volvo, Philips, NATO, JV LKSoft Baltica-Boeing and NASA. The best results of R&D are obtained within the fields of biotechnology, biochemistry, laser optics, chemistry and physics.

4.3

Textile and Apparel Industry

Lithuanian Development Agency

The Lithuanian textile and apparel industry is recognized as one of the most developed industries with long-standing traditions. The textile and apparel industry is one of the major local exporters successfully competing in European Union (EU) markets. Recently the Lithuanian–EU trade in textile articles and apparel has been undergoing a rapid development.

The Lithuanian textile and apparel industry consists of:

- manufacture of textiles;
- manufacture of wearing apparel, dressing and fur dyeing;
- manufacture of leather and leather products.

Growth of textile and apparel industry

A constant growth tendency can be observed in the Lithuanian textile and apparel industry from 1997 (Table 4.3.1). During 2001, as compared to 2000, the sales volume of the country's textile and apparel industry grew by 5.4 per cent and, in comparison to 1997, by 21.6 per cent.

In 2001 textile production amounted to 422 million euros. During 2001, compared to 2000, the sales volume of the country's textile industry grew by 17 per cent and, according to export forecasts, was set to grow by 5.8 per cent in 2002. The sales of textiles account for 6.2 per cent of the total sales of industrial products in Lithuania.

Wearing apparel, dressing and fur dyeing production accounted for 586 million euros in 2001. Compared to 1997 the industrial output of the country's apparel industry grew by 47 per cent. Exports forecast that the sales volumes of the country's apparel industry increased by 5.5 per cent in 2002. According to the statistical data the total output in 2002 increased by 11 per cent. The sales of apparel account for 8.6 per cent of the total sales of industrial products in Lithuania. In 2001 the

Table 4.3.1 Sales of textile and apparel industry production (million euros)

Textile and apparel industry	1998	1999	2000	2001	2002*
Manufacture of textiles	401	339	359	422	446
Manufacture of wearing apparel, dressing and fur dyeing	457	554	584	586	618
Manufacture of leather and leather products	71	62	67	59	61

Source: Statistics Department of Lithuania
*estimate

leather and leather products industry accounted for 66 million euros. Compared to 2000 the industrial output of the country's leather industry decreased by 4 per cent.

Concentration of industry

The textile and apparel industry accounts for approximately 15 per cent of the total output of Lithuania's industries. There are 551 enterprises, of which 319 are small, 167 medium-sized, and 65 large-scale. The large-scale enterprises sell approximately 72 per cent of all textile and apparel produced in the country.

Based on data from 1 January 2002 the textile industry was represented by 159 enterprises (personal excluded); this number accounts for 29 per cent of the total number of textile and apparel industrial enterprises in which 20,900 individuals are employed; it constitutes 36 per cent of the total number of those employed in the textile and apparel industry.

Based on data from 1 January 2002 the apparel industry was represented by 358 enterprises (personal excluded). This number makes up 65 per cent of the total number of textile and apparel industrial enterprises in which 34,100 people are employed and it constitutes 53 per cent of the total number of employees working in the textile and apparel industry.

In 2002 the leather industry was represented by 34 enterprises (private excluded). This number makes up 6 per cent of the total number of textile and apparel industrial enterprises wherein there are 2,600 employees. The largest leather industry enterprises realize 72 per cent of the leather and leather products produced in the country.

Growth of domestic market

Since 1997 a steady growth tendency has been observed in Lithuania's textile and apparel industry. Between 1997 and 2001 the domestic market of textiles and apparel grew by 31.2 per cent with the average annual growth being 7.2 per cent. In 2001, compared with 2000, the domestic market grew by 10.1 per cent. The share in GDP was evaluated at 6.5 per cent in 2001.

Since 1997 a growth tendency has been observed in Lithuania's textile industry. Between 1997 and 2001 the domestic textile market grew by 44 per cent, with the average annual growth being 10 per cent. In 2001, compared with 2000, the domestic market grew by 19.4 per cent and amounted to 610 million euros.

Between 1997 and 2001 the domestic wearing apparel and dressing market increased by 25 per cent, the average annual growth being 8 per cent. In 2001 the domestic market amounted to 174 million euros.

In 2001 the domestic market of leather and leather products increased by 19 per cent. In the same year this market amounted to 81 million euros.

Export potential

The Lithuanian textile and apparel industry is the leader in national exports. Based on the data of 2001 the value of exported production comprised approximately 19.5 per cent of all Lithuanian exports. The total export volume of the textile and apparel industry output makes up 87.4 per cent. Approximately 83 per cent of all textiles and apparel is exported to the European Union (EU).

In 2001 the export of textiles and textile articles was valued at 382 million euros. Compared with 2000 the export of textiles grew by 2.4 per cent. In 2001 86 per cent of textiles produced in Lithuania was exported. The export of textile articles of apparel and clothing accessories, knitted or crocheted, constitutes 53 per cent of all textile export. In total, 89 per cent of textile articles of apparel and clothing accessories and 62 per cent of fibre and yarn were exported to the EU.

In 2001 the export of wearing apparel and dressing articles was valued at 499 million euros; compared with 2000, export grew by 8 per cent. In 2001, 93 per cent of the apparel produced in Lithuania was exported. Between 1997 and 2001 the export of apparel dressing articles grew by 47 per cent with an average annual growth of 9 per cent. Of all the exported wearing apparel and dressing articles, 92 per cent was exported to the EU in 2001.

In 2001 the value of leather and leather products export was estimated at 67 million euros. Compared with 2000 the export of leather and leather products increased by 8 per cent. In 2001 65 per cent of the leather and leather products produced in Lithuania was exported. Between 1997 and 2001 the export of leather and leather products grew by 9.8 per cent; the average annual growth was 2 per cent. Of all the exported leather and leather products 60 per cent was exported to the EU in 2001.

Producers successfully cooperate with international companies such as Ikea, Nike, H&M, Zara, C&A and Laura Ashley.

Capital investment in manufacturing

According to the data of the Lithuanian Apparel and Textile Industry Association an allocation of 34.8 million euros capital investment was made into the textile and apparel industry from own financial resources. In 2000, compared with 1995, capital investments in the textile and apparel industry grew by 73 per cent.

The technological lines and equipment functioning in the textile industry are steadily renovated and modernized. In order to achieve the aforementioned improvements the enterprises use their own funds as well as direct foreign investments. In 2000 21.6 million euros of capital investments were made into the textile industry. In 2000, compared to 1995, capital investments in the manufacturing of textiles increased by 44 per cent. In 2002, according to the data of the Lithuanian Apparel and Textile Industry Association, investments in textile industry amounted to 23.2 million euros. The biggest investment is planned in the linen industry.

In 2000, 14.6 million euros of capital investments were made into the apparel industry. In the same year, compared with 1995, capital investments in the manufacture of wearing apparel, dressing and fur dyeing increased by 168 per cent. In 2002, according to data from the Lithuanian Apparel and Textile Industry Association, investments in the apparel industry amounted to 17.4 million euros. Leather industry capital investments amounted to 1.4 million euros.

Foreign investment

Foreign investment made into the manufacture of textile products amounted to 125 million euros. In 2001, compared with 1998, foreign investments grew by 151 per cent

Investments in the manufacture of textile products amounted to 96.8 million euros in 2001. The main investor countries were Germany and Great Britain; Germany's foreign investments constituted 28.2 per cent, Great Britain's 19 per cent.

Investment in the manufacture of wearing apparel, dressing and fur dyeing amounted to 27.8 million euros in 2001. The main country investors were Denmark, Germany and Great Britain. From Denmark foreign investments made up 33.3 per cent, from Germany 12.9 per cent and from Great Britain 19.7 per cent. Investments made in the manufacturing of leather and leather products amounted to 385,000 euros in 2001.

In 2002 the main investors were Tuch Fabrik Wilhelm Becker (17 million euros) and Marzotto SPA (13 million euros).

The experience and competitive costs

The experience required to ensure product quality has been improving. Both product quality and cost relation is becoming more and more acceptable to partners and investors. In the textile and apparel industry, production per employee ranges from 19,900 euros to 21,300 euros. In 2001 employees earned an average of 222–291 euros per month.

In the textile industry, production per employee amounts to 21,300 euros per year. Capital investments accounted for 65 per cent, earnings were 20.7 per cent and depreciation accounted for 5.6 per cent in the structure of the textile industry's production costs. In 2001 average monthly earnings of employees were 290.5 euros.

In the wearing apparel and dressing industry production, per employee is 19,900 euros annually. Of the production costs, material expenditure and services rendered by the enterprises constituted 43 per cent, earnings 40 per cent and depreciation 4.1 per cent. In 2001 average monthly earnings of employees was 222.4 euros.

In the leather and leather products industry, production per employee amounts to 23,500 euros annually. Material expenditure constitutes 71 per cent and earnings account for 20 per cent in the structure of production costs of the manufacturing of leather and leather products. In 2001 average monthly earnings of employees was 244.1 euros.

With the exception of product quality and the term between order taking and completion, there is a very important factor in competitiveness enhancement. Systematic term-shortening allows the enterprise to take advantage of the competence and organizational skills of its staff, and the fact that the work process is becoming more efficient.

Structure of assets

The accumulated fixed assets of the textile industry constituted 10 per cent of the assets held by the quarrying and manufacturing enterprises in 2000. The textile fibre processing and spinning industry accumulated

18 per cent of the total long-term tangible assets held by the textile industry; the weaving industry accounted for 57 per cent. The knitwear and knitted production industry represented 24 per cent of the total long-term tangible assets held by the textile industry. According to the data of the Lithuanian Apparel and Textile Industry Association the clothing and fur dressing and dyeing industry accumulated long-term tangible assets amounting to 86.9 million euros or 3 per cent of the total industry assets. About 80 per cent of the long-term tangible assets were accumulated by the wearing apparel enterprises.

Skills and qualifications of employees

Lithuania has a tradition for high professional training of engineering and technically educated staff, so enterprises employ a sufficient number of competent employees. Highly professional textiles and apparel industry specialists are trained in eight vocational schools (the number of students is around 5,000), professional colleges and universities such as the Kaunas University of Technology (which is an Eastern European Member of the Association of Universities for Textiles (AUTEX)), Vilnius Academy of Fine Arts and others

High technology textiles

The Lithuanian Textile Institute creates, designs and manufactures technical textile fabrics and protective clothes. The product range is the result of research and technological development in close cooperation with leaders in the field from Western Europe. High-tech materials and technologies result in the development and manufacturing of a wide range of garments including personal protective equipment and protective clothing for military, police and civil application that meets the requirements of EN, NATO and NIJ. A modern testing laboratory provides efficient analysis of textile garments according to EN and ISO standards.

In the near future the Lithuanian Textile Institute will issue 'European certificates for textile fabrics'. In 2002 the last accreditation procedures were completed in the Lithuanian Textile Institute for the accreditation that will be valid in all European countries. Exporters will be able to receive this certificate more quickly and cheaply than their peers in other countries.

Customer standards and requirements

Lithuanian companies seek to compete in both domestic and foreign markets, so they certify their production according to ISO standards. The leaders in the country's textile and apparel industry have either implemented, or are in the process of implementing, ISO quality standards such as ISO 9000, ISO 14000 and others.

4.4

The Woodworking Industry

Lithuanian Development Agency

The woodworking industry employs over 32,000 people in over 1,000 companies. The industry accounts for 10 per cent of all Lithuanian exports. Since 1999, wood and furniture industry branches were steadily growing and in 2002 the growth of those branches was estimated to be the fastest in the manufacturing industry on the whole.

The dominating role in the industry belongs to the wood and wood products branch (Figures 4.4.1–4.4.3).

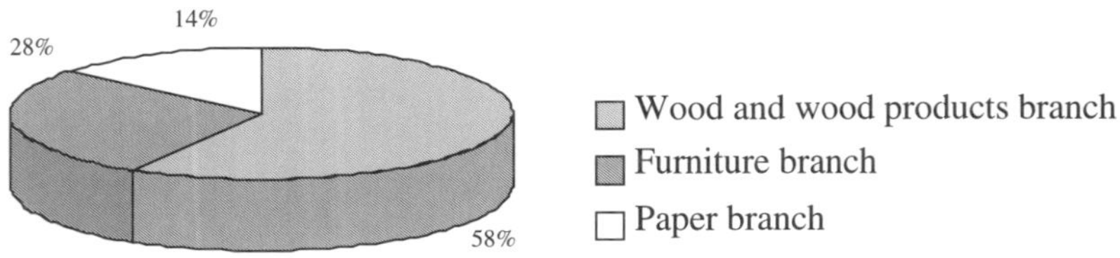

Figure 4.4.1 The distribution of income in wood and furniture industry branches in 2001 (%)

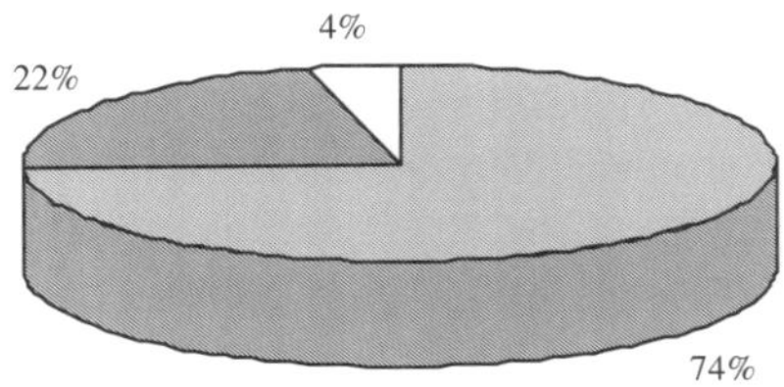

Figure 4.4.2 The distribution of companies in wood and furniture industry branches in 2001 (%)

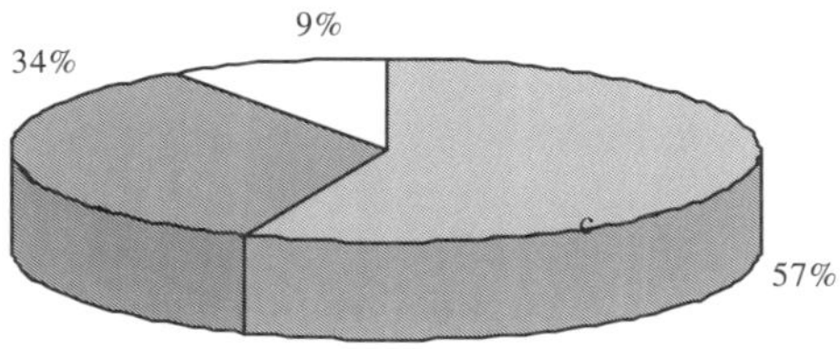

Figure 4.4.3 The distribution of employees in wood and furniture industry branches in 2001 (%)

Estimated results for 2002 show that growth of the wood and wood products branch is slower than that of the furniture and paper branches. A particularly rapid progress is observed in the paper branch (up to 35 per cent) compared to the previous period.

Lumbering

A total of 31 per cent of Lithuanian territory was covered with forests in 2002. The forests area amounts to 2.2 million hectares. According to the Lithuanian Statistic Department the lumbering level remains rather stable in Lithuania and amounts to 5.5 million cubic metres per year. Wood is lumbered in private and state-owned forests. The current growth in lumbering comes from private forests. In 1999 lumbering in private forests amounted to 1.02 million cubic metres, in 2001 to 1.76 million cubic metres. Lumbering in state forests remains rather stable. According to different prognoses lumbering within 10 years should reach 6.7 million cubic metres. Later it could go up to 8.9 million m^3 annually.

Round timber market

The amount of imported round timber constitutes only 1–2 per cent of all the supplies. However, it should be noted that the amount of imported round timber is constantly decreasing; in 1997 100,000 cubic metres of round timber was imported but thus was reduced to 60,000 cubic metres in 2000. State-owned enterprises supply approximately two-thirds of all round timber. However, a share of these enterprises is slightly decreasing each year. The share of state-owned enterprises declined from 69 per cent to 65 per cent between 1998 and 2000. Of all round timber, 20–28 per cent is still exported. In spite of the declining supply in 1998 and 1999, the export of round timber increased; 786,000 cubic metres were exported in 1998 and the export grew to 1.3 million cubic metres in 2001.

The increase in lumbering in 2000 enabled an increase in round timber export, which has been growing over the last three years. Export increased by 28 per cent and reached 1.2 million cubic metres. More than a half of the round timber was exported to Sweden and almost all of the remaining half went to Poland and Russia. Although export increased most considerably to Russia and Poland (50 per cent and 39 per cent), Sweden consolidated its position by export volumes most significantly.

Wood and wood products

The wood and wood products branch grew twice as fast as the country's total industry in the period from 2000 to 2001 (Figure 4.4.4).

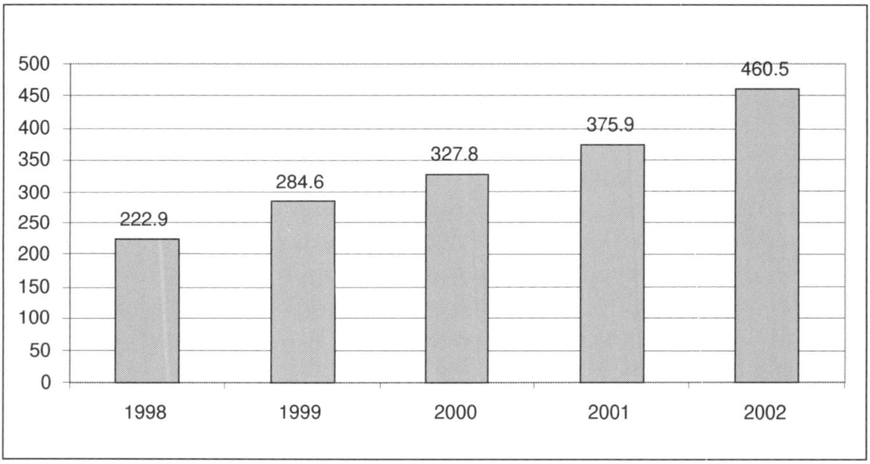

Figure 4.4.4 The total sales of the wood and wood products branch (million euros)

Even if the growth of the wood and wood products branch was significant, this increase was due to the growing number of employees engaged in the industry. Meanwhile labour productivity in this branch grows rapidly only in lumber milling, plywood and panels production. Labour productivity in lumber milling, plywood and panels production in 2000 was more than twice as high as that in 1996. The labour productivity in other production branches is very insignificant.

The main export country is Germany although it should be noted that its part in the structure of exports decreased from 32 per cent in 1999 to 23 per cent in 2001. Of all wood and wood products 10–12 per cent is exported to Sweden. At present exports to Poland and the USA are growing. Exports to Great Britain and Denmark remain constant at 8 per cent and 5.5 per cent respectively. There is a slight increase in exports to Russia and Latvia and exports to Norway and Finland increased considerably in 2001. There is a significant decrease in exports to Holland.

Raw wood dominates in the export of Lithuanian wood and wood products production. The export of round timber increased by almost 40 per cent from 1999 to 2001 and was 1.3 million cubic metres in 2002. The export of sawn wood grew rapidly in 2000 and was almost 830,000 cubic metres, though it declined by almost 80,000 cubic metres in 2001. The export of low value timber (firewood, chips and timber waste) increased significantly from 1999 to 2001. This group of products, however, constitutes only a small part in the structure of exports where value is concerned. During this period (1999–2001) the export of production with a larger added value increased rapidly. The export of plywood increased by more than 50 per cent to 38,200 cubic metres. The export of shaving panels during this period increased to almost twice as much as its previous amount at 97,600 cubic metres in 2001.

The number of companies in the wood and wood products branch in 2000 increased by 11 per cent and reached a total of 781 in comparison with the previous year. This number, however, reduced to 760 in 2001. The size of companies in the wood and wood products branch can be described as small because more than a third of them employed between one and nine individuals in 2001 and almost 90 per cent had fewer than 50 employees. Only 28 companies had 100 or more employees in 2001. This means that the number of such companies increased four-fold in comparison with 2000.

There were 18,100 employees in the wood and wood products branch in 2001. The biggest proportion of employees (more than 80 per cent) worked in non-personal enterprises. From 1999 to 2001 the number of workers in the wood and wood products branch increased by 15 per cent, although this was not achieved as a result of the growth of personal enterprises.

There were 760 enterprises in the wood and wood products branch in 2001, 62 of whom had attracted foreign direct investments. The size of these investments grew until 2000 but decreased in 2001 and settled at 38.1 million euros. Enterprises using other financing sources (mostly profit and loans), however, gained long-term property for almost 30 million euros in 1999, 24.8 million euros in 2000 and 32.6 million euros in 2001.

The furniture branch

The furniture branch, as well as the wood and wood product branch, grew rapidly after the crisis of 1999. The growth rate for the 1999–

2000 period was 24.2 per cent and that for 2000–2001 19.3 per cent. In 2002 the furniture branch increased by 30 per cent.

From 1999 to 2001 furniture sales increased from 117.3 million euros to 179.6 million euros, which gives a rise of more than 50 per cent. According to preliminary data sales of furniture in 2002 amounted to 230 million euros (Figure 4.4.5).

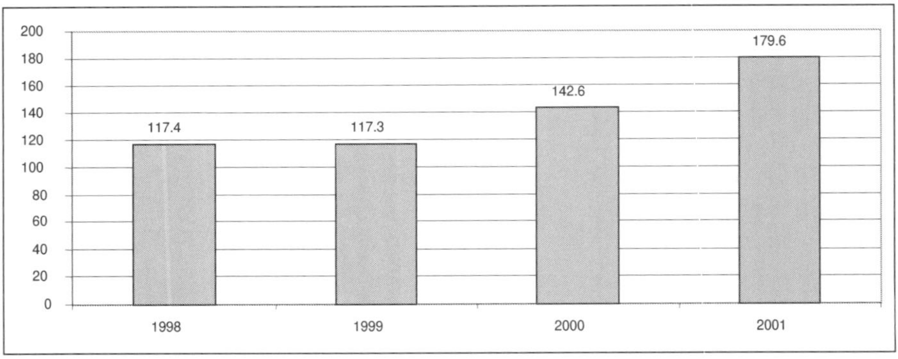

Figure 4.4.5 Total sales of the Lithuanian furniture branch (million euros).

Although Lithuanian furniture production sizes are growing rapidly, in the European context the Lithuanian furniture branch exceeds only its Latvian counterpart. Production by German and Italian furniture branches is more than 100 times bigger.

Labour productivity is not high in the furniture branch. Between 1996 and 2000 labour productivity increased from 9,300 euros per employee per year to 13,000 euros. However this growth was primarily during 1997–1998, as between 1998 and 2001 the labour productivity increased by less than 10 per cent.

Labour productivity in the furniture branches of other countries was significantly higher in 2000. In Sweden, Italy, Germany and Denmark productivity was about 141,900 euros per employee. In other European Union (EU) countries this index is a little lower (eg in Greece and Portugal it is 33,900 euros and 28,100 euros respectively). In comparison with some other countries however, the labour productivity of the Lithuanian furniture branch does not appear so bad – Latvian, Bulgarian and Romanian furniture branch labour productivity was even lower.

The Lithuanian furniture branch is export-orientated. A total of 41.8 per cent of production was exported in 1998 but exports in 2001 were almost three-quarters of all furniture sales (Figure 4.4.6).

Almost a quarter of exported furniture and its components are exported to Germany. At present furniture exports to Sweden, Great Britain, Holland and Norway are rapidly increasing.

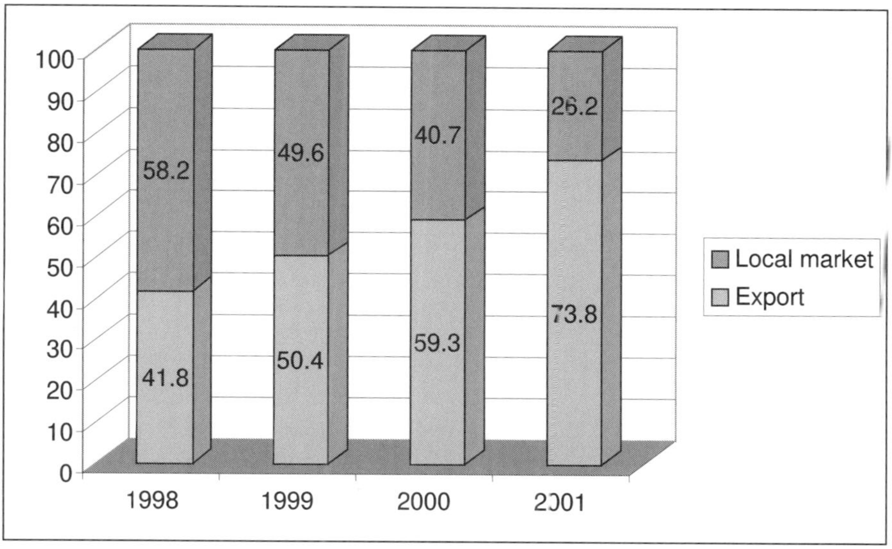

Figure 4.4.6 Sales structure of the Lithuanian furniture branch (%)

In the furniture branch the number of enterprises changes relatively little. The number increased in 2000, then decreased a little in 2001 leaving 225 enterprises.

Almost a third of furniture industry enterprises are very small, having fewer than nine employees. Enterprises with 10–99 employees constitute more than half of the companies in this branch and only 15 per cent of these enterprises have more than 100 employees. It must be noted that the number of enterprises with more than 100 employees is quite stable.

The number of employees in the furniture branch grows constantly, each year increasing by almost 500 workers. If, in 1999, there were a little more than 10,000 employees, this number would have grown to over 11,000 in 2001. This growth is much more rapid in companies other than personal and state enterprises.

Small companies (with fewer than 10 employees) constitute almost a third of all furniture branch enterprises and only 3 per cent of the employees of this branch work in them. A total of 70 per cent of furniture branch employees work in enterprises with more than 100 workers.

The wages of all furniture branch employees declined in 2000; however it increased last year and was higher than in 1999. The average monthly salary (excluding personal enterprises) constantly increased, finishing at 270.8 euros in 2001.

Small enterprises (with fewer than 10 employees) sold less than 2 per cent of all furniture branch production, whereas big companies (with more than 100 employees) sold three-quarters of all branch production.

The sales of enterprises with 10–99 employees constituted 20 per cent of all branch sales.

The Lithuanian furniture branch attracted relatively few foreign direct investments though they are constantly increasing. By the end of 1999, 6.7 million euros were invested in this branch; this figure had increased to 7.5 million euros by the end of 2001. Despite small foreign direct investments, furniture branch companies use other financing sources for gaining long-term property. In 1999 furniture branch enterprises made capital investments of almost 10.1 million euros; in 2001 the amount reached 12.7 million euros.

The paper branch

The smallest growth in the paper branch was from 1998 to 2001 in comparison with other wood and furniture industry branches. The paper branch declined in the period from 1998 to 1999; however there was a rapid growth in 2000 by almost 20 per cent. In 2001 this growth decreased (12 per cent) but a rapid growth (31 per cent) was noticed in 2002.

Sales of the paper branch from 1998 to 2002 increased constantly – 86.9 million euros in 2001 and approximately 115 million euros in 2002 (Figure 4.4.7).

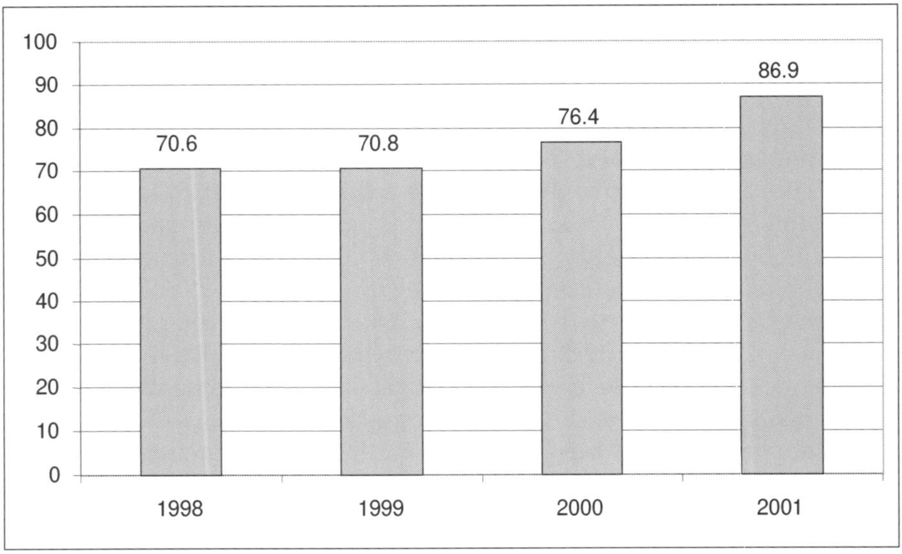

Figure 4.4.7 Total sales of the Lithuanian paper branch (million euros)

The production of cardboard increased rapidly in the paper branch In 1999 27,600 tonnes of cardboard were produced and in 2001 this figure almost doubled to 54,300 tonnes. The production of paper was reduced significantly in 1999, and 1998's volume was reached only in 2001. The production of toilet paper is constantly growing and increased significantly in 2001 when production went up by 30 per cent. The production of exercise books also grew. Meanwhile the production of fibre plate decreased significantly in 1999. In 2001, 15.8 million square metres of splint panel were produced – only 80 per cent of 1999's quantity.

The export of paper is constantly growing. The export value of 1999's production was 37.8 million euros, a figure which rose by 42 per cent to 53.8 million euros in 2001 (Figure 4.4.8). Paper branch exports constitute 53–62 per cent of all the branch production.

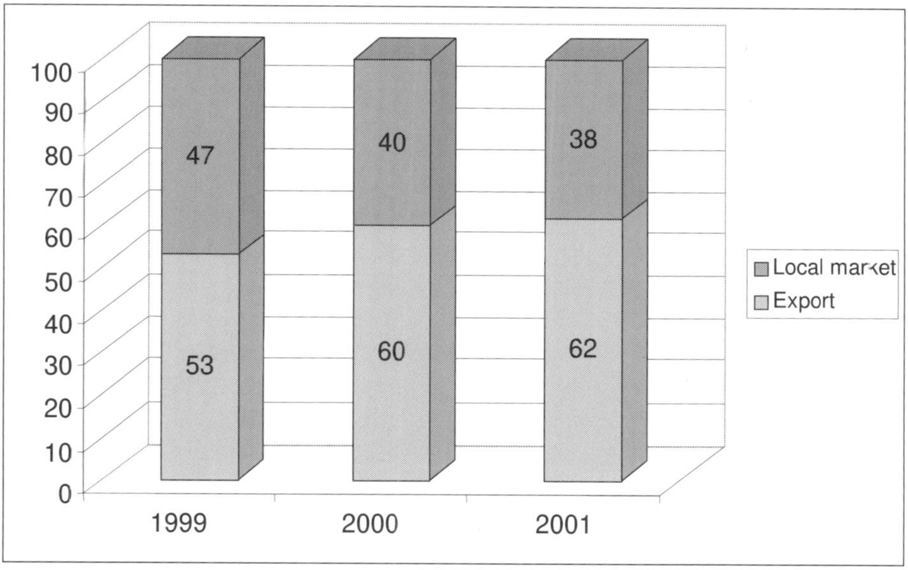

Figure 4.4.8 Sales structure of Lithuanian paper branch (%)

The main share of export is paper and cardboard. The export of products doubled during the 1999–2001 period and amounted to 67,700 tonnes. Splint panel exports also increased; in 2001 this had grown by a third compared to levels in 1999.

In 2000–2001 32 companies were working in the paper industry. Almost 40 per cent of these enterprises (excluding personal enterprises) were small (having a maximum of nine employees). Less then 20 per cent were enterprises with over 100 employees. During 1998 and 2000 the number of these enterprises diminished, but the number of those with 20 to 49 employees increased. In recent years the number of employees has decreased; between 1998 and 2000 the number of employees working in the paper industry was reduced by 1000. Analysis of the dynamics of employees in different kinds of enterprises shows why the number of employees has diminished. In total, three-quarters of the branch's employees work in big enterprises (those with more than 200 employees).

Compared with salaries in the wood branch, paper branch employees' salaries were bigger in the 1999–2001 period. In the paper branch the salary was stable, and over recent years has increased to 319 euros a month from 304 euros.

Foreign direct investments in the paper branch, publishing and printing enterprises amounted to 32.7 million euros in 2001.

4.5

The Plastics and Rubber Industry

Lithuanian Development Agency

General overview

During the period of 1995–2002, Lithuania's industry underwent a stage of growth, the tendencies of which also influenced the development of the country's plastic and rubber products industry. During 2001, compared to 2000, the increase in sales of plastic and rubber products was over 20 per cent. The estimated growth in 2002 is at the same level and is expected to reach 18 per cent. In 2001, Lithuanian manufacturers of plastic and rubber products sold 67 per cent of their total production in the domestic market and exported 33 per cent.

There are 186 companies working in the country's plastic and rubber industry, of which 168 engaged in the production of plastics and only 18 in the production of rubber products. The industry employs over 5,500 individuals; annual production per employee in 2001 reached 35,900 euros. At the moment this indicator is among the highest in Lithuania's manufacturing industry, but still retains potential for further growth. The average monthly gross salary in 2001 was 264 euros.

Over 60 per cent of companies in the plastic and rubber industry are small and medium-sized businesses. They are specialized, flexible, easily able to respond to market developments and implement all the stages of the production process – from the design and casting of forms through to delivery of the final product.

Product groups

Lithuanian plastic and rubber goods manufacturers offer a wide range of finished or semifinished industrial and household products. During the period of 1995–2002 the major directions in which the Lithuanian plastic and rubber products industry could go were formed. This included the production of:

- plastic building materials: PVC profiles; PVC pipes; PVC constructions, windows, window frames, doors, and blinds; polymer roofing, rain pipes, windowsill; PE insulation foam;
- automotive components from plastic: hulls for cars and yachts; panels for trailers and semitrailers; small plastic details for cars;
- plastic packaging: various-sized polyethylene bags; PET bottles, plastic containers, and other production; plastic film; plastic boxes;
- various household goods from plastic: plastic barrels and pots; plastic dishes; plastic toys;
- automotive components from rubber: axle shaft protection products, fenders, charge removers, spacers, seal rings, belts, etc;
- industrial rubber products: manshet sealings, rubber pipes etc;
- non-standard rubber products.

Access to raw materials

Lithuanian plastic and rubber product manufacturers have a well-developed access to raw materials. The main sources of primary raw materials in 2001 were Russia (approximately 39 per cent), Belarus (approximately 11 per cent), and Poland (approximately 11 per cent).

Many Lithuanian plastics companies have gained experience in the plastic recycling area, which gives an opportunity, after equipment modernization, to recycle plastic waste and produce secondary raw materials locally, thus reducing the production costs of plastic goods. As can be seen in Table 4.5.1, the use of recycled waste is increasing.

Quality control

The main guarantee of the quality of plastic and rubber products made in Lithuania is a strict mechanism of quality control and manufacturers'

Table 4.5.1 Recycling and use of plastic and polymer waste in production (tonnes)

Plastic and polymer waste	1994	1995	1996	1997	1998	1999	2000
Produced	505	280	288	949	1,234	12,410	14,040
Recycled and used in production	3,961	4,083	6,424	10,618	11,445	12,557	13,147

Source: Lithuanian Department of Statistics

orientation to International Organization for Standardization (ISO) standards. In total, 10 per cent of Lithuanian plastics manufacturers, including all major producers and exporters of plastic products, are certified according to ISO 9000 requirements.

The orientation of the plastic and rubber goods industry toward ISO standards goes along with the general tendencies in the country's industries. According to the Lithuanian Standards Board, by December 2002 270 Lithuanian companies obtained ISO 9000 quality control certificates and 27 companies acquired certificates of environmental management standards ISO 14001.

Exports

One of the major factors determining the growth of the plastic and rubber industry was finding new attractive markets and the rapid development of export. Based on statistical data of 2001, the value of exported plastic and rubber production comprised roughly 2 per cent of total Lithuanian export. Approximately 20 per cent of all exported plastic and rubber industry products were imported by European Union (EU) countries, 31 per cent by Commonwealth of Independent States (CIS) countries and 3 per cent by CEFTA.

The current export growth is based on the increasing export to the Baltic countries, Russia and Ukraine (Figure 4.5.1). Lithuanian companies are regaining Eastern markets and this is one of the factors indicating the further potential of this industry.

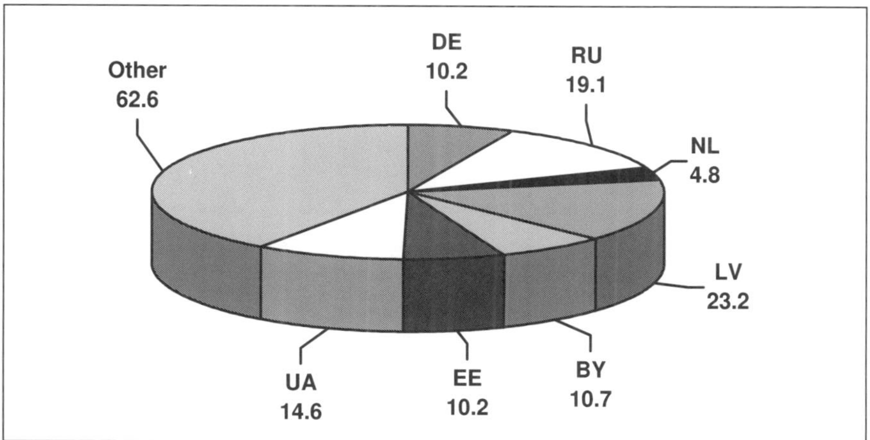

Figure 4.5.1 Exports of plastic and rubber products, 2001 (million euros)

Source: Lithuanian Department of Statistics

Domestic consumption

From 1995 to 2001 the domestic market for plastic and rubber goods in Lithuania increased more than seven-fold, and its average annual growth amounted to approximately 25 per cent. The increase in the market share of Lithuanian producers demonstrates that the plastic goods made in the country are successfully competing with imports, in terms of both quality and technical characteristics. Such a market structure also indicates the opportunities for investments in areas where imports could be replaced by local products. The most attractive fields for investment are considered to be the production of plastic profiles and piping systems, plastisol roofing, plastic parts for automobiles, PET containers and their semi-finished goods and products from HDPE.

Investments

Foreign direct investments (FDIs) in the plastic and rubber goods industry in Lithuania at the beginning of 2002, compared to 1998, grew by 53 per cent and amounted to 31.3 million euros (Table 4.5.2). At present, 17 per cent of companies producing plastic and rubber products have attracted FDIs. International companies, like Wavin, Schmitz Cargobull, British Vita and Aluplast are successfully operating in Lithuania and plan to expand their activities further.

Table 4.5.2 Foreign direct investment in the plastic and rubber industry, 1997–2001

	1997	1998	1999	2000	2001
Total in Lithuania	1,205.5	1,882.9	2,389.9	2,704.2	3,087.9
Manufacturing industry	441.6	609.9	760.3	777.9	790.3
Plastic and rubber industry	14.5	26.0	28.0	30.9	31.3
Plastic and rubber industry, % of total FDI in manufacturing industry	3	4	4	4	4

Source: Lithuanian Department of Statistics

Research and development

A number of institutions related to research and development (R&D) activities in the plastic and rubber industry provide the infrastructure for the development of new products and technologies. R&D activities in the area of plastic and rubber are very important for retaining competitiveness in the industry. Two main institutions working in this area are:

- Packaging Research Centre at Kaunas University of Technology (KTU);
- Institute of Architecture and Constructions.

Other R&D institutions are not directly related to the plastic and rubber industry, but to some extent are facilitating its development. These include:

- Institute of Materials Science;
- Institute of Environmental Engineering and other scientific institutions and centres under KTU;
- Institute of Thermoisolation at Gediminas Technical University;
- Institute of Material Science and Applied Research at the University of Vilnius;
- Lithuanian Institute of Chemistry;
- Lithuanian Institute of Physics.

In September 1994, the country's packaging companies established the Lithuanian Packagers Association. In 1995, it became a full member of the World Packaging Organization (WPO). The Association supplies information, training and professional development of specialists, organization of seminars, presentations, shows and other events and provides solutions to various problems related to the packaging industry, eg ecological and legal issues, standardization and certification.

The relatively large number of technical specialists sets the stage for the high qualification of employees as well as for the possibility to make use of advanced technologies.

Prospects for branch development

Lithuanian producers explore world trends in the development in the plastic and rubber branch, which are:

- the growing use of plastic components in plastic branch: automobile producers are increasing the use of plastic in automobile manufacturing, seeking to make use of the following advantages of plastic auto parts: longevity, resistance to corrosion, ease of processing and painting, little weight etc. Successful investments of Schmitz Cargobull, the development of JSC Swedlit AB Baltic, JSC Stikloplastika,

JSC Plastic Formo, JSC Stigma and other local companies demonstrate the opportunities in this market in Lithuania;

- the growing demand for plastic packaging materials: in the Lithuanian market, and especially in the food industry, more and more plastic containers are being used. The Lithuanian industry is becoming stronger and is investing in a new generation of high-quality packaging. On the basis of data from the research carried out by Market Tracking International, it is expected that within the next two years, plastic packaging will replace cardboard and paper in the world market. The sales of plastic packaging should comprise 38 per cent of the world market for packaging goods;
- the growing use of secondary raw materials in the plastic sector: current developments in the world market for plastic products indicate the increasing use of recycled plastic and secondary materials, especially in the area of plastic packaging.

At present, plastic constitutes approximately 10 per cent of all household and technological waste; therefore the collection and recycling of plastic rubbish is economically promising from the point of view of both environmental protection and production cost reduction. In Lithuania the recycling and use of secondary plastic raw material in manufacturing almost quadrupled between 1994 and 2000. Over 10 companies like SC Plasta, JSC Polivektris, PE Maldis are recycling plastic waste at present.

All the above listed trends in the development of Lithuania's plastic and rubber industry enable a prediction of further reasonable growth in this sector. The presented characteristics support the prognosis that the growth level in this industry will remain at the level of 15–20 per cent.

4.6

The Chemical Industry

Lithuanian Development Agency

General information

The chemical industry emerged in Lithuania in the nineteenth century. Paints and varnishes, various acids and salts, as well as pharmaceutical and cosmetic products, were manufactured from the beginning. The Union factory, founded in 1869 and manufacturing superphosphate, was one of the largest enterprises of the chemical industry in Lithuania. In 1908 there were 28 chemical industry factories operating in Lithuania (not including the region of Klaipeda), the output of which comprised 1.4 per cent of all the industrial production. In 1907, 11 chemical industry factories were operating in the region of Klaipeda. The growth of Lithuania's chemical industry reached its apex in 1960–1965.

In 2002, 67 enterprises were operating in Lithuania's chemical industry, of which 27 per cent should be ascribed to the category of small businesses and 48 per cent medium-sized or big business entities. At the beginning of 2002, chemical industry enterprises employed 5,900 people, whose average monthly wage was 428 euros.

The sales volume of chemical products has increased by 6 per cent since 1997 and at the end of 2001 consisted of 305 million euros (Figure 4.6.1). Enterprises employing over 500 employees sold the biggest part of the production (73 per cent).

The chemical industry is one of Lithuania's economic sectors, the sales volume of which, as a consequence of industrial reorganization and the Russian crisis, fluctuated between 1997 and 2002. In 2002 the sales volume had increased by 6 per cent over 1997. Meanwhile, the volume of production sold by Lithuania's extraction and processing industry during this period increased by 33 per cent. The monetary expression of the production sold by the enterprises of the chemical industry in 2002 comprised 5 per cent of the entire volume of the country's processing industry.

The domestic market of Lithuania's chemical industry had increased in 2002 by 21 per cent in comparison to 1997. According to 2002 data,

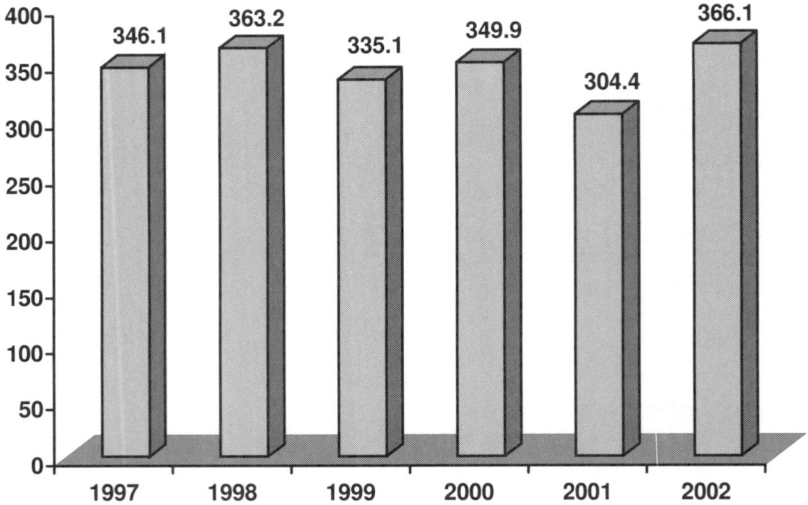

Figure 4.6.1 Product sales of Lithuania's chemical industry (million euros)

Source: Lithuanian Department of Statistics

the manufacturers of Lithuania's chemical industry products sold 55 per cent of their total output on the domestic market.

Main products

The chemical industry sector in Lithuania encompasses the following main branches:

Basic chemical production (enzymes, organic and non-organic chemicals)

Basic chemical production in Lithuania includes the production of enzymes as well as organic and non-organic chemical products (sulphur, nitric acid, carbamide, methanol, ammonia etc). The basic chemical domestic market in Lithuania makes up approximately 13 per cent (133 million euros) of the entire chemical industry. Basic chemical exports comprise some 13 per cent of all chemical product exports.

The main leaders of this branch are Achema AB and Lifosa AB. The biggest enzyme production enterprise, Fermentas AB, sells only 1 per cent of its products in Lithuania. Fermentas AB presently controls approximately 10 per cent of the global market, exporting to 42 countries world-wide. Branches of the enterprise have been opened in the USA, Canada, and Germany.

Fertilizer production

In 2001, the domestic market of the fertilizer industry comprised the biggest part, (approximately 36 per cent or 356.2 million euros) of the entire chemical industry in Lithuania. Of the products produced, 56 per cent are exported. Two big fertilizer producers exist at the present time in Lithuania, namely Achema AB and Lifosa AB.

The pharmaceutical industry, medicinal chemical products and botanical products (pharmaceutical products)

Lithuania's pharmaceutical enterprises have successfully continued their activities in recent years. On the basis of data for 11 months in 2002, the production of pharmaceutical products increased by 10 per cent. Lithuania's pharmaceutical industry grew by over 30 per cent in 2001 in comparison to 2000. According to the data of the international rating agency, Fitch, the pharmaceutical enterprises of Central and Eastern Europe are continuously increasing the strength of their positions in the region. This is mostly due to enterprises understanding the local markets and the willingness of consumers to select medicines manufactured in their own country. In 2001 the domestic pharmaceuticals market constituted approximately 25 per cent (243 million euros) of the entire chemical industry.

Soaps, detergents, cleansers, polishes, fragrances and toiletries (household chemicals, solvents, varnish, body care products, perfumes, cosmetics)

At this time, imported household chemicals and cosmetics account for approximately 70 per cent of the country's entire market. Meanwhile, the country's manufacturers are using only 5–20 per cent of their capacities. Specialists assert that after creating more favourable conditions for businesses and by using only 50 per cent of their capacities, local manufacturers could increase their sales volumes and sell twice as many products. The domestic market of the household chemical and body care product industry accounted for some 18 per cent (170.9 million euros) of the entire chemical industry in Lithuania in 2001. At present, the biggest Lithuanian enterprises active in this branch are Koslita UAB, Naujoji Ringuva AB, Alytaus Chemija AB, Baltic Chemical International UAB, Baltchem UAB, Biok UAB and Higeja AB.

Semi-synthetic fibre manufacturing (acetate thread)

There exists at the present time only one enterprise in Lithuania manufacturing semi-synthetic fibres, namely Dirbtinis Pluostas AB. The long manufacturing experience of Dirbtinis Pluostas AB and their qualified specialists guarantee consumers not only a diverse assortment of thread but also competitiveness in Western markets. The enterprise manufactures products worth 29 million euros per year. The principal realization market of Dirbtinis Pluostas AB is the countries of Europe (87 per cent), namely, England, Italy and the Netherlands. Approximately 7 per cent of its production is realized in Lithuania. The sale of the production of Dirbtinis Pluostas AB is affected by seasonality.

Raw materials

The main primary raw materials of Lithuania's chemical industry sector are sulphur, sulphuric acid, hydrates and soda-ash. Part of the raw materials is purchased from local manufacturers but the biggest part is imported from countries of the Commonwealth of Independent States (CIS).

Foreign sales

Even growth is characteristic of the chemical industry's exports. Exports of Lithuania's chemical industry's production in 2001 comprised 341.7 million euros (or 6.4 per cent of the country's total exports). Of the chemical products, 65 per cent were exported to European Union (EU) countries, 18 per cent to the CIS and 12 per cent to the countries of the Baltic region.

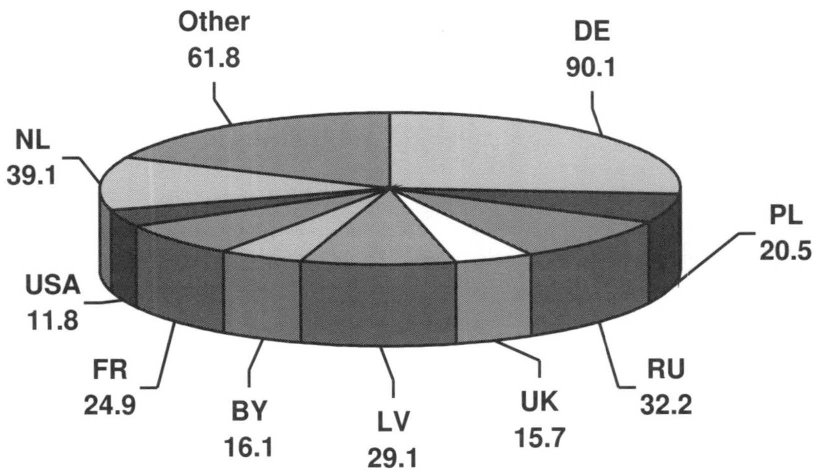

Figure 4.6.2 Exports of chemical products, 2001 (million euros)

Source: Lithuanian Department of Statistics

In 2001, Lithuania imported chemical products worth 677.3 million euros (or 9.2 per cent of the country's total imports), ie twice the amount of that manufactured in Lithuania. As Lithuania's chemical product market is dominated by imported products, there is a possibility of developing local production in order to replace those products being imported.

Domestic market

Between 1997 and 2002, the domestic market in Lithuania for chemical industry products grew by 21 per cent while annual domestic growth for the country as a whole reached 5 per cent. According to 2002 data, the manufacturers of Lithuania's chemical industry sold 55 per cent of their output on the domestic market. The greatest part of the chemical industry's products in the domestic market consists of the manufacture of fertilizer and pharmaceutical products (Figure 4.6.3).

Fluctuations in sales volumes have been observed in Lithuania's chemical industry sector since 1998: in 2001, in comparison with 1998, the volume of production sold in the country's chemical industry sector declined by 15 per cent. However, in the first half of 2002, in comparison with the same period in 2001, sales of the chemical industry's products grew by 13.5 per cent. An overview of sales in the period from 1999 to 2002 is given in Figure 4.6.4. The increase in the share of Lithuanian production shows that the products of the chemical industry that are domestically manufactured are successfully competing with imported production both in terms of quality and technical characteristics.

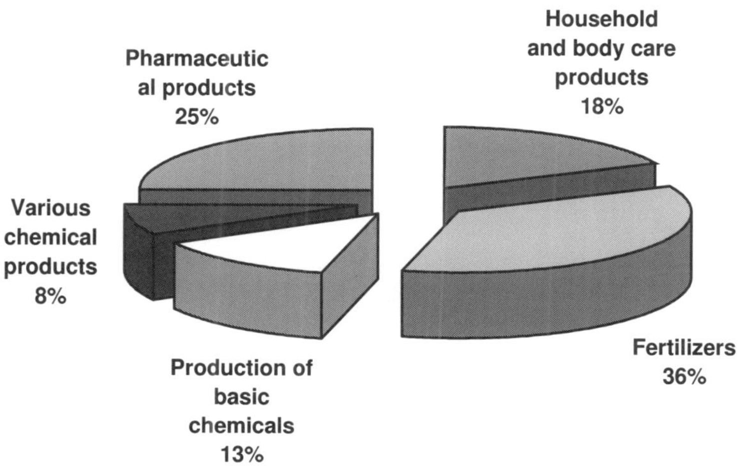

Figure 4.6.3 The domestic market for chemical industry products

Source: Lithuanian Department of Statistics

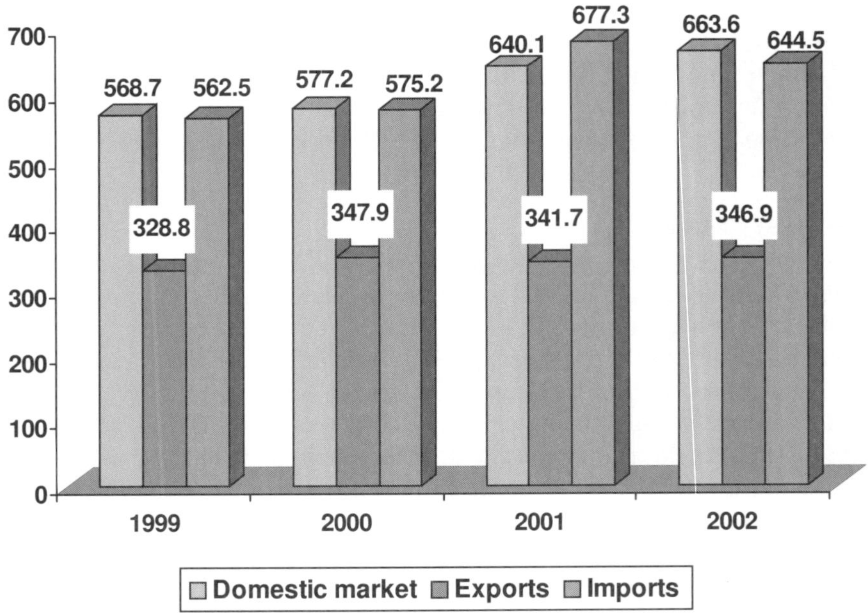

Figure 4.6.4 Domestic consumption, exports and imports of chemical products 1999–2002 (million euros)

Source: Lithuanian Department of Statistics

Foreign direct investment

At the beginning of 2002 foreign direct investments in the chemical industry sector in Lithuania declined by 17 per cent, in comparison to 1998, and amounted to 26.7 million euros. Of the 67 enterprises presently producing chemical industry products, 20 have attracted foreign capital. The principal countries that have invested are Denmark (8 million euros), USA (4.1 million euros), Sweden (4 million euros) and Estonia (0.3 million euros).

The areas of the chemical industry that are most attractive for investments are considered to be the manufacture of pharmaceutical products and chemical ingredients, the latter being used in the chemical industry.

Scientific research

There are currently 15 active institutes/centres in Lithuania that are able to carry out scientific research for the chemical industry. In 1997, the enterprises active in the chemical industry sector founded the

Association of Lithuanian Chemical Industry Enterprises (ALChIE). Over 80 per cent of the country's chemical industry products are produced in enterprises that are Association members. ALChIE is a member of the Lithuanian Confederation of Industrialists and an associate member of the European Chemical Industry Council (CEFIC).

The amassed technological base and experience in the area of the production of technological fixtures and equipment enable the manufacturers of the chemical industry sector in Lithuania to more effectively organize the production process. The potential for research and development is strongly developed in Lithuania. Scientific research centres have been founded in almost all the enterprises that lead the Lithuanian chemical industry sector. In 2001, 133 employees engaged in scientific research were employed in the chemical industry (Table 4.6.1).

Table 4.6.1 Employees engaged in scientific research (2001)

Industry	Scientists and engineers		Technicians and similar personnel		Other service staff		Total
	Women	Men	Women	Men	Women	Men	
Chemical industry	58	29	11	6	14	15	133

Source: Lithuanian Department of Statistics

Lithuania also has a well-developed education system able to prepare some 300 highly qualified chemical specialists per year.

Quality control

According to 2002 data, 14 enterprises active in the chemical industry sector have International Organization for Standardization (ISO) quality control certificates and one enterprise, Achema AB, has introduced the ISO 14001 environmental protection standard. The enterprises of the chemical industry sector in Lithuania are also gradually preparing to introduce the 'Responsible Care' standard. Lithuania's future EU membership is now forcing pharmacists to inculcate the requirements of 'good manufacturing practice' (GMP), which will become mandatory for Lithuania's pharmaceutical enterprises in 2004.

4.7

The Automotive Component Manufacturing Sector

Lithuanian Development Agency

The design and manufacturing of automotive components has deep roots in Lithuania; electronic devices, metal parts, windows, automotive compressors, agricultural machinery and other metalworking have been developed in the country for decades.

The automotive component industry in Lithuania is focused on manufacturing, among others, the following products:

- automotive wire and cable bundles;
- fuel pumps;
- automotive electronics;
- automotive electronic wiring;
- automotive compressors;
- diesel engines;
- oil and air filters;
- brake systems;
- cargo containers;
- car hitches;
- car windows;
- ornamental parts.

Lithuanian companies also have experience in equipping and assembling special purpose motor cars as well as in fully assembling stock motor vehicles.

An analysis of the automotive component sector in Lithuania has revealed that small or medium-sized manufacturing enterprises of up to 50 employees predominate. However, as previously mentioned, automotive components are manufactured by enterprises that are diversely classified according to the NACE activities classifier; therefore it is difficult to determine the precise number of enterprises engaging in this activity. It would be possible, according to the nature of their activities, to group the enterprises manufacturing automotive components into the following main areas (at the same time also presenting the main manufacturers):

- development in the automotive component sector;
- plastic and rubber automotive part manufacturing;
- spare and maintenance parts;
- chemical and electrochemical capabilities;
- mechanical and other non-chemical metal processing capabilities.

Development in the automotive component sector

In the area of automotive electronic wiring and electronic devices, the following products are manufactured:

- wire assemblies for Renault passenger cars;
- automotive wire bundles for Volvo lorries;
- automotive comfort system components;
- automotive liquid petroleum gas (LPG) equipment components, etc.

The largest enterprise in the area of electric wiring products is SY Wiring Technologies Lietuva UAB in Klaipeda, a private capital enterprise belonging to the Siemens group of companies (Germany) and Yazaki (Japan). The enterprise manufactures the latest generation of electrical wiring assemblies (ignition system wires) for Renault passenger cars. Since the beginning of its activities, it has already invested 24 million euros in Lithuania and now employs 2,700 people. Over 1,000 new workplaces had been created by 2002 because production of electrical wiring assemblies for the Renault Megane model had begun.

All of the enterprise's production is exported to France and Spain. The enterprise is the sector leader with an annual sales turnover amounting to 74 million euros in 1999, 74 million euros in 2000, 63 million euros in 2001 and 71 million euros in 2002. The enterprise's sales are expected to consist of 99 million euros in 2003 and over 90 million euros in 2004. A contract with Renault for the supply of electrical wiring assemblies until 2008 has been concluded.

Lietkabelis AB, being the largest wire and cable manufacturer in the region, has excellent development possibilities in the area of wire and cable bundle assembly. The enterprise can supply suitable components for many kinds of automotive cable bundles. The automotive bundle manufacturing division, which was founded back in 1997, manufactures engine and feed system electrical bundles for the Swedish bus and lorry manufacturer, Volvo. Approximately 230 employees presently work in this area. At this time, it manufactures about 800 different kinds of cable bundles and power cables. The volume of bundle production is steadily growing. In 2001 its production was sold for 12.5 million euros and in 2000 for 11.3 million euros.

Accel Elektronika UAB predominates in the area of electronic devices. This subdivision, which was founded by the Swedish electronic company, Accel, specializes in the creation of electric comfort systems for motor cars and carries out not only manufacturing but also research and design activities. Accel Elektronika UAB designs and manufactures devices intended for automotive air conditioning systems. At the present time, the enterprise manufactures photo-optic sensors, which are used to maintain a constant temperature in a car's air circulation system, relays, universal sensors and electronic thermostats etc. The enterprise's clients include such world-famous companies as Volvo, Saab, NedCar and Valeo.

Auregis UAB was founded in 1997 by reorganizing the Kaunas Scientific Research Institute of Radio Measurement Technology. The enterprise presently designs and manufactures electronic devices for automotive LPG equipment. High quality, competitive prices and a big market demand forecast a bright future for this enterprise. Quality, flexibility and an orientation towards the client's needs are the company's main objectives – this plays its part in constantly increasing the number of the company's steady clients.

Plastic and rubber automotive part manufacturing

This area includes the production of car body shell parts, car roofs, spoilers, undershields/underside panelling, plastic door locks and plastic boot and window components for lorries and tractors etc. Axles, axle housings/spare parts, wings, belts and weather-stripping, to name but a few, are successfully manufactured from rubber. There is a growing tendency to use more plastic materials in automotive manufacturing as they have a number of advantages, such as being long lasting, resistant to erosion, easy to process and dye and lighter than those made from other materials.

Schmitz Cargobull Baltic UAB is a subsidiary company of the German trailer and semitrailer manufacturer, Schmitz Cargobull. The enterprise was founded with the aim of breaking into Eastern European markets. At present, the enterprise manufactures sandwich-type isothermal panels, freezing chambers, plastic automotive panels and prefabricated semitrailers. In 2001 the enterprise sold production worth 6 million euros, in 2002 worth 9.8 million euros, and in 2003 it plans to sell production worth 14.5 million euros.

Swedlit AB Baltija UAB is a Swedish company that manufactures parts for plastic door locks, luggage compartments, sunroofs and the like for Volvo passenger cars. Sales between 1997 and 2001 grew four-fold and in 2001 amounted to 4.5 million euros. Its entire production is exported to the countries of the European Union (EU).

Spare and maintenance parts

In this area the following are produced: laminated three-ply windscreens for motor cars, lorries, vans and buses as well as side and rear car windows. The windscreens produced meet the international vehicle safety standards that are compulsory for all vehicle manufacturers. The certificates are registered with the Vehicle Registration Centre in Helsinki, Finland. Panevezio Stiklas UAB has mastered two types of automotive glass manufacturing: laminated and tempered – laminated three-ply windscreens for motor cars, lorries, vans and buses as well as tempered side and rear automotive windows. The automotive glass, manufactured using the new Finnish production line in the enterprise, is oriented towards the secondary market for this automotive component production, ie replacement glass. The enterprise can manufacture roughly 300 different kinds of windows for cars, lorries, vans and buses.

The main production of the company, Panevezio Aurida UAB, is one- and two-cylinder brake system pneumatic compressors for lorries (MAZ, KAMAZ, ZIL, KrAZ), buses (LAZ and IKARUS), and wheeled tractors (K-701) that are produced in countries of the Commonwealth of Independent States (CIS). Using Bühler (Swiss) automated casting equipment, aluminium castings weighing 0.05–1.5 kilograms and covering an area of up to 1,040 square centimetres are made. The capacity of the casting division is 1,500 tonnes of castings per year. The compressors have been certified with a mark of conformity in the Russian Federation, Ukraine and Belarus. The rules for its activities are based on the International Organization for Standardization (ISO) quality control standard ISO 9000. The authorized capital consists of 10.2 million euros. A total of 220 employees work in the company; the annual sales turnover in 2001 was approximately 3 million euros.

Chemical and electrochemical capabilities

Chemical and electrochemical capabilities include galvanizing, simple and chemical oxidation, phosphating, steel and cast iron oxidation, anodizing, electrochemical burnishing of stainless steel, copper, nickel, bronze, chromium, or tin plating, aluminium metalworking, covering and plating with tin-bismuth, tempering, powder painting, rubberizing and coating metal surfaces with polymers.

Mechanical and other non-chemical metal processing capabilities

Mechanical and other non-chemical metal processing capabilities include mechanical cutting, plasma-arc and laser cutting, metal extrusion, milling of claws, carousel-grinding work, longitudinal and level grinding, coordinate grinding, electric arc spot welding and arc cutting.

Automotive component sector

When talking about the individual possibilities of specific enterprises to accept orders from foreign manufacturers and to work with them, it is possible point out several enterprises. However Vingriai AB is the only company in the Baltic States able to offer component assembly services under 1,000 class clean-room conditions. These can be electrical engineering wiring components, components or mechanisms that must have a vacuum or other high tech components.

The Auridos group designs and manufactures various metal parts (bevel gears, seals, rings etc) many of which are already being used in the automotive industry. Rokiskio Autogamykla UAB and Radviliskio Masinu Gamykla UAB have accumulated experience in assembling Lada passenger cars as well as Gazel and Sobol minibuses and lorries.

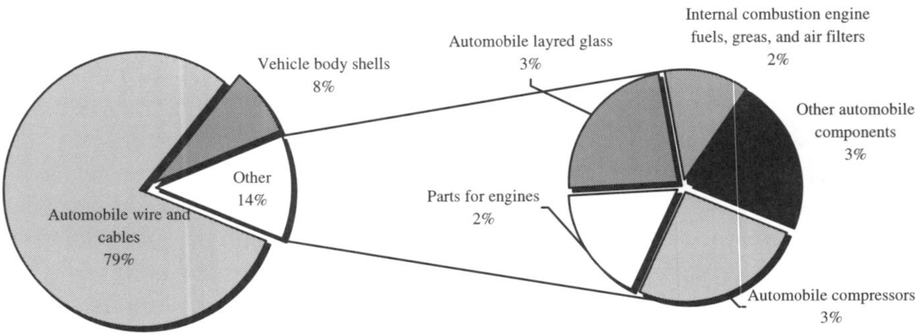

Figure 4.7.1 The structure of the automotive component sector in 2002 (%)

Soure: EKT Group, 2002

The equipment possessed and the experience accumulated by the employees can be realized in one or more automotive assembly processes.

The achievement of companies to work according to ISO standards is an important factor when evaluating their activities.

According to the Lithuanian Department of Statistics, at the beginning of 2001 the Lithuanian science and research system consisted of 175 institutions: institutions of higher education and academies (20), public scientific research institutes, institutions, and other entities (67), as well as over 80 private structures. The most important of these research institutes, which are the most significant in the expansion and development of the automotive component sector being examined, include:

- Semiconductor Physics Institute: the Institute's Semiconductor Device Construction Laboratory works in the field of the creation and testing of semiconductor mechanical-sized (pressure, fluid level, vibration etc) sensors;
- Kaunas University of Technology (KUT) Institute of Automation and Control Systems: the Institute carries out scientific research oriented towards the search for, testing of, and realization of controlling algorithms conserving the resources of technological equipment operating under conditions of optimal capacity;
- Kaunas University of Technology Institute of Piezomechanics: the main aims of the Institute are to create theoretical and practical foundations for constructing and introducing new types of products and equipment components to the Lithuanian industry, to introduce new research results into higher education and to improve the existing modules and laboratory base. In 2001, this Institute became a partner (GTC1-2000-28021) of PolEcer (Polar Electroceramics), a growth programme of the EU's Framework V Thematic Network).
- Vilnius Gediminas Technical University Institute of Welding and Material Science Problems;
- Vilnius University Institute of Material Science and Applied Research.

Researchers and scientists of the technical sciences who have a doctor of science or scientific researcher degree comprise 20 per cent of all the scientists.

Between 2000 and 2002, approximately 95 per cent of the automotive components manufactured in Lithuania were exported. In 2002, exports of automotive components increased by 10 per cent in comparison to 2000. Approximately 80 per cent of all the automotive components manufactured in Lithuania were exported to EU countries, 7 per cent to CIS countries, and 9 per cent to European Free Trade Association (EFTA) countries. In 2002, 84 per cent of all the exports of automotive components manufactured in Lithuania were automotive wire and cable assemblies. These amounted to 70.8 million euros.

The investments of such international companies as Siemens, Yazaki, Accel and Schmittz Cargobull into Lithuania's automotive component sector were very successful. It should be noted that even such well-known companies as Volvo, Saab, Renault, Nedcar, Valeo, Autolive, Jonsons Control, GAZ and others buy automotive components manufactured in Lithuania.

4.8

The Metalworking, Machinery and Appliance Industry

Lithuanian Development Agency

Metalworking and the production of machinery and appliances have long-standing traditions in Lithuania; shipbuilding, the manufacture of agricultural machinery and other metalworking have been developed since the beginning of the century. Currently about 600 enterprises operate in this sector, some of which have many years of experience. This sector employs over 41,000 people, which accounts for 20 per cent of all the employees in the manufacturing industry.

The metalworking, machinery and appliance industry is one of the sectors that, due to timely privatization, has successfully adjusted to market economy conditions. Since the market share of metalworking, machinery and appliance products is comparatively small in Lithuania, most of the products manufactured are sold on foreign markets.

According to the areas of economic activities, the products manufactured and the services provided as well as the metalworking, machinery and appliance production sector can be divided into the following main divisions:

- processing of base metals;
- production of metal articles, other than for machinery and appliances;
- production of machinery and appliances.

Based on the results of the most successful enterprises (particularly in the area of exports), the following promising groups of products can be discerned in this sector:

- processing of non-ferrous metal waste and scrap (processing of base metals);
- sheet metal and other small products (production of metal articles, other than for machinery and appliances during economic activities);

- heating and refrigeration equipment (production of machinery and appliances during economic activities).

Production and sale of the base metals

It is necessary to mention the recycling of secondary raw materials separately. The recycling of non-ferrous metal (aluminium, copper, lead etc) and ferrous metal scrap and diverse production from these raw materials (cast iron castings and various boilers, containers, and other articles of ferrous metal) is very well developed in Lithuania. Secondary non-ferrous metal raw materials are a saleable product on the market. Statistical data also shows the successful dynamics of the growth in the sales of the enterprises in this sector: sales grew by 11 per cent in 2000 and by 38 per cent in 2001 over the previous year. Sales in the first half of 2002 exceeded the corresponding period of the previous year by 22 per cent. It is possible to enumerate the factors determining the success of this product and its future prospects:

- The use of secondary raw materials by metal recycling and metal article factories saves over 20 times more energy in comparison to primary metal production (for example, in the aluminium industry);
- Wider use of secondary raw materials has a big ecological significance in addition to being a more rational use of natural resources, therefore public institutions are promoting this activity.

In order to successfully sell scrap metal products on the foreign market, they are sorted according to the individual non-ferrous metal groups, cleaned of undesirable contamination (ferrous metal, plastic, rubber etc), pressed if the client so desires and packed according to the needs of each client. At present, mostly aluminium castings are exported. In the main, metals are exported to Germany, Poland, Sweden, China, India and Hong Kong.

Baltical UAB, founded in 1999, is a foreign capital enterprise with 95 per cent of its capital from the USA and 5 per cent from Germany. Baltical UAB exports almost all of its output (standard 5 kg aluminium ingots satisfying EN AB 46000 and EN AB 47000) to Germany, Sweden, France, Switzerland and Austria. The enterprise buys up scrap in Lithuania and ships it to Western Europe. In 2001 the enterprise's turnover was 1 million euros; in 2002, this increased to 6 million euros. The enterprise's success has been caused by the general need in Europe for secondary aluminium produced from scrap – a need that currently amounts to 2 million tonnes per year. This should increase in the future. The amount of aluminium in cars is constantly increasing and this metal is being ever more widely used to manufacture window frames and decorative elements.

Production of metal articles other than machinery and appliances

The production of metal articles other than machinery and appliances includes the manufacture of metal articles and metal constructions. The demand for shaped aluminium articles and other metal constructions is directly related to the growth in the machinery and appliances. The biggest buyers of shaped articles made of aluminium and other metals are Lithuanian companies that have broken into foreign markets. The products with the highest demand are non-standard metal constructions including shaped metal articles.

Baltijos Laivu Statykla AB is a leader in the area of metal constructions. In 2001, the enterprise's sales turnover amounted to 153 million euros and it exported 95–97 per cent of its total production. The main export countries were Denmark, Germany and the Netherlands. The enterprise specializes in the manufacture of metal constructions for the shipbuilding industry.

Baltijos Laivu Statykla AB has allocated large investments to renovate its equipment, to erect new scraping and painting shops and to found a ship design centre. As a consequence, its steel construction manufacturing capacity was increased. Recently the enterprise's production has been concentrated on the production of equipped superstructures and large blocks intended for the construction of container ships at Odense. The modernized and developing Lithuanian shipbuilding enterprise has been able to sign contracts with foreign shipbuilding companies and, at the time of writing, is the only shipbuilding enterprise in the three Baltic States (Lithuania, Latvia, and Estonia) that offers a full assortment of shipbuilding and other services.

Production of machinery and appliances

The production of machinery and appliances includes the manufacture of production equipment and heating and refrigeration equipment and the like for various branches of industry and personal use. The success of the enterprises engaging in this activity is shown by statistical data: sales grew by 1.8 per cent in 2000 and by 26 per cent in 2001 over the preceding year and in the first half of 2002 they exceeded the corresponding period for the previous year by 8.6 per cent.

Snaige AB is without a doubt the leader of this sector, having achieved a 57.9 million euros annual turnover in 2001. It exports over 90 per cent of its production to Western, Eastern and Central European markets. It presently sells its products in 30 countries.

The quality control and environmental protection control systems introduced by the enterprise have been evaluated by International

Organization for Standardization (ISO) standards ISO 9000 and ISO 14001. Each year, the enterprise invests an average of 15 million litas in new technologies. The enterprise is striving to create products that will not only satisfy the consumers' needs but also completely satisfy ecological requirements. Each year the enterprise creates several new refrigerator models.

A considerable number of enterprises in this sector successfully produce intermediate products, semi-manufactured products, complex construction components and other similar products intended for the creation of the final product in the fields of such Western European industries as furniture, electronics, machinery and equipment. Exports in 2001 consisted of:

- 70 per cent in the area of base metals;
- 66 per cent in the area of machinery and equipment;
- 76 per cent in the area of electric machinery and appliances;
- 93 per cent in the area of recycling metal waste and scrap.

The total of all the types of economic activities ascribed to the sector in question comprised 8 per cent of Lithuania's entire export turnover in the first half of 2000–2002.

The amount of foreign investments in Lithuania's metalworking, machinery and appliance sectors in the first quarter of 2002 included approximately 30 million euros (4 per cent of all foreign investments) in the Lithuanian manufacturing industry. In general, according to the total volume of investments, Denmark occupies first place (579 million euros), Sweden second, and Estonia third. In the first quarter of 2002, Denmark and Sweden invested the most in the metalworking and machinery and appliance manufacturing sectors with investments of 12 million euros and 7.6 million euros respectively. This comprises approximately 65 per cent of the foreign investments in these sectors. According to first quarter data for 2002, German investments in the sectors consisted of some 5 million euros. Such countries as Austria and Finland have also invested in the sector's enterprises.

An analysis of the export results in the metalworking, machinery and appliance production sector shows that the most active international trade has been taking place between Lithuania and the European Union (EU). Exports to the EU amounted to 140.6 million euros (48.36 per cent) while imports from it were 581.2 million euros (67.68 per cent). Exports to countries of the Commonwealth of Independent States (CIS) amounted to 124.5 million euros (42.81 per cent) while imports were 189 million euros (22.02 per cent). Exports to CEFTA countries amounted to 25.6 million euros (8.82 per cent) while imports were 88.4 million euros (10.30 per cent).

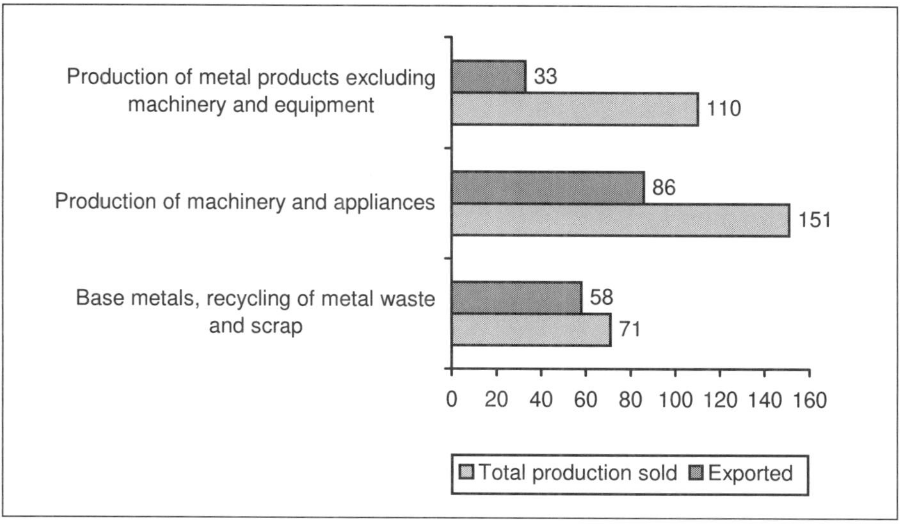

Figure 4.8.1 Export volumes of the production manufactured by the sector's branches (million euros)

In order to operate successfully in the EU and all the world's markets, the international rating of the products being exported is very important. Thus, the achievements of enterprises and the success of the market in certifying their activities in accordance with ISO standards for both quality control (ISO 9001, 9001) and environmental protection (ISO 14001) are a vital component in the successful rating of their activities.

The training of specialists and the application of research findings in Lithuania have deep-rooted traditions and good potential. The annual number of university graduates per 1,000 inhabitants is the largest in the region. Between 1997 and 2001 Lithuanian institutions of higher education prepared a relatively large number of technology specialists – approximately 1,800 per year. Last year the number of technology students in Lithuania comprised 23 per cent of all higher education students as compared to 15 per cent in Europe. A relatively large number of technology specialists results in a situation where highly qualified specialists are available to work in the country's metalworking and machinery industry sector and, at the same time, advanced technologies are used.

Lithuania's main research and development (R&D) capabilities are concentrated in the activities of higher education and scientific research institutions. The metalworking, machinery and appliance sectors in part include several laboratories, which are comparable to small and medium-sized enterprises and offer high tech products that are competitive on the global market. Of these, the research services firm, GTV, should be mentioned. This creates and manufactures various purpose automated and computerized technological equipment and machinery with sensor systems; monitoring and emergency stopping systems for machinery, lines, and factories; equipment, machinery, stations and pipe lines with thermal insulation for manufacturing; multi-point fast and accurate measuring machinery and operatorless measurement lines and technologies, machinery, and lines for cleaning metal surfaces.

Of the 29 active public institutions of scientific research, it is possible to distinguish several, which are the most significant in the development of the metalworking and machinery and appliance production sector in question:

- Kaunas University of Technology Institute of Piezomechanics: the main aims of the Institute are to create theoretical and practical foundations for constructing and introducing new types of products and equipment components in Lithuanian industry, to introduce new research results into higher education and to improve the existing modules and laboratory base. In 2001 the Institute became a partner (GTC1-2000-28021) of PolEcer (Polar Electroceramics), a growth programme of the EU's Framework V Thematic Network);
- Kaunas University of Technology Institute of Automation and Control Systems: the Institute carries out scientific research oriented towards the search for, testing of, and realization of controlling algorithms conserving the resources of technological equipment operating under conditions of optimal capacity;
- Semiconductor Physics Institute: the Institute's Semiconductor Device Construction Laboratory works in the field of the creation and testing of semiconductor mechanical sized (pressure, fluid level, vibration etc) sensors.

These institutions are creating an environment for developing globally competitive products through the use of advanced technologies. In general, there about 9,500 R&D specialists, 20 per cent of whom work in the field of technology. One of the most significant research areas promoting the development and expansion of the metalworking, machinery and appliance sector is mechatronics. Mechatronics is defined today as technology combining such fundamental branches of science as mechanics, electrical engineering or electronics, computers and management theory, in which the achievements of all these areas synergistically complement each other.

The Lithuanian metalworking, machinery, and appliance sector can boast quite a number of internationally recognized enterprises, which produce high tech products and services. Vingriai UAB is the only company in the Baltic States that can offer component assembly services under 1,000 class clean-room conditions.

The successful investments of such international companies as ACG-Nystrom, Rautaruukki, ABB, VAE AG, Odense Steel Shipyard Ltd (AP Moller Group) in the Lithuanian metalworking, machinery and appliance sector prove the attractiveness of this sector and the prospects for further investments.

4.9

The Oil Industry

Vita Markevičiūtė, Financial Analyst Association and AB Mažeikių Nafta

Production and demand outlook

In aggregate the Lithuanian oil industry, both directly and indirectly, inflicts a great impact on the national economy. The primary source of such an impact should be attributed to Mažeikių Nafta, the only refinery in the Baltic region that provides for 15–20 per cent of tax revenues to the state budget. In addition, consumption of fuel comprises a substantial part of the consumer basket of an average citizen. Mažeikių Nafta has immense power in setting the prices in the country, since it is the dominant, and for the most part only, fuel supplier. Due to both economic and political reasons oil issues in Lithuania deserve a lot of attention from regulators, investors and consumers. In this chapter we will aim to provide an overview of the industry's most current developments, industry infrastructure, as well as highlighting the status of privatization.

Oil products constitute the largest proportion of the balance of primary energy resources in the country. In 2001 national consumption of oil products reached 2.5 million tonnes or 31 per cent of the total energy resources consumed by the economy. Future demand will be determined by the trends, which are no different from those of Western Europe.

Lithuania has been invited to become a full member of the European Union (EU) in 2004. EU membership will require a harmonization of national fuel specification with EU norms. The quality of refined products required in the European marketplace will play a key role in future refining investment decisions and supply/demand balances. The decision by the EU to move to higher quality fuels will require either investment in refineries that intend to compete in the marketplace or the closure of those refineries that do not make the investments.

Overall, oil demand is expected to increase as the economy develops. Consumption of heavy oil products will decrease, whereas demand for

Table 4.9.1 Lithuanian oil industry production†

	1996	1997	1998	1999	2000	2001	2002
Extraction of crude petroleum* (million litas)	103.5	134.2	98.3	131.3	169.2	186.1	184.5
Share in total industry sales (%)	0.5	0.6	0.4	0.6	n/d	n/d	n/d
Oil extraction (million tonnes)	0.161	0.212	0.277	0.232	0.316	0.471	0.434
Manufacture of refined petroleum products* (million litas)	2,654	3,488	3,120	2,372	2,194	3,311	3,085
Share in total industry sales (%)	12.8	14.7	12.5	10.3	n/d	n/d	n/d
Petrol (million tonnes)	3.75	5.03	6.43	4.51	4.66	6.45	6.54

† prices correct at time of writing without value added tax or excise
* Financial Analyst Association (FAA) estimates for 2000–2002
n/d – no data available
Source: Lithuanian Department of Statistics

light products, mostly used for transportation purposes, will grow. Specifications in the fuels marketplace are changing quickly. Even though 50-ppm fuels are not mandated until 2005 in the EU markets, many markets have moved more quickly by means of tax incentives. The use of heavy fuel oil is expected to remain essentially static until 2005, depending mainly on the demand for district heating.

There are plans to expand the natural gas network and most heating plants will have the capability to be dual fuelled with oil and gas. Some of the more remote plants will continue to use oil. This could change depending on the EU accession decisions regarding low sulphur fuel oil. Moving to 1 per cent fuel oil will have significant financial and economical consequences on the Lithuanian economy and on Mažeikių Nafta in particular. Demand for diesel and gasoline is expected to recover as overall oil prices fall. Vehicle growth is expected to be modest as more efficient vehicles replace the aging car fleet and diesel engine cars start to become more widely used. In the short term, conversion of gasoline-engine cars to liquid petroleum gas (LPG) was popular; the trend peaked in 2000 and is now moving to a more stable demand profile. Diesel demand is expected to grow strongly as industry and commerce develops.

Infrastructure

Lithuania's geopolitical location, which connects two major economic regions, should bring its merits by stimulating higher demand for significant volumes of transport and logistics services. Consequentially, consumption of light oil products will grow. Lithuania does not expect to face any serious difficulties to meet such a demand. The infrastructure of transportation, refining, storage and retailing is well matched against current and future economy needs.

Capabilities of separate units of the Mažeikių Nafta complex – refinery, terminal and pipeline – are well balanced so that they can be utilized both independently and as an integrated complex. The design capacity of the pipeline connected to the refining unit is 16 million tonnes per annum; design capacity of the refinery is 15 million tonnes per annum, although only a third of the capacity is utilized. There are attractive ways to solve the underutilization problem. Given current high prices in the world crude oil market, it would be worth constructing a pipeline to connect the Mažeikių refinery and the Butinge terminal and export Russian crude, in excess of refinery needs, to Western markets.

The transportation system and import–export terminals for oil and oil products were developed in the first Energy Strategy prepared by the Government of Lithuania in 1994. Construction of the Butinge terminal linked by pipeline to the Mažeikių refinery and reconstruction of the Klaipeda terminal, which handles waterborne exports of oil products, completed a very important phase of the infrastructure development. It provides for an independence of the industry from one source of crude oil and creates an efficient transit basis for exporting oil and oil products from countries with excess supply to countries with excess demand.

Table 4.9.2 Transportation of oil and oil products in Lithuania by pipelines

	Year (million tonne-km)					
Production	**1997**	**1998**	**1999**	**2000**	**2001**	**2002***
Crude petroleum	2,399	2,685	2,315	3,148	4,430	3,409
incl. transit	1,271	1,269	1,195	2,184	2,994	2,467
Petroleum products	258	279	312	309	350	256
incl. transit	258	279	312	309	350	256
Total	2,656	2,964	2,627	3,457	4,780	3,665
incl. transit	1,529	1,548	1,507	2,493	3,344	2,723

*Based on first 9 months of the year
Source: Lithuanian Department of Statistics

Storage and distribution

Another important part of the Lithuanian oil industry is the storage and distribution of oil products. Following EU requirements Lithuania will have an obligation to store 90 days worth of the annual consumption of all oil products as state strategic reserves. In 2002 the Lithuanian parliament passed the Law on Strategic Reserves and established procedures for industry participants. The state, at its expense, will be responsible for the accumulation of 50 per cent of total reserves, and producers and importers will hold the remaining 50 per cent of state reserves. In Lithuania there is an overabundance of storage capacity; however not all meet quality requirements.

The distribution network for the delivery of refined products to consumers has followed the fastest path of development and modernization. Before 1992 the state company Lietuvos kuras had the largest retail network and could dictate the rules of monopolistic game. In 1992 Lietuvos kuras lost its monopoly rights of trading in oil products and soon afterwards international companies, such as Shell, Statoil, Neste and Lukoil as well as local players, entered the market. In 1995 the total number of fuel stations increased several times on account of the newcomers who either established their own companies or formed joint ventures. At that time foreign capital owned 6 per cent, local public and private companies owned 48 per cent, and personal companies 25 per cent of the total retail network. Such a structure implied that even in 1995 competition verses monopoly had started shaping market development.

It is interesting to note that from 1990 to 1995 although the overall consumption of oil products decreased, a number of wholesale and retail companies grew significantly (Table 4.9.3).

Table 4.9.3 Lithuanian retail trade in automotive fuel†

Retail trade	**1997**	**1998**	**1999**	**2000**	**2001**	**2002***
Retail sale of automotive fuel (million litas)	1,267.5	1,370.9	1,532.1	1,671.9	1,686.0	1,460.1
Share in total retail sales (%)	10.9	10.4	13.1	12.7	12.0	12.7

†prices correct at time of writing without value added tax
*Based on first 9 months of the year
Source: Lithuanian Department of Statistics

There were a number of reasons for such imbalances, namely poor regulation of the market by the state, breaches in the mechanism of tax collection and restrictions on investment of capital into other economy sectors. At the end of 1994 the state tightened trading regulations and tax collection control. Together with intensifying competition from foreign capital, such measures yielded mass bankruptcies of small market players and withdrawal of criminal capital from the business. By 1998 the oil business in Lithuania had become a domicile for large, financially strong and, for the most part, international companies. During the last five years Lukoil, Statoil, Shell, Neste, Hydro Texaco and Uotas have developed modern retail networks that meet the high requirements of client service.

To complete the picture of the Lithuanian oil industry, local oil exploration and production should not be forgotten. The first 12,500 tonnes of oil were extracted from the earth of Lithuania in 1990. In 2001 this figure reached 471,000 tonnes, and in 2002 434,000 tonnes. Although Lithuania is not a rich country in terms of oil resources, it can still meet 15 per cent of local needs. The production capacities of the industry are 0.3–0.5 million tonnes of crude per annum. Such a level is expected to hold through until 2015. The State Office of Geology has estimated that there are about 60 million tonnes of oil in the depths of Lithuania. Despite the high crude price in the world markets, the scale of small business does not encourage larger investments into exploration. The largest oil producer is Minijos nafta, a Lithuanian–Danish joint venture. In 2002 Minijos nafta extracted 264,000 tonnes of oil. Another three companies engaged in oil exploration and production are Geonafta, Genciu nafta, and Manifoldas.

To summarize the overview of the infrastructure of the Lithuanian oil sector we should distinguish three major features:

- refining and transportation capacities of the system are excessive;
- the country's retail network has already undergone major development stages;
- the geopolitical position of the country provides for attractive opportunities for exports of Russian crude to Western European and other undersupplied markets.

Mažeikių Nafta

Mažeikių Nafta was constructed, originally as a hydroskimmer, by Russian engineers and constructors in 1980. The refinery was upgraded several times by installing new units. Its design capacity is 16 million tonnes per annum, making it one of the largest in Central and Western Europe. Mažeikių Nafta was originally conceived and constructed as a key part of the military and civilian infrastructure in the Baltic region of the FSU. It historically served the needs of the three Baltic countries, adjacent parts of Belarus, Ukraine, Poland and the Russian enclave of Kaliningrad. It continues to directly tie into the FSU's crude oil pipeline system and, until the recent construction of an import terminal, it was completely reliant on crude oil supplies from Russia.

From its inception, the Butinge terminal was a political project built in reaction to Lithuania's fear of the consequences of being dependent on Russia for its crude oil supply. The terminal facilities were built by German and US contractors in 1998 and 1999 and were certified by Russian and Lithuanian authorities in November 1999. Originally it was conceived as an import terminal (and it can perform this function) but it has more economic value as a crude oil export route for Russian oil producers. The terminal consists of three 50,000 cubic metre storage tanks and a 36-inch crude oil pipeline, which runs 7.4 kilometres offshore to a single-point mooring loading system. The terminal can handle up to 150,000-tonne tankers. Three additional storage tanks are planned to enhance operational capabilities.

Mažeikių Nafta also owns the entire crude oil products pipeline system located in Lithuanian territory, which Lithuania inherited from the FSU's Transneft system. The pipeline system consists of three pipelines: one crude oil line which supplies the Mažeikių Nafta refinery and the Butinge terminal, another crude oil line which supplies crude oil exports to the Latvian seaport Ventspils, and a smaller diesel products line. The pipeline assets and pump stations currently move over 15 million tonnes per year to Western markets. A total of 13 million tonnes per year can be shipped through the spur that extends to Ventspils, Latvia. With the Butinge terminal fully operational, the Lithuanian pipeline assets have the capacity to transport both the existing 15 million tonnes per year plus an incremental 9 million tonnes of Russia's crude oil, representing almost a quarter of all Russia's crude oil exports. This is in addition to the volumes supplied to the refinery. In reality, however, such capacity will hardly be utilized when the Russian pipeline operator Transneft completes the third phase of the Primorsk terminal in Russia, which is designed to handle 30 million tonnes of export crude oil per annum.

Privatization of Mažeikių Nafta

Following Lithuania's independence in 1991, the Lithuanian Government inherited the Mažeikių Nafta refinery complex, which had a capacity far in excess of the needs of Lithuania and its Baltic neighbors. Moreover, following the FSU collapse, Russian crude oil exporters required cash-in-advance payment terms from all refineries in Russia's former satellites. The cash-strapped Mažeikių Nafta faced the double impact of a dramatic reduction in its market and an inability to purchase crude oil at reasonable prices and terms. It also faced the threat of politically motivated embargoes of Russian crude in retaliation for Lithuania's efforts to leave Russia's economic sphere. By 1996 the Lithuanian Government recognized that the only hope for the continued operation of the loss-making Mažeikių Nafta refinery would be to sell it to a strategic investor.

In 1998 the Government of Lithuania merged the Mažeikių Nafta refinery with the majority state-owned pipeline and terminal companies into a single surviving company, AB Mažeikių Nafta. Concurrent with the merger, new shares in the company were approved for sale to a strategic investor. The combined company received all the assets of its predecessor companies as well as all of their debt. The debt burden included over 200 million US dollars of state guaranteed debt used to finance the new terminal, direct loans by the Ministry of Finance and a major working capital deficit. The challenge faced by the Government was to find a strategic investor that would purchase a stake in the company despite its extensive debt burden, turn the separate units around and commercially integrate them and allow the Government to retain a significant investment upside.

After extensive and controversial negotiations that caused a resignation of the Prime Minister and its cabinet, on 29 October 1999 Williams International and the Government signed the detailed agreements whereby Williams International, USA, became a 33 per cent shareholder of AB Mažeikių Nafta. The subscription price for the purchased shares was 150 million US dollars. Williams International paid half of this amount in cash and issued a promissory note for the balance. It also funded a long-term subordinated loan of 75 million US dollars to the company, guaranteed by the Lithuanian Government. Williams International inserted a senior management team and developed a modernization programme for business turnaround.

The worst times, however, were not over. Despite cash injected by the Government and Williams, AB Mažeikių Nafta suffered from a lack of capital investment, lack of working capital, low refinery utilization, product quality issues and inefficient yields. Because of the political reasons mentioned above, AB Mažeikių Nafta was still not able to buy crude oil at market prices and in line with payment terms. Williams realized that the only way out was to attract a Russian crude supplier to become a shareholder of AB Mažeikių Nafta.

In June 2002 Yukos Oil Corporation signed agreements with the Government of Lithuania and Williams International Company. Yukos has become both a long-term crude supplier and a 26.8 per cent shareholder of AB Mažeikių Nafta. Yukos injected 150 million US dollars in new money into AB Mažeikių Nafta by transferring 75 million US dollars as payment for the shares and giving the same amount in the form of the loan guaranteed by the Government of Lithuania. The cash injection allowed AB Mažeikių Nafta to start a 400 million US dollars modernization programme without further delay.

This modernization programme has been developed to make improvements to economic performance while meeting changing product specifications in the markets that are served by AB Mažeikių Nafta. The main areas of focus for Phase One (years 2002–2006) are:

- meeting EU product specifications for gasoline, jet and diesel fuel;
- increasing production and sales of higher value products;
- making significant environmental improvements;
- improving processing reliability;
- reducing operating expenses through an overall efficiency upgrade programme.

Prior to 2002, approximately 10 million US dollars was expended for the plan. The remaining funding for Phase One is currently estimated at approximately 400 million US dollars. The first stage of the modernization programme will last for five years and involve the completion of 12 separate projects.

On 20 August 2002 the parent company of Williams International – the Williams Companies of Tulsa, Oklahoma, which had been experiencing financial difficulties in recent months – made a strategic decision to divest AB Mažeikių Nafta. As a result of its previous involvement with Mažeikių Nafta, Jukos was the logical choice to acquire Williams' stake and the two companies were soon able to reach a mutually beneficial agreement. This involved Jukos, through its subsidiary, paying 85 million US dollars to acquire Williams' 26.85 per cent stake as well as its management control over the company. Jukos now owns 53.7 per cent and the Government owns 40.6 per cent of AB Mažeikių Nafta. Both shareholders have agreed on the strategy for AB Mažeikių Nafta to become a major regional refiner and transporter in the changing energy business of Europe.

4.10

The Retail Market

Viktorija Trimbel, Suprema, Evli Group

Market development and outlook

The current retail system started to emerge from the system owned and operated by the state in the late 1980s. Prior to that, all retail trade was conducted through state-owned shops and a retail cooperative that connected the majority of rural and urban retailers. Aside from that, any intent to sell goods privately was considered speculation and was punished.

In the late 1980s, the first private enterprises were allowed. A lack of adequate goods led to a number of traders entering the market who could procure goods from abroad or through their connections to the state distribution system. Since state retailers did not offer external goods (goods not offered through the state-controlled retail system), the best way to sell these products was at open markets. Increasing sales at these markets led to the creation of the first independent shops.

After gaining independence in 1990, the Lithuanian Government started to privatize state-owned assets, including retail outlets. Since this time there has been no Government ownership within the retail sector. Modern retail philosophies began to emerge in the second half of the 1990s, retail chains developed and the first hypermarkets and discount stores opened, with an ongoing and increasing shift from open markets and groceries to more Western-style formats.

The market has witnessed increased success regarding discount stores, as they were able to offer better prices than open markets to the price-sensitive population. However, the growth of super/hypermarkets is very impressive, due to their ability to offer service of a high quality, entertainment and competitive prices due to a strong bargaining power. The leading retail groups are deemed to be shaping consolidation trends in the producer market, as fragmented producers are not able to sustain the bargaining power of retailers, requiring significant discounts and sales credit, on their own.

Table 4.10.1 Retail trade turnover (value added tax included)*

	1995	1996	1997	1998	1999	2000
Total retail incl. open market and catering† (million litas)	9,235.2	12,039.1	14,529.0	16,202.0	15,356.2	16,752.0
Real annual change (%)	108.0	105.0	112.9	109.2	95.0	110.9
Retail trade excl. catering (million litas)	8,801.1	11,586.5	13,923.5	15,569.9	14,762.8	16,199.2
Real annual change (%)	107.6	106.1	112.5	109.7	95.0	111.5
Restaurants and other public catering‡ (million litas)	434.1	452.6	605.5	632.1	593.4	552.8
Real annual change (%)	117.2	93.6	119.6	99.6	92.1	93.3
Stocks of commodities in retail trade, eop	616.0	749.9	1,545.3	1,551.6	1,555.9	1,530.0

*This table is based on the retail trade data only, including sales on the open market, but excluding non-retail activities of retail companies.
†Data on all trading enterprises including restaurants and other public catering enterprises.
‡Including catering in other activities' enterprises
Source: Department of Statistics

The Lithuanian retail sector has expanded significantly over the past few years (Table 4.10.1). The growth has further accelerated in recent years, especially 2002, with the growing economy, positive future outlook and development of a consumer credit market.

Turnover of retail enterprises, excluding value added tax (VAT) and catering, reached 15.6 billion litas, ie 4,500 litas per capita in 2002. The market grew by 12.4 per cent in comparable prices. Part of this growth is attributable to the 22.6 per cent increase in retail trade in automobiles, their maintenance and repair and fuel, which has been influenced by the change in VAT taxation. Other retail turnover grew by 8 per cent. Turnover of restaurants and other catering enterprises grew by 17.1 per cent and reached 430 million litas, VAT excluded (Table 4.10.2).

The growth in the market has also been backed by a change in purchasing habits – newly established super/hypermarkets are becoming more popular, while grocery stores are becoming less so. Due to the specific circumstances of urban development, super/hypermarkets are located within urban areas with a high population density, making little room for the convenience store concept.

Lithuanian retail space still lags behind that of the EU. Table 4.10.3 gives details of the retail space in Lithuania; per capita, it forms only around 30 per cent of the EU-15 average. A significant amount of retail space opened in 2002 – in Vilnius 180,000 square metres of new shopping space was built.

Table 4.10.2 Turnover of retail enterprises (million litas) VAT excluded*

	1997	1998	1999	2000	2001	2002[1]
Retail (excl. motor vehicles and catering)	8,309.2	9,213.3	8,441.7	9,412.7	9,800.0	10,467.0e
Real annual change (%)	n/a	–108.7	93.2	114.8	103.4	108.0
Retail trade in motor vehicles, repair and fuel	3,364.6	3,969.9	3,214.6	3,728.7	4,266.3	5,172.7e
Real annual change (%)	n/a	115.4	77.8	111.7	119.8	122.6
Total retail (excl. catering)	**11,673.8**	**13,183.2**	**11,656.3**	**13,141.4**	**14,066.3**	**15,639.7**
Restaurants and other catering	354.5	379.1	381.1	350.0	362.1	430.0
Real annual change (%)	n/a	102.1	98.7	92.0	102.1	117.1
Total retail (incl. open market and catering)	**12,028.3**	**13,562.3**	**12,037.4**	**13,491.4**	**14,428.4**	**16,069.7e**

*This table is based on the turnover of enterprises, engaged in retail trade, including sales on the open market and other activities, but excluding VAT.
Source: Department of Statistics. Suprema's estimates (e)

EU convergence trends, increasing disposable income and improving living standards should result in strong future retail growth in Lithuania. The outlook for 2003 is very positive – retail sales in January 2003 of the leading retailer, VP Market (Vilniaus Prekyba), grew over 26 per cent on the annual basis.

Table 4.10.3 Retail space in Lithuania*

	1995	1996	1997	1998	1999	2000
Number of shops (year end)	22,112	19,421	18,275	19,153	19,401	19,211
Shopping floor space (000m^2)	1,674	1,523	1,480	1,632	1,735	1,790
Average floor space of one shop (m^2)	76	78	81	85	89	93
Number of restaurants and catering enterprises (year end)	4,359	4,287	4,502	4,998	5,013	5,142
Capacity of restaurants and catering enterprises (000 seats)	153.9	168.9	180.0	202.2	204.3	207.8
Average number of seats per catering enterprise	35	39	40	40	41	40

*This table is based on the retail trade data only, including sales on the open market, but excluding non-retail activities of retail companies
Source: Department of Statistics

An additional boost for organized retail will be given in the form of a reduced VAT rate for fresh meat products. The 18 per cent rate has dropped to just 5 per cent, helping to move meat retail from the open market (currently estimated at around 50 per cent) to the retail chains, increasing sales of other consumer staples.

The majority of retail sales consist of food products; the share of non-food consumer goods, however, is increasing every year with economic development (Table 4.10.4).

Table 4.10.4 Retail trade composition (VAT included)

	1995	**1996**	**1997**	**1998**	**1999**	**2000**
Retail goods turnover (total)	**9,235.2**	**12,039.1**	**14,529.0**	**16,202.0**	**15,356.2**	**16,752.0**
Food products (total)	**5,515.3**	**6,536.0**	**7,727.8**	**7,540.9**	**7,052.3**	**7,863.2**
Meat, poultry and fish	1,176.4	1,601.6	1,672.6	1,542.6	1,590.5	1,771.8
Milk and dairy products	676.0	697.7	982.8	754.2	631.7	672.6
Bread, confectionery, pasta and other pastry products	563.0	607.4	893.2	803.7	801.7	808.9
Fruit and vegetables	502.0	517.7	653.8	614.9	527.2	614.9
Other food products	1,117.2	1,374.2	1,527.6	1,688.8	1,235.9	1,895.5
Alcoholic beverages	1,480.7	1,737.4	1,997.8	2,136.7	2,265.3	2,099.5
Non-food commodities (total)	**3,719.9**	**5,503.1**	**6,801.2**	**8,661.1**	**8,303.9**	**8,888.8**
Tobacco products	242.2	282.0	348.4	359.5	358.1	373.8
Clothing, underwear, fur, knitwear and footwear	605.3	895.0	931.4	785.9	795.4	380.9
Furniture, carpets and other floor coverings	177.5	256.4	449.9	316.5	255.0	242.4
Electric appliances, cookware and household goods	120.2	184.9	346.7	416.9	465.8	475.9
Pharmaceutical, medical and orthopaedic goods	351.0	450.3	517.6	676.3	731.1	765.1
Television sets, video recorders, radio equipment	48.7	91.3	167.0	287.8	241.4	234.5
Cars, motorcycles, other transport vehicles	126.1	227.1	293.8	897.1	611.5	723.9
Press, notebooks, paper, office goods	151.3	174.2	180.7	206.7	254.3	261.3
Personal hygiene goods	91.4	162.0	308.9	312.5	301.5	313.8
Other commodities	1,806.2	2,779.9	3,256.8	4,401.9	4,289.8	4,617.2

Units – million Litas
Source: Department of Statistics

Market players

The Lithuanian retail market is dominated by three major players – VP Market, IKI and ICA/Ahold (Rimi) – that together are estimated to control over 50 per cent of the total market.

VP Market has successfully competed against both local and international competitors, emerging as pan-Baltic leader. It has entered Latvian and Estonian markets and is considering expansion to Russia and Ukraine. In 2002, VP Market operated the largest shopping and leisure centre in the Baltic, Akropolis, which occupies over 53,000 square metres. VP Market operates 214 trade centres in total – 165 in Lithuania, 48 in Latvia and one in Estonia. The company plans to invest 300 million litas in 2003, open 20 new stores and reach 3.45 billion sales through its network in Lithuania, Latvia and Estonia – up by 13.5 per cent compared to 2002. VP market operates five different store formats under the trade names of:

- Hyper Maxima/Maxima Baze (hypermarkets/cash and carry);
- Maxima (large supermarkets);
- Media (supermarkets);
- Minima (convenience stores);
- T-Market (discount stores).

IKI is the next largest player, attempting to focus on the high-end segment with their supermarkets and pursuing a domestic expansion strategy. IKI Group is owned and managed by three brothers – George, Oliver and Nicolas Ortiz – who moved from Belgium to Lithuania in 1991 following the collapse of the Soviet Union. Not finding grocery goods to their taste, they opened their first store in 1992 in Vilnius. IKI chain ownership will be consolidated under a single operator, Palink, in 2003. Currently the IKI retail chain consists of 106 stores under three different formats:

- IKI (54 stores, primarily supermarkets);
- Pigiau Grybo (49 discount stores);
- the newly launched Ikiukas (three convenience stores).

In 2003, the IKI retail chain plans to open 20 new stores under these formats. Non-audited chain sales in 2002 reached LTL 1 billion.

Attracted to high growth in nearby markets and a stability in the economy that has reduced the risk of investment, Scandinavian retailers started entering the Baltic and Lithuanian retail markets. ICA/Ahold is the only foreign player with a pan-Baltic presence. ICA/Ahold acquired the entire Ekovalda retail chain in the middle of 2002. Up to date, the chain had approximately 40 stores in four different store formats, whose identity and brand names have been partially influenced by the historical consolidation processes:

- Rimi (hyper/large supermarkets);
- Eko (supermarkets);
- Vikonda (convenience stores);
- Sustok ir pirk (discount stores).

In 2003 all store formats will be readjusted to meet the standard ICA/ Ahold store formats. They plan to open 11 new hypermarkets and supermarkets in 2003. Chain sales in 2002 reached LTL 440 up by 27.5 per cent.

Due to the dominant market influence by these three key players, small retail shops started consolidation processes and several local retail chains emerged. The Norfos mažmena retail chain has 38 retail stores in Lithuania and plans to open 15 new stores in Lithuania and five in Moscow in 2003. Norfa has three store formats:

- Norfa XXL (over 2,000 square metres of shopping space);
- Norfa XL (600–2,000 square metres of shopping space);
- Norfa L (less than 600 square metres of shopping space, currently 16 such stores).

Norfos mažmena plans to reach sales of 500 million litas in 2003.

A network of small and medium-sized retail stores, Aibes mažmena unites some 376 retail outlets. Its sales grew by 6.9 per cent in 2002 and reached 420 million litas. The network aims to achieve sales of 500 million litas in 2003 and become the third largest retail chain in Lithuania. Aibes mažmena has organized a retail chain Aibe in Latvia, together with the local retailer's association, uniting 145 retail outlets by the end of 2002.

Several northern Lithuanian retailers, having the trade names of Tau, Kubas and Gruste, have formed their own retail network with a total of 36 stores and 15,000 square metres of shopping space. Their consolidated turnover in 2002 amounted to 94 million litas.

4.11

The Media Market

Viktorija Trimbel, Suprema, Evli Group

Market trends

Lithuanian advertising spending is growing faster than gross domestic product (GDP) and, based on preliminary estimates, reached 0.48 per cent of GDP in 2002 (Figure 4.11.1). The advertising market follows general economic cycles and is closely related to the status of the economy in each individual country – it is rapidly developing in emerging countries, while the spending and GDP ratio in developed countries remains virtually the same.

Lithuanian advertising spending per capita is the lowest in the Baltic region; however the size of the consumer market and the economy structure indicate a higher potential for growth. As Figure 4.11.2 shows, the advertising market grew in 2002 at an annual rate of 18.2 per cent

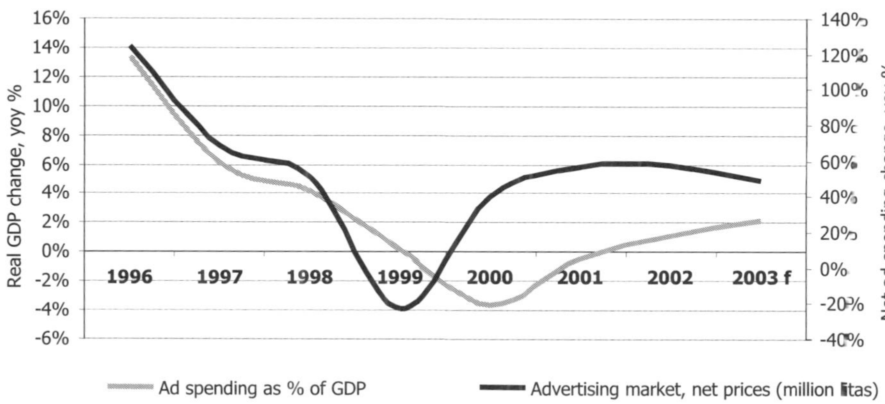

Figure 4.11.1 Lithuanian advertising market and GDP development

Source: BMF Gallup Media and Sic Gallup Media, Media House, Department of Statistics. Suprema's estimates (f)

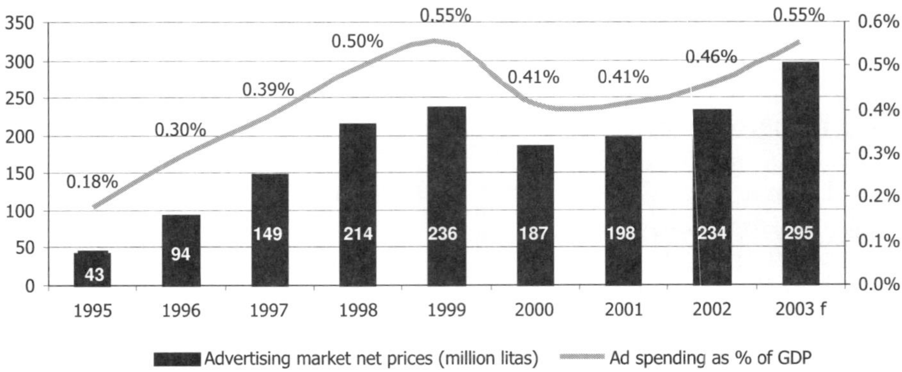

Figure 4.11.2 Advertising market in net prices

Source: BMF Gallup Media and Sic Gallup Media, Media House. Suprema's estimates (f)

and amounted to 234 million litas or 67 litas per capita (68 million euros and 19.3 euros respectively). The main market drivers have been increasing purchasing power and domestic demand.

The market dropped notably in 2000 following the Russian crisis, but the recovery came the next year and the market continues to grow. Fierce competition in the market, however, and limited corporate budgets for marketing expenses after the economy contraction in 1999, resulted in the increasing gap between advertising market development in gross prices and net income of media providers. Customers are now used to discounts in the market reaching as high as 80 per cent on TV channels, therefore the actual (net) advertising revenues fail to catch up with the rapid increase of the quantity of advertising materials displayed and broadcasted (Table 4.11.1).

It is expected that gross and net advertising market prices will gradually converge towards a sustainable equilibrium. At the beginning

Table 4.11.1 Advertising market in gross and net prices (million litas)

	1995	1996	1997	1998	1999	2000	2001	2002
Gross prices	102	217	360	464	503	514	699	914e
Annual change (%)		113	66	29	8	2	36	31
Net prices	43	94	149	214	236	187	198	234
Annual change (%)		119	59	44	10	-32	6	18

Source: BMF Gallup Media and Sic Gallup Media, Media House. Suprema's estimates (e)

of 2003 net market prices grew by 10 per cent compared to the previous year. The market itself is estimated to grow at double digit rates in the medium term with the main growth drivers being integration into the European Union (EU) and the North Atlantic Treaty Organization (NATO), general economic recovery, increased purchasing power and consumer spending. Demand for marketing communications services will primarily come from telecommunications, banking, insurance and IT industries as well as retail in consumer goods and durables in particular.

At the time of writing the total public relations market was valued by unverified sources at approximately 12–15 million litas with marketing communications strategic consultancy services estimated to equal around 3 million litas. However, reliable statistics are not yet available. The public relations market is expected to experience a major boost in demand in 2003 due to the surprise results during the elections of the new president in December 2002. This victory was to a large extent attributed to the successful implementation of public relations applications in his campaign. In addition, advertising agencies are increasingly expanding their scope of services and offering more lucrative strategic advisory services in the marketing communications business, renaming some of their services that are currently recorded as advertising revenues.

Advertising channels

Advertising market channels are different in different countries. This could be explained, to a large degree, by cultural differences, market maturity and country specific factors. Visual media channels, such as television and print, have the greatest role in Lithuania (Figure 4.11.3). Based on the 2002 figures, by channels the largest advertising spending

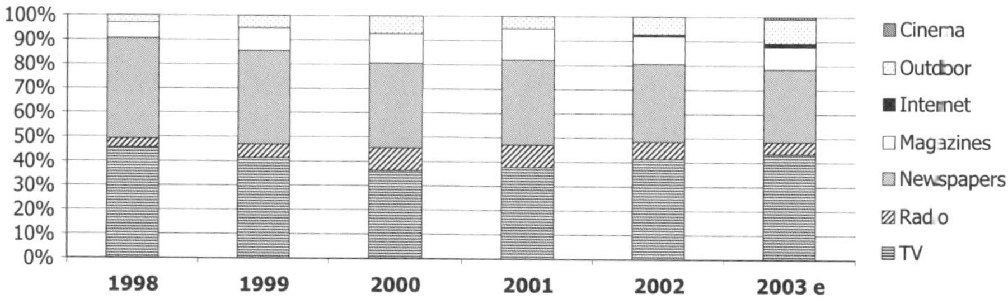

Figure 4.11.3 Advertising channels (net prices)

Source: BMF Gallup Media and Sic Gallup Media, Media House. Suprema's estimates (e)

Table 4.11.2 Advertising market channels in net prices (million litas)

Channel	1998	1999	2000	2001	2002	2003e
TV	98.4	97.2	68.0	75.0	96.0	127.8
Radio	6.4	14.3	17.0	17.7	18.0	13.8
Newspapers	89.9	91.2	66.0	69.0	74.0	87.4
Magazines	12.8	21.6	23.0	26.0	28.0	26.9
Internet	n/a	n/a	n/a	n/a	1.5	4.0
Outdoor	6.4	11.7	13.0	10.0	16.0	29.0
Cinema	n/a	n/a	n/a	n/a	0.2	2.8
Total	**213.9**	**236.0**	**187.0**	**197.7**	**233.7**	**291.7**

Source: BMF Gallup Media and Sic Gallup Media, Media House. Suprema's estimates (e)

in net prices is in television (96 million litas or 41 per cent of total), newspapers (74 million litas or 32 per cent) and magazines (28 million litas or 18 per cent). Market estimates for 2002–2003 imply an even larger share of advertising on television (Table 4.11.2).

As already mentioned, the Lithuanian advertising market has quite large discrepancies in pricing (ie market value in net prices amounts for only 30 per cent of the gross prices) – this difference is even greater with regard to television channels. Preliminary estimates for 2002 indicate that the gap increased even more last year, especially on the radio broadcasting channels (Table 4.11.3); due to the pricing deficiencies, advertising through a more influential media agent such as a television channel was offered at rates close to that of radio advertising. However, as already mentioned, gross and net prices started to converge slowly in 2003. A double digit growth is expected in the new advertising market channels such as Internet and video displays.

Table 4.11.3 Key advertising market channels in gross prices (million litas)

Channel	1997	1998	1999	2000	2001	2002e
TV	132.8	211.4	238.9	213.7	420.3	632.1
Radio	n/a	n/a	20.7	18.5	17.8	29.8
Print	n/a	137.6	145.0	120.5	136.3	206.0

Source: BMF Gallup Media and Sic Gallup Media, Media House. Suprema's estimates (e)

Table 4.11.4 Presence and revenue of global media agencies (million litas)

			1999	2000	2001	2002
Omincom group	Optimum	OMD Lietuva	6,400	13,600	17,500	30,416
	TBWA	Creative Media Services	10,000	16,340	25,016	20,452
WPP group	Mindshare	Media Bridge	n/d	8,380	8,548	n/d
Interpublic	Initiative	VIA Media	25,668	24,092	25,124	26,129
Publicis/ Bcom3 group	Zenith Media	Mediapool	10,000	9,500	8,400	n/d
	Starcom	VRS, Leo Burnett - Starcom	n/d	25,640	16,319	14,914
Aegis	Carat	Baltic Media Services	6,640	8,200	n/d	n/d
Tempus	CIA / MQI	Media House	24,284	22,516	26,300	25,245

Source: Verslo Žinios, agency data, Suprema's estimates

Table 4.11.5 Presence and revenue of global agencies networks (million litas)

			1999	2000	2001	2002
Omincom group	BBDO worldwide	Lukrecija BBDO	13,688	1,801	7,955	6,300
	DDB Worldwide	Brand Sellers DDB Vilnius, UAB	2,617	4,162	4,162	n/d
	TBWA Worldwide	Videvita Vilnius, UAB	7,046	9,729	10,346	10,441
WPP group	J. Walter Thompson	J.Walter Thompson SAN Vilnius	n/d	n/d	n/d	n/d
	Oligvy & Mather	Tatura, UAB	n/d	650	900	n/d
	Young & Rubicam	Garažas 4x4, UAB	n/d	n/d	37,883	n/d
Interpublic group	Foot, Cone & Belding	Baltic FCB, UAB	4,290	5,124	5,350	4,589
	Lowe Lintas & Partners	Age reklama, UAB	6,620	6,435	6,972	7,331
	McCann-Erickson	Astos dizainas, UAB	5,435	4,053	7,010	13,713
Publicis/Bcom 3 group	Publicis worldwide	Kredo R, UAB	14,100	12,000	5,900	4,950
	Saatch&Saatchi	Adell reklama, UAB	5,435	5,342	3,872	4,201
	Bates worldwide	ADM group, UAB	3,572	4,100	5,624	n/d
	Leo Burnet	Leo Burnet Vilnius	7,225	6,134	12,000	n/d
Other	Euro RSCG Worldwide	MIA	2,424	3,610	7,640	7,800
	Inorek & Grey	Havera, UAB	n/d	n/d	n/d	n/d
	ACE Baltic	MAP/ACE Baltic, UAB	6,572	7,120	3,550	2,160

Source: Verslo Žinios, Association of Estonian Advertisement Agencies, Latvian Round Table (JIC) 2002, agentūrų duomenys

Competitive environment

The main global media holdings originating from the USA, ie Interpublic, Publicis, WPP Group and Omnicom Group, have their presence in Lithuania through agency agreements and direct ownership interests. These global players expanded aggressively to other markets following their clients' business development and aim to maintain key accounts while utilizing local resources. There are also representatives of several other global networks and some local pan-Baltic groups.

Information given in the tables below is based on figures that differ in their accuracy and reported revenue composition and therefore should be used with caution. As an example Garage 4 × 4 data for Lithuania include results of the whole pan-Baltic creative and media operations, some companies, like MIA, include billings paid by their clients directly to the media providers, while the other companies are engaged in a variety of activities. In general, media operations have been distributed to separate companies by the majority of industry players.

The Lithuanian advertising market has gone through a series of consolidation and mergers, particularly affected by the market crisis in 2000 following the Russian crisis and bans on tobacco advertising, as well as the consolidation of foreign partner agencies. As mentioned above, media businesses have generally been distributed to separate companies, while traditional agencies increasingly turn to providing complex marketing communication solutions. It is worth mentioning that the largest advertising agency (with 2002 revenues amounting to 22.8 million litas) was only established in 2000. It is, however, affiliated with the retail market leader VP Market (its main client) and accumulates advertising and marketing activities of consumer staples sold through this retail chain.

The public relations market started developing between 1997 and 1999; the number of agencies grew to between 25 and 30 last year. However, in many cases these are 'one-man-show' agencies that should go through consolidation in the foreseeable future. In 2000 two agencies, Viešuju ryšiu partneriai and Taukacikas ir partneriai, merged, making pan-Baltic partnerships or affiliating with international agencies.

Table 4.11.6 Public relations agencies' revenue (million litas)

Local agency	Global network	1999	2000	2001	2002
A.Jonkus ir partneriai	Hauska, Fleishman-Hillard	0.38	0.86	1.25	1.88
Viešųjų ryšių partneriai	n/a	n/a	0.96	1.21	n/a
Komunikacija ir konsultantai	PR Net Baltic	1.40	1.41	1.00	
PM Consultants	Hill & Knowlton	n/a	n/a	0.92	0.99
DDB&Co Katkevičius	DDB&Co, Omnicom	n/a	0.09	0.76	1.13
Vox Populi	n/a	n/a	n/a	0.72	n/a
Guliverio tinklas	Network Guliver	0.57	0.54	0.71	n/a
Komunikacijos tiltai	VIA Media, Initiative media/ Universal	0.05	0.15	0.30	0.50

Source: Verslo Žinios, corporate data

FINANSŲ ANALITIKŲ ASOCIACIJA

Association of Financial Analysts (FAA) is non-for-profit professional organisation established in January 1999 while its initiative group has been active since 1997. Currently, there are almost 30 regular members and a wide network of interested finance and investment professionals.

Focus of FAA activities – is to raise members' awareness on the current topics in Lithuanian economy and other issues of interest to its members through the series of discussions with guest speakers, advocate on professional ethics and best practices, comment on draft laws and other important events in Lithuanian financial markets. Finance and investment professionals, as well as a group of leading journalists and reporters, covering finance and economic topics, also take part in FAA discussion series.

FAA puts a lot of emphasis on the continued education of finance and investment professionals, their ethical and high quality professional practice. Our members must to comply with the Code of Ethics and Standards of Professional Conduct, as well as with all applicable laws. In order to promote professional education, FAA has introduced and awards annually a LTL 1,000 grant for the CFA® Level 1 candidate.

CFA®, Chartered Financial Analyst, is the professional designation, awarded by the Association for Investment Management and Research (AIMR), based in USA. The Chartered Financial Analyst Program is a globally recognized standard for measuring the competence and integrity of financial analysts. Its curriculum develops and reinforces a fundamental knowledge of investment principles. Three levels of examination measure a candidate's ability to apply these principles at a professional level. The CFA exam is administered annually in more than 70 nations worldwide.

Contacts:
Ms. Viktorija Trimbel
President, Association of Financial Analysts
A.Goštauto St. 40, 5th floor
2001 Vilnius Lithuania
+3705 2362 714
+3705 2362 771
www.finansai.lt

4.12

The Commercial Real Estate Market

Andrius Stonkus, Rimvydas Baranauskas, Prime Real Estate

Historical overview

The inception of the Lithuanian real estate market goes back to 1991 when the then Supreme Council of Lithuania adopted a resolution allowing the population to purchase their living premises from the state. During the first privatization stage from 1991 to 1995 a total of 29,000 houses and 500,000 flats were transferred into private ownership.

The prices for flats and commercial premises, which between 1991 and 1993 were approximately 50–80 US dollars per square metre, started growing in the autumn of 1994. This was mainly driven by an unstable economy (decline of gross domestic product (GDP), hyper-inflation), stagnating construction of dwelling houses and, consequently, a shortage of flats.

In 1996 the prices for living premises surged to the levels of 150–350 US dollars per square metre as a result of numerous bankruptcies of banks and the following economic crisis in the country. As investment into real estate seemed the best value for money, the demand for properties increased which in turn pushed the prices up. With the start of the financial turmoil in Russia in the autumn of 1998 the prices for real estate in Lithuania skyrocketed by an average of 30 per cent within several months to reach approximately 450 US dollars per square metre. However, in 1999 the total turnover of real estate declined by almost half, although prices continued to follow an upward trend. Commercial land and land lots for private housing maintained the largest transaction volumes.

With the recovery of the national economy in 2000 the Lithuanian real estate market stabilized and started showing signs of growth. The activity of market participants increased in line with expanding volumes of loans and investment into real estate projects and the steeply growing construction of commercial premises. Compared to 1991, the prices for real estate boosted by almost 1,000 per cent to reach 500–1000 euros per square metre in the largest cities of Lithuania: the capital city Vilnius as well as Kaunas and Klaipeda. In smaller towns the development of the real estate market has been slower although countrywide expansion of large shopping centres gives a serious impetus to market growth outside of the main cities.

Back in 1996 no hyper/supermarkets were present in Lithuania. Today there are more than 350 stores that belong to different food, do-it-yourself (DIY) or home appliances retail operators. The largest food retailers in Lithuania are VP Market, Palink, RIMI Lietuva and Norfos Mažmena; the main DIY chain is Senukai and those selling home appliances are Topo Centras, Ogmina and Elektromarkt. The first new construction supermarket was opened by VP Market in 1998 in Vilnius.

The first A-class, 4,000 square metre office building was built in 1999 in Vilnius by Hanner, a Lithuanian real estate developer. Currently, the total area of A-class office buildings in Vilnius exceeds 30,000 square metres and is expected to triple by the end of 2004.

The first modern 20,000 square metre warehouse was constructed in the middle of 2002. Naturally, some modern warehouses of 2,000–3,000 square metres existed earlier; however they were built by companies to serve their own needs. The same year a new 10,000 square metre warehouse was opened in Klaipeda, the third largest city in Lithuania.

The recent construction boom and large volumes of new commercial real estate coming to the market have caused some decline of rent prices in these properties. Also, strong growth in the supply of new modern premises has influenced a significant decline in the occupancy of old premises. However, as in Western and Central Europe, real estate on average is priced 30–100 per cent higher in this segment of the market. Lithuania's expected accession to the European Union (EU) in 2004 should significantly boost the prices for real estate in the country as a result of accession arbitrage.

Foreign investment

Foreign investors have just discovered the Lithuanian real estate market. Until recently, investment with the aim of speculation was most common in the market – this has, however, become less attractive due to declining returns. Although Lithuania has not yet attracted large foreign investors into real estate looking for stable, long-term oriented returns, the small investors – mostly Scandinavian construction companies, some international real estate funds and a handful of developers – have already completed a number of commercial real estate projects.

Publicly available information is not sufficient to determine the total amount of investment into real estate; however individual projects are valued up to 20 million euros with the majority being in the range of 3–10 million euros. It is expected that new investment projects on infrastructure development in the capital city of Vilnius may exceed 50 million euros and attract larger foreign real estate developers and funds.

According to the Lithuanian Department of Statistics a sum of over 270 million euros was invested in real estate by foreign investors as of 1 October 2002. Among the largest investors is Great Britain with approximately 20 per cent of all foreign direct investment (FDI) into real estate; the USA is the second largest with 15 per cent (Figure 4.12.1).

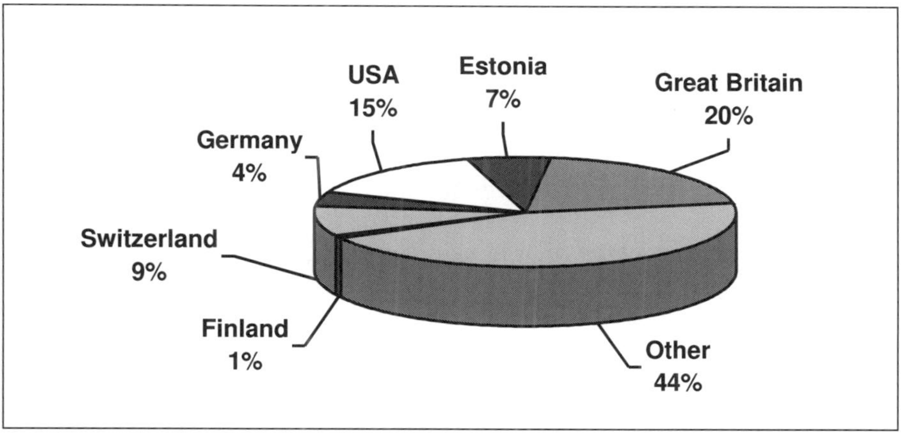

Figure 4.12.1 Foreign investors in real estate

Source: Lithuanian Department of Statistics

In light of Lithuania's shortly expected accession to the EU and the North Atlantic Treaty Organization (NATO), increasing foreign investment into real estate is largely driven by the Lithuanian Government's policy of integration with Europe. In addition, emerging pension funds and other larger institutional investors are viewed as potential buyers of current local and foreign investors, thereby increasing the liquidity of the commercial real estate market in the medium to long term. Given the currently prevailing trends in the country, foreign investment into the Lithuanian real estate market is expected to increase substantially between 2003 and 2005.

Market participants

The number of active local and foreign real estate investors such as investment or pension funds is still low in Lithuania. Laws and other legal acts restrict the volumes of investment into real estate of insurance companies, which usually are among the largest investors in commercial real estate. Moreover, Lithuanian insurance companies have little experience regarding this type of investment. At present the commercial real estate market has rather limited appeal to large international institutional investors due to its relatively small size, limited number of available attractive properties with long-term prospects and low liquidity.

The largest Scandinavian and Estonian construction and real estate developers, namely Skanska Statyba, NCC Statyba, Merko Statyba and SRV Development, have already established a presence in Lithuania. Due to the abundant supply of cheap local contractors capable of delivering acceptable quality at a low price, they prefer to act as general contractors responsible for overall project management and quality assurance while subcontracting specialized local construction companies. Lithuanian construction companies, on the other hand, are often too small to compete in general contractor's tenders and therefore focus on investing their own funds in the construction of office buildings, commercial or trade centres, warehousing or logistics centres and apartment blocks and private housing.

Pinus Proprius and Linstow are among the most active foreign real estate developers while Hanner, MG Valda, Invalda and Ogmios Centras are local companies, each of which has completed at least one project. The most active real estate investment funds include Baltic–American Enterprise Fund, Baltic Property Trust and Moller Real Estate.

Currently, the size of real estate projects ranges from 5–15 million euros although there are some projects in progress, as well as plans for such, exceeding 30 million euros. At present a joint project is being carried out by Hanner and Skanska real estate developers and the lease company VB Lizingas (a member of SEB Group) on the construction of a commercial and office buildings complex in Vilnius. The total area of the complex is estimated to exceed 56,000 square metres with a total investment of over 30 million euros.

Companies are also expanding their core business (eg retail, logistics) which requires substantial investment into real estate in various parts of Lithuania. It appears that today there are numerous businesses in Lithuania that are still slow to move from the model of owning the properties to leasing them on a long-term basis.

Two years ago, an average of 40 per cent of all transactions related to real estate in Lithuania were financed by long-term bank loans. Recently, with a sharp drop in annual interest rates to 5.5–7.5 per cent, improved financing terms and more transparent procedures, the share of transactions financed by long-term bank loans has climbed to 60 per cent.

Office space market

In the last three years the Lithuanian office market has witnessed significant growth. This comes as a result of an increasing demand for modern offices by international companies and fast-growing local enterprises, coupled with the construction of new office buildings and the reconstruction of old ones. Over this period of three years a distinct segment of A-class office space emerged in Vilnius, substantially diminishing the occupancy of old office buildings that were often very inconvenient and unsuitable for office purposes. The inception of the Lithuanian office market is related to the opening of the first A-class office building (4,000 square metres) by Hanner in Vilnius at the end of 1999. A great shortage of new modern office space in the capital facilitated the development of other high class office buildings exclusively for rent. By the end of 2002, it was estimated that in Vilnius alone 30,000 square metres of new modern office premises had been brought to the market with the majority of office buildings claiming occupancy rates of up to 100 per cent (Table 4.12.1).

On average, occupancy rates in this segment approached 85 per cent by the end of 2002. During the period 2003–2004 another 70,000 square metres are expected to hit the market in Vilnius. Also plans for the construction of modern office buildings are underway in other major cities including Kaunas, Klaipeda, Šiauliai and Panevėžys. At the end of 2002, the total area of new modern office premises countrywide amounted to 140,000 square metres; this includes properties constructed by banks and companies specializing in information technology (IT), telecommunications and insurance to be used for their own purposes.

In Vilnius, the only city where A-class premises are available, rent prices for this type of property have decreased slightly over the last couple of years. However, they are still relatively high compared with Central and Eastern Europe, where prices are in the region of 15–18 euros per square metre per month. Demand for A-class premises remains high with most of them rented out during the construction phase.

With a substantial share of companies moving from the old town and the city centre to adjacent areas, the price of office premises in the old town and city centre has dropped to 6–14 euros per square metre. Difficult access, limited parking space and comparatively poor quality of offices are the main reasons behind 'the migration' of the corporate community to outside the historic centre of Vilnius. Office premises of old construction are still the most expensive in the old town followed by the city centre with monthly rent in fully refurbished premises

Table 4.12.1 Most significant high class office projects (end 2002)

Building	Class	Date	Developer	Office area (m^2)	Total area (m^2)	Occupancy rate (%)
Hanner I	A	1999	Hanner	4,000	4,000	100
International Business Center	A	2000	Invalda	8,200	8,200	90
Verslo centras 2000	A	2000	Pinus Proprius	14,000	19,000	35
Hanner II	A	2001	Hanner	4,800	5,500	100
Ogmios Hanner Center	B	2003	Hanner and Ogmios Centras	4,500	15,100	n/a
Baltic Center	A/B	2003	MG Valda	10,000	16,200	80*
Baltic Business Center	A	2003	Eika	7,850	8,000	85*
Europa Center	A	2004	Hanner	15,700	21,000	40*
Municipality Center	A	2004	Skanska	25,000	35,000	n/a
MVC Center (in Kaunas)	A	2004	Mikrovisata	5,000	5,000	n/a
Total				**99,050**	**137,000**	

*Not yet opened
Note: All projects of A-class office space for rent were completed in Vilnius
Source: Prime Real Estate, 2003

Table 4.12.2 Price of office premises (end 2002)

	Rent prices per month (euro/m^2)			Sales prices (euro/m^2)		
Location	**New construction**	**Reconstructed**	**Old construction**	**New construction**	**Reconstructed**	**Old construction**
Vilnius	17.5–19.0	10.5–17.5	3.5–11.5	580–1,300	400–580	230–400
Kaunas	7.0–11.5	4.3–7.2	1.5–4.3	460–3,100	240–460	145–240
Klaipeda	8.5–11.5	7.2–8.7	4.3–7.2	900–925	405–520	290–520

Source: Prime Real Estate, 2002

reaching 10–14 euros per square metre. Office premises situated further from the main streets of the old town and the city centre are priced at 6–10 euros per square metre per month. Sales prices for this type of real estate fall within the range of 800–1,200 euros per square metre. Premises in old construction buildings in areas other than the city centre remain the cheapest with a monthly rent of 5–7 euros per square metre and a sales price of 250–450 euros per square metre.

Different to the situation in Vilnius, the market of A-class office premises in other Lithuanian cities is just starting to develop. By mid-2004 local investors plan to offer a total of 5,000 square metres of A-class office space in Kaunas. Some plans have also been disclosed for Klaipeda. However, large real estate companies have no plans yet regarding other cities due to weak demand, small office space requirements per tenant (typically ranging between 100 and 200 square metres) and low rent prices. Currently, the rent price for office premises in other larger Lithuanian cities other than Vilnius is approximately 4–10 euros per square metre per month. Most in demand is the office of approximately 100–150 square metres with a traditional configuration of the floor including a reception, separate rooms for an executive and chief accountant, a common working space, a meeting room and often a small kitchen.

At present, international companies and their representative offices in Lithuania (pharmaceutical, insurance, legal, IT and telecommunication and banks) are the main tenants of A-class office premises. Companies moving to new premises with the aim of improving working conditions and enhancing their corporate image make up around 60 per cent of the tenants while the remaining share consists of companies expanding their activities, start-ups or representative offices of foreign companies entering the market.

It is estimated that in the next couple of years the prices for A-class office premises in Vilnius will remain rather stable with some probability of a slight decrease if the construction of new, large office buildings is only driven by the market's growing demand. A decline in prices for A-class premises would occur only subject to surplus volumes of office space brought to the market which would force real estate developers to compete fiercely in price; however this is unlikely in the next few years. Appearance on the market of new comparatively small office buildings is not likely to have any significant influence on price levels. However, the prices of old office buildings, the occupancy of which has been constantly declining, are likely to continue in their downward trend.

Retail space market

The retail sector has experienced substantial growth over the last couple of years with local companies dominating the sector. However, many changes lie ahead, such as the further development of hypermarkets and shopping malls and the entry of Western department and food retailing stores, DIY hardware and electronics and apparel chains into the market. Having gone through the stages of privatization and commercialization since the early 1990s, retailers are growing at a fast pace, rationalizing their operations, striving to differentiate from competitors and developing local and pan-Baltic chains. Some well developed local chains with significant market shares are potential acquisition targets for Western Europe's prominent retailers who are gradually increasing their importance in shaping Eastern Europe's retail landscape.

Having been the most active real estate segment in the last two years, the market of retail space is expected to retain its growth patterns in the near future. Although the overall number of shops has been declining, the total retail area has been on the increase. In one year the number of trade points decreased by 10 per cent and at the end of 2002 there were 16,500 trade points selling fast-moving goods.

Fast expansion of large supermarket chains is a driving force in consolidating the food retail market. Back in 1996 no hyper/supermarkets were present in Lithuania. Today there are more than 350 stores, which belong to different food retail operators (the largest food retailers in Lithuania are VP Market, Palink, RIMI Lietuva and Norfos Mazmena, of which only RIMI Lietuva is an international food chain). The estimated turnover of these stores comprised some 60 per cent of the Lithuanian retail market in 2002 compared to less than 5 per cent in 1996.

Compared to Central and Western Europe the shopping mall market is still in its inception. Akropolis, which opened in the first half of 2002 in Vilnius and has a total area of over 50,000 square metres, is the only shopping and entertainment complex in Lithuania. Plans for opening the shopping malls, Mecca (in 2003) and Europa (in 2004) are under way. TK Development, one of the largest real estate developers in Scandinavia and Central Europe has also declared plans to enter the Lithuanian shopping mall market by opening two shopping malls in the next two years (Table 4.12.3).

Rent prices in different shopping centres are similar, ranging from 11.5 euros per square metre per month to 30 euros per square metre per month depending on the total area rented and the location of the shop. Companies that rent large trade areas pay up to 15 euros per square metre per month with the exception of large food retailers that pay on average 6–8 euros per square metre per month. The average rent price for a 200–300 square metre shop falls within 20–25 euros per square metre per month, while it will cost 40 euros per month for a 50–100 square metre shop.

In the prestigious streets of Vilnius rent prices start at 30 euros per square metre per month and reach 60 euros per square metre per month

Table 4.12.3 Existing and planned shopping malls

Shopping mall	**Town**	**Date**	**Developer**	**Trade area (m^2)**	**Total area (m^2)**
Akropolis	Vilnius	2002	NDX Development	50,000	50,000
Europa Centre	Vilnius	2004	Hanner	5,300	21,000
Mecca	Vilnius	2003	VUP	16,000	16,000
Akropolis	Kaunas	2003	NDX Development	40,000	40,000
Baltic Shopping Centre	Kaunas	2004	Objekt-Entwicklung	70,000	70,000
Myla	Vilnius	2004	TK Development	26,000	28,000
North	Vilnius	2004	TK Development	25,000	27,000
Total				**232,300**	**252,000**

Source: Prime Real Estate, 2003

for smaller shops or exceptional locations. Rent prices on Gediminas Avenue, which was listed in 2002 as the 53rd most expensive street in the world, are the highest in Vilnius and the rest of Lithuania; they can easily reach 50–60 euros per square metre per month. On the high streets of Kaunas and Klaipeda prices are lower, amounting to 36 euros per square metre per month and from 5–10 euros per square metre per month on other streets.

The trade area per 1,000 residents in the largest cities of Lithuania represents less than 100 square metres, which is at least twice as low as the countries of Western Europe. The growing purchasing power of the population and steadily increasing spending on consumer and durable goods will continue to stimulate an increase in the number of shopping centres, although at a slower pace compared to the growth rates over the last two to three years. In addition, notable changes in the market are anticipated due to the expected significant investment activity declared by large international retail giants such as Kesko Group, Ica-Ahold and Lidl.

In the short term, a number of large shopping malls coming to the market in Vilnius over the next two years may temporarily press down rent prices. In the longer term, however, the prices in conceptually cohesive and well managed shopping malls, as well as on the best retail streets in the largest cities of Lithuania, are unlikely to decline. This is primarily due to the fast growing disposable income, increasing competition between retailers and yet numerous unexplored retailing opportunities left on the table. Moreover, with the entrance of large foreign real estate developers and Lithuania's forthcoming accession to the EU and NATO, rent prices may even increase slightly; at present they are 30 to 100 per cent lower than those of Western and some Central European countries.

Warehousing premises

The Lithuanian warehousing premises market is in its early stage of development. Renovated old Soviet-type warehouses prevail; most of them are old constructions situated on the premises of former large Soviet factories that went out of business or old warehousing centres. Often they are located in the vicinity of the city centre, which makes them very difficult to access by heavy load trucks. Recently, interest for logistics and warehousing centres jumped significantly although no major projects have been realized yet.

There are only two modern warehousing complexes meeting the requirements of the EU in Lithuania at present. One of them is located in Vilnius (20,000 square metres) and the other in the port city of Klaipeda (10,000 square metres); both have been fully rented out. Given the acute

Table 4.12.4 Price of trade premises (end 2002)

	Rent prices per month (euro/m^2)			Sales prices (euro/m^2)		
Location	**New construction**	**Reconstructed**	**Old construction**	**New construction**	**Reconstructed**	**Old construction**
Vilnius	17.4–46.3	11.6–17.4	5.2–10.1	3,378–6,940	1,200–3,380	463–580
Kaunas	15.9–34.7	5.8–15.9	3.5–7.5	1,050–3,470	810–1,050	320–810
Klaipeda	17.3–23.1	8.6–17.3	4.5–8.5	1,180–1,750	540–1,200	405–540

Source: Prime Real Estate, 2003

shortage of new warehousing space for rent some foreign companies have launched the construction of 2,000–5,000 square metre warehouses to serve their own needs even though it is not in line with their strategies and corporate policies in general. In the five largest cities of Lithuania rent prices in warehouses of old construction fall to between 1.5 euros per square metre and 3 euros per square metre depending on the rented area and condition of the warehouse. Due to the shortage of modern warehousing space, in newly constructed warehouses rent is 4–5 euros per square metre regardless of the area rented (Table 4.12.5).

Due to the fact that developers have been slow at bringing to the market new warehouses constructed in line with EU requirements, in the short term those developers that manage to offer modern warehouses over the next year or so should be in a position to demand premium rents.

Land

Approximately 2,500 transactions are conducted monthly on purchase/sale and rent of private and state land in Lithuania. At present, non-residents and legal persons are allowed to acquire land for non-agricultural purposes only. In line with the Constitution, namely the amendment of section II of Chapter 47, after Lithuania's accession to the EU non-residents and legal persons will be allowed to purchase agricultural land, although some restrictions will apply for a certain period of time. These changes are expected to encourage the concentration of ownership of land and attract larger local and foreign players to a market that is currently very fragmented and of low liquidity.

In 2002 agricultural land in Lithuania was priced, on average, at 510 euros per hectare. The Vilnius district was at the top of the price range where one hectare on average was priced at 730 euros per hectare. Meanwhile, agricultural land located close to the city, surrounded by beautiful landscape and purchased mostly for summer houses and leisure purposes, was priced in the range of 1,500–8,500 euros per hectare and ever higher. The price for forest has also been increasing in recent years. Most expensive was forest in southern Lithuania where the average price reached 1,800 euros per hectare while in other regions it stood at 480–1,340 euros per hectare. Mature forest was more expensive and cost on average 3,000 euros per hectare; a hectare of oak forest cost 6,000 euros.

In terms of the structure of land-related transactions, agricultural land occupied the lion's share (60 per cent) while the rest was split between forest land (6–10 per cent) and other land (30–35 per cent). The private housing market was most active in the five largest cities of

Table 4.12.5 Price of warehousing premises (end 2002)

Location	Rent prices per month (euro/m^2)			Sales prices (euro/m^2)		
	New construction	Reconstructed	Old construction	New construction	Reconstructed	Old construction
Vilnius	5.8–8.7	3.0–5.8	1.2–3.0	150–289	100–150	58–100
Kaunas	n/a	2.3–5.8	1.2–3.0	260–434	100–260	51–90
Klaipeda	n/a	1.7–3.5	1.2–3.0	87–104	70–90	46–70

Source: Prime Real Estate, 2002

Lithuania (Vilnius, Kaunas, Klaipeda, Šiauliai and Panevėžys). These cities accounted for more than 30 per cent of all land lots sold for private housing.

Based on 2002 data, statistically the average land lot for private housing was 18,600 square metres in size while the average lot of agricultural land totalled 3 hectares. Private land lots of 900–1,000 square metres were purchased most often. In line with existing legislation the smallest permissible size of land on which private house can be built in town cannot be smaller than 400 square metres, while the maximum is set at 2,000 square metres. In suburban areas land lots are bigger as a rule, reaching up to 3,000 square metres. In Soviet-style garden house complexes located in the vicinity of the towns, land lots of 600 square metres prevail.

Demand for commercial land is peaking in Vilnius, Kaunas, Klaipeda, Šiauliai and Panevėžys. Depending on the location, a square metre of commercial land in these cities is priced at 30–100 euros, with Vilnius taking the lead as the city where prices for land are the highest. In Vilnius the price per square metre easily jumps to 200–300 euros for lots situated in the proximity of the city centre and old town. In other large towns the prices for commercial land lots are, on average, lower by at least 15–20 per cent.

Municipalities play a major role in shaping the supply of land through auctions of municipal land for sale or lease (up to 99 years). Currently the largest purchasers and/or lessees include office developers, shopping centre developers and operators and companies engaged in the construction of houses.

Real estate in 2003 and beyond

Overall, in Lithuania most of the traditional commercial real estate segments continue to grow well above Western European rates. Retail, new office space and hotel sectors have been experiencing a very steep growth over the last two or three years, although the hotel sector now seems to be slowing down (Figure 4.12.2).

This growth deceleration is primarily as a result of the great number of new hotels due to open in Vilnius in 2003 and 2004. These new hotels are expected to add up to 2,500 new beds to the city's hotel market. It is estimated that in the longer term, the economy class hotel segment will remain attractive to real estate investors because there is still an insufficient number of beds offered. In terms of locations, the growth of the hotel market is primarily taking place in the capital city of Vilnius, while other cities in this segment are experiencing a lack of demand. In the short term the situation does not seem to change to any significant degree.

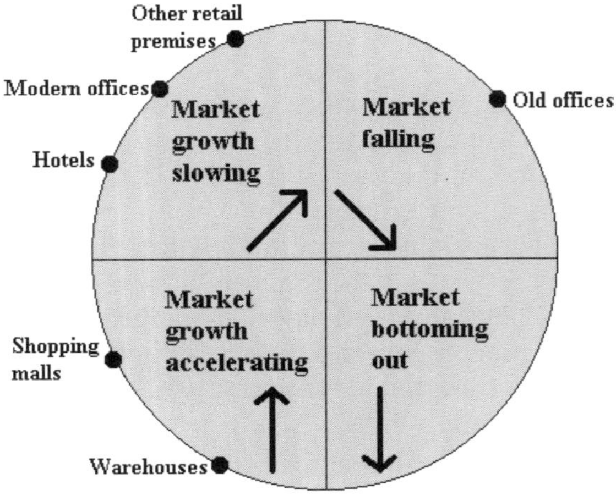

Figure 4.12.2 Real estate sector clock

Regardless of the fact that all A-class office space developments have so far taken place in Vilnius, this segment does not appear to be completely filled. It would seem that creative office space developers in Vilnius should look for new opportunities in B-class office space developments in more remote but convenient locations as well as in tailor-made office spaces built to suit the specific needs of large successful corporations in the country that are willing to rent. In the short to medium term other large cities seem to offer rather limited opportunities for A-class developments but may have good prospects for a limited number of B-class office developers.

Due to the great shortage of modern warehousing in Lithuania, warehouse developers are most likely to enjoy the attractive returns that can be obtained over the next couple of years. Although the shopping mall sector seems to be very promising at present, the completion of a great number of new shopping malls in Vilnius in 2003 and 2004 will boost supply to the extent that the construction of additional shopping malls in the city may have a negative effect on rent levels. It is believed that great potential remains in Lithuania's other large cities as well as in Vilnius itself but not for well focused shopping malls.

At present the only contracting segment appears to be old office space. However, as a result of the substantial modern office space that is coming to the market, this trend takes place primarily in Vilnius. In other large cities contracting old office space appears to be rather stable but is expected to decline as soon as modern office space buildings come to the market.

4.13

The Electricity and Gas Sectors

Lideika, Petrauskas, Valiūnas ir Partneriai

The electricity sector: overview

The Lithuanian electricity sector has traditionally been structured as a vertically integrated public monopoly. In 2000 the *Seimas* (parliament) passed the law to expedite the reorganization of the stated-owned electricity generating, transmission and distribution company, SPAB Lietuvos energija (Lithuanian Energy). The reorganization was fully implemented at the beginning of 2002, along with bringing into force the new Law on Electricity of 20 July 2000. This law established regulation of the electricity market in line with the requirements of the European Union (EU) Directive 96/92/EC.

The reorganization of Lithuanian Energy resulted in the emergence of two electricity generating companies, one electricity transmission company and two electricity distribution companies (AB Rytų skirstomieji tinklai and AB Vakarų skirstomieji tinklai). At present the electricity distribution companies – the major shareholders of which are the Government (85.72 per cent of shares in each of the companies) and EON Energie AG (10.9 per cent of shares in each of the companies) – are on a list of companies to be privatized. The Government intends to sell at least 51 per cent of its shares in each of the companies and expects the privatization to be consummated by the end of 2003. According to experts' expectations, the total price for the shares of AB Rytų skirstomieji tinklai and AB Vakarų skirstomieji tinklai may exceed 1 billion litas (approximately 289 million euros).

Lithuania may be characterized as a net exporter with a large reserve margin. The total installed electricity generating capacities in 2003 and 2004 will remain at approximately 6,156 megawatts, resulting in an overcapacity of more than 1,550 megawatts. Therefore, the present generating capacities will fully satisfy the demands of Lithuanian customers. It is expected that consumption of electricity in 2003 and 2004 will be approximately 14.8 TWh, including export of electricity to the amount of approximately 5.7 TWh. Currently Lithuania exports electricity to Russia and the Kaliningrad region, as well as neighbouring Latvia and Estonia. Plans to export electricity to Poland and Ukraine are being considered.

Presently, coverage of electricity transmission and distribution grids meets the demands of Lithuanian electricity customers. However, significant investments will have to be made in the near future to renew most of the grid in order to meet security requirements and those regarding the stability of the transmission of electricity. Strategic objectives in the electricity sector include linking the Lithuanian power grid to the Western systems, in particular by interconnecting the power grids of Lithuania and Poland, as well as establishing a common electricity market of the Baltic States. Although the initiatives concerning these objectives are clear, because of the large investments required it is unreasonable to expect their implementation to commence in 2003.

One of the factors that will have a significant impact on the generation of electricity in Lithuania is the foreseen shutdown of the Ignalina Nuclear Power Plant. Nuclear power generating capacities currently amount to 42 per cent of all the installed electricity generating capacities and between 1998 and 2002 the Ignalina Nuclear Power Plant supplied approximately 76–90 per cent of all the electricity consumed in Lithuania. The full shutdown of the plant comes as a result of negotiations to become a member of the EU and will be gradually implemented until completion in 2009. It is estimated that, as a result of the shutdown of this power plant, the investments necessary for the reorganization of the electricity generation sector will initially reach 2.8 billion litas (approximately 810 million euros).

In line with the requirements of the EU directives, the National Energy Strategy (adopted in 2002) sets forth an objective to increase the share of renewable energy sources by up to 12 per cent of the aggregate balance of primary energy sources in 2010. Therefore, the Government will maintain an interest and support the construction and operation of electricity generators using the renewable energy sources that are available.

Regulation of the electricity sector

Authorizations

Under current legislation, most of the activities in the electricity sector are subject to prior authorization of state institutions in the form of a licence or a permit. The Law on Electricity provides that the following activities in the electricity sector are licensable:

- activity of the market operator;
- electricity transmission;
- electricity distribution;
- electricity supply.

Activities for which a permit from an authorized state institution is mandatory are:

- electricity generation;
- expansion of electricity generating capacities;
- electricity export;
- electricity import;
- construction of the direct line.

A permit for the generation of electricity should be issued for every legal or natural person requesting it, provided that such person ensures the intended activity will conform to requirements of safety and security, environmental protection, use of land and planning of constructions and those related to the nature of the primary sources.

Regulation of tariffs

In general, tariffs for electricity are either contractual or regulated by the state. Only the tariffs for electricity (and reserve capacity) offered by electricity producers and independent suppliers are not subject to regulation, provided that the market share of electricity sales of such producers or suppliers does not exceed 25 per cent. In all remaining cases tariffs for electricity and the prices of the respective services are regulated; this is based mainly on three objectives:

- to ensure the availability of electricity for household customers at a reasonable price;
- to prevent the abuse of significant influence in the electricity market, including abuse of naturally existing monopoly rights to transmit and distribute electricity;
- to promote the use of alternative energy sources in generating electricity.

In each case the electricity tariffs comprise the price of electricity as the product, the prices of the supply and, depending on which level of voltage the customer receives electricity from, transmission and/or distribution services. As mentioned, the prices of electricity and reserve capacity are not regulated but determined by the auction or negotiations between the parties. However, producers and independent providers whose share is over 25 per cent of the market must follow mandatory methodologies to calculate the tariffs as approved by the state authorities.

The prices of electricity transmission and distribution services, as well as public tariffs for electricity, are regulated by the state authorities who set ceilings on the prices and tariffs. The ceilings are calculated by estimating the initial level of income of a transmission or distribution company or a public electricity supplier for a period of three years and adjusting it every year by four coefficients (contingency, volume adjustment, indexation and correction factors). Particular prices and tariffs are established by electricity utilities; however they may not exceed the established ceilings. Price regulation, through the establishment of the ceilings, is based on certain objectives that include:

- inducing electricity utilities to provide services to customers at the lowest costs;
- ensuring sufficient income of electricity utilities;
- ensuring the stability of tariffs;
- ensuring that the tariffs are not cross-subsidized.

Aiming to promote the use of renewable energy sources when generating electricity, the Government established a public service obligation for electricity suppliers to purchase a certain amount of electricity generated using renewable sources. However, as the direct costs of such electricity generation are comparatively high and it would be difficult for producers to sell the electricity in line with competitive market conditions, the legal acts provide that the purchase price of electricity generated using renewable sources will be established by the state authorities.

Liberalization

Legislation seeks to implement an electricity market model based on bilateral agreements between electricity producers, suppliers and eligible customers by applying the principle of regulated third party participation in the delivery of purchased electricity. Based on current regulations, the right to conclude contracts on the direct purchase of electricity with producers will be granted gradually as follows:

- from 1 January 2003 – to customers who consumed more than 9 million kilowatt hours of electricity in the previous year;
- from 1 January 2004 – to customers who may apply for the status of eligible customer in accordance with the degree of openness of the

market which should be established and published by the Government annually;

- from 1 January 2010 – to all customers.

In accordance with legal acts, eligible customers have the right to negotiate, without restrictions, electricity supply agreements with national and foreign electricity producers and suppliers having licences for such activity. However, eligible customers may import electricity only following the conditions established by the Government or its authorized institution. In addition, permission to import electricity should be issued in accordance with the established quotas and only if the exporting state provides to its eligible customers and suppliers an adequate possibility to import electricity from Lithuania.

Public service obligations

Current regulations provide for the following obligations for public and independent electricity suppliers as well as for eligible customers who import electricity:

- to purchase and sell electricity generated using renewable and waste energy sources;
- to purchase and sell electricity generated at CHP plants that provide heat to the district heating systems of towns;
- to purchase and sell electricity generated at the specified power plants wherein electricity generation is necessary to assure energy system reserves;
- to cover the costs related to nuclear power safety improvement measures as well as the storage and burial of nuclear waste.

Certain public service obligations are also established for transmission and distribution operators, namely:

- to ensure that all customers who have implemented respective technical requirements have the possibility to be connected to the transmission or distribution networks and receive a reliable supply of electricity;
- to ensure the high quality of the electricity supplied;
- to develop the infrastructure of the state energy system and inter-system connections in order to satisfy the growing demand for electricity in the country.

Natural gas sector

Lithuania is fully dependent on the import of natural gas from the Russian Federation. The share of natural gas in the aggregate balance of the primary energy sources of Lithuania amounts to approximately 28 per cent. Statistically, the import of natural gas has been increasing by 1.1 per cent per year since 1998. It is expected that in 2003 imports will reach the level of 2.8 billion cubic metres.

The Lithuanian pipeline system comprises over 1,600 kilometres of main pipelines, over 6,000 kilometres of distribution pipelines and has the capacity to transport 6 billion cubic metres of gas per year. The gas supply grid is interconnected with the grids of neighbouring Latvia and the Kaliningrad region but is not linked with the grids of Western Europe.

Until 1992 the only company allowed to import natural gas into Lithuania was the state company, AB Lietuvos dujos (Lithuanian Gas). On 31 August 1992 the Government adopted Resolution No 642, which abolished the monopoly in supplying Lithuanian customers with natural gas and allowed private companies to import and sell natural gas without any quantitative restrictions. In 2002, 70–80 per cent of all the imported natural gas was purchased by eligible customers from newly established gas suppliers.

At present Lithuanian Gas remains the sole owner of the main grid and owns approximately 75 per cent of the distribution grids. In 2002 the company was partially privatized; a consortium of Rhurgas AG and EON Energie AG acquired 35.6 per cent of company shares, 58.4 per cent remained in the ownership of the state and 6.0 per cent remained with the minority shareholders. Another 34 per cent of state shares will be sold during the second stage of the company's privatization, which is intended to be consummated in 2003.

The legal acts establish the right of natural gas suppliers and eligible customers to use the main pipelines and distribution pipelines on a contractual basis. The prices of transportation and distribution pipelines are fixed and may not exceed the ceilings established by the state authorities in accordance with the approved methodologies.

Part Five

Appendices

Appendix 1

Business Risk Assessment

Coface

(A) Lithuania

Rating: A4

Assets

- prospect of European Union (EU) membership in 2004 continues to drive reforms;
- skilled manpower and low labour costs;
- hub of East–West trade;
- sound economic fundamentals and fiscal consolidation ensured the successful re-pegging of country's currency to the euro in early 2002;
- ethnic homogeneity promotes stability.

Weaknesses

- large external account deficit due to economic modernization;
- exports highly dependent on transit trade;
- low domestic savings;
- transition to market economy could heighten social tensions against a background of high unemployment.

Risk assessment

In 2002 the country posted strong economic growth on the back of buoyant domestic demand. However, the sluggish recovery in the EU should affect growth in 2003, despite exports to countries of the Commonwealth of Independent States (CIS) holding firm. Furthermore, inadequate fiscal revenues and accession costs could prevent the government from meeting its fiscal objectives.

Soaring imports, buoyed by a healthy domestic demand, are keeping the current account in the red, the country's main weakness. Lithuania remains heavily dependent on international capital markets, but favourable terms of access to these markets, along with rising foreign direct investment (FDI), have helped cover the country's external financing requirement without difficulty.

The country needs to step up structural reforms in public (especially municipal) financial management, pensions, business environment, labour legislation and energy and transport privatization.

Econometric data

Source: Bank Austria (Table A.1.1).

MIG analysis

Introduction

Lithuania's centre-left coalition, in power since June 2001, has made good progress in implementing reform, pushing through an austere fiscal programme, sound tax reforms and keeping EU accession on track.

The economy has held up well in the present downturn, registering 5.7 per cent growth in the first half of 2002 with low inflation. However, unemployment remains high at around 13 per cent, which will continue to restrain domestic consumption growth in the medium term. Foreign direct investment remains buoyant, growing by 13 per cent in the first half of 2002.

Fourth quarter 2002 grey area dynamics™: 49
(Europe and FSU GAD Rating: 60.87)

- fighting index: low
- crime levels: medium
- bureaucracy: medium to high
- cultural integration: medium
- religious extremism: low

Table A.1.1 Econometric data

Change from previous year	**1999**	**2000**	**2001**	**2002**	**2003 (forecast)**	**2004 (forecast)**
GDP (real) (%)	–3.9	3.8	5.9	5.0	3.5	4.5
Industrial output (real) (%)	–11.2	5.3	16.9	4.5	5.0	6.0
Gross fixed capital formation (real) (%)	–6.3	–3.9	10.6	12.0	8.0	10.0
Consumer prices (yearly average %)	0.8	1.0	1.3	0.2	1.0	2.5
Unemployment (yearly average %)	14.1	15.4	17.0	16.6	16.0	15.2
Budget balance (% of GDP)	–5.6	–2.7	–1.9	–1.8	–1.9	–1.8
In %:						
Merchandise exports (€ million)	2,950	4,382	5,456	5,990	6,300	6,800
Merchandise imports (€ million)	4,266	5,576	6,693	7,450	7,900	8,400
Current account (€ million)	–1,119	–730	–640	–884	–870	870
Current account (% of GDP)	–11.2	–6.0	–4.8	–6.0	–5.7	5.3
FDI (inflow, net, € million)	448	406	498	696	680	720
Gross foreign debt (end of period, € million)	4,256	5,284	5,879	6,290	6,500	6,600
Gross foreign debt (% of GDP)	42.6	43.3	43.9	43.0	42.5	40.5
Import cover (months)	2.8	2.8	3.0	3.2	3.0	2.8
Average exchange rate: litas/euro	4.27	3.70	3.58	3.45	3.45	3.45
Average exchange rate: litas/US dollar	4.00	4.00	4.00	3.65	3.34	3.38

Source: IMF, Bank Austria Creditanstalt Economics Department

Practice

Corruption and bribery

Lithuania is generally seen as 'cleaner' than neighbouring Latvia, but the same problems associated with a weak and underpaid state apparatus exist. Corruption is particularly serious in the customs and police services, although tangible progress has been made in the past year.

Mechanisms include 'greasing palms' to speed up the unwieldy bureaucracy, paying for information or security guarantees from state agencies and 'buying' protective regulations and decisions from government departments.

Regulation and judiciary

As in Latvia, the regulation of banking and securities has improved thanks to EU pressure. Insurance and data protection remain problem areas, particularly on the question of regulatory independence. The past year has seen significant judicial reform, encompassing the training of judges themselves in addition to new procedural codes and structural reform. Nonetheless, undertrained judges and prosecutors operating in a new system has led to a heavy case backlog.

Organized crime

Lithuania is unique among the Baltic States with regard to the degree to which it remains economically integrated with the CIS. The latter accounted for over 25 per cent of its trade in 2001. Organized crime groups have seized on this to exploit the East–West transit trade, both legal and illegal. Counterfeiting in particular remains a growth industry against which little progress has been made, partly due to a lack of cooperation between the responsible authorities.

EU enlargement

Lithuania is set to join the EU in 2004, following the likely conclusion of negotiations this year. Russia's increasingly close relations with the USA have eased the tensions associated with accession to the North Atlantic Treaty Organization (NATO), also due in 2004.

Essentials

Denmark and Sweden remain the most prolific investors in Lithuania, registering 17 and 16 per cent of the cumulative total respectively. However, some of the most prominent recent investments have been German. German energy companies have been buying up utilities across Eastern Europe. In Lithuania, energy giants Ruhrgas and EON Energie paid 116 million litas (33 million US dollars) for a 34 per cent stake in the natural gas company, Lietuvos Dujos (Lithuanian Gas).

The US Undersecretary of Commerce, Grant Aldonas, informed the government during a visit in October that the USA expects to recognize Lithuania as having a functioning market economy in the near future, which will further encourage US foreign direct investment.

The country has a large, well-trained and relatively low wage workforce.

Concerns

Lithuania is a major refining centre for Russian crude oil, a position that generates tension. Supply conflicts with Russian oil giants Lukoil and Yukos have hit refined oil exports since 2000. The latter acquired a controlling stake in the state oil company, Mažeikių Nafta, in October 2002.

The government has also been thrashing out the terms of sale of a 34 per cent stake in the natural gas company Lietuvos dujos (Lithuanian Gas) to Russian gas giant Gazprom. This control opens Lithuanian energy to possible manipulation by Russian interests in the future and makes further disagreements on supply issues very likely.

Tensions are high over the issue of transit between Russia and the Kalingrad enclave on Lithuania's south-western border. Lithuania is obliged to rescind visa-free access to the enclave under its EU obligations in 2003, which Russia is determined to resist. A temporary compromise involving a simplified visa system is likely, but the issue will continue to raise tensions with Russia as EU accession approaches.

Unemployment remains stubbornly high, acting as a drag on private consumption growth. Public finance and social security reform, which have been largely avoided so far, remain essential if the country is to maintain its impressive growth rates.

Appendix 2

Useful contacts

Government ministries

Government of the Republic of Lithuania
Gedimino pr 11
2600 Vilnius
Tel: +370 5 2629 038
Fax: +370 5 2663 877
Web: www.lrvk.lt
Email: kanceliarija@lrvk.lt

Ministry of Agriculture
Gedimino pr 19
2600 Vilnius
Tel: +370 5 2391 032
Fax: +370 5 2124 440
Web: www.zum.lt
Email: zum@zum.lt

Ministry of Culture
Basanaviciaus 5
2683 Vilnius
Tel: +370 5 2619 486
Fax: +370 5 2623 120
Web: www.muza.lt
Email: culture@muza.lt

Ministry of Economy
Gedimino pr 38/2
2600 Vilnius
Tel: +370 5 2629 412
Fax: +370 5 2623 974
Web: www.ekm.lt
Email: kanc@po.ekm.lt

Ministry of Education and Science
Volano 2/7
2600 Vilnius
Tel: +370 5 2743 126
Fax: +370 5 2612 077
Web: www.smm.lt
Email: smmin@smm.lt

Ministry of Environment
Jaksto 4/9
2600 Vilnius
Tel: +370 5 2663 661
Fax: +370 5 2663 663
Web: www.gamta.lt
Email: info@aplinkuma.lt

Ministry of Finance
J Tumo-Vaizganto 8a/2
2600 Vilnius
Tel: +370 5 2390 005
Fax: +370 5 2791 481
Web: www.finmin.lt
Email: finmin@finmin.lt

Ministry of Foreign Affairs
J Tumo-Vaizganto 2
2600 Vilnius
Tel: +370 5 2362 444
Fax: +370 5 2313 090
Web: www.urm.lt
Email: urm@urm.lt

Ministry of Health Care
Vilniaus 33
2001 Vilnius
Tel: +370 5 2661 400
Fax: +370 5 2661 402
Web: www.sam.lt
Email: ministerija@sam.lt

Ministry of the Interior
Sventaragio 2
2600 Vilnius
Tel: +370 5 2717 130
Fax: +370 5 2718 551
Web: www.vrm.lt
Email: spaudavrs@vrm.lt

Ministry of Justice
Gedimino pr 30/1
2600 Vilnius
Tel: +370 5 2628 001
Fax: +370 5 2625 940
Web: www.min.tm.lt
Email: tminfo@tic.lt

Ministry of National Defence
Totoriu 25/3
2001 Vilnius
Tel: +370 5 2735 745
Fax: +370 5 2126 082
Web: www.kam.lt
Email: vis@kam.kam.lt

Ministry of Social Security and Labour
Vivulskio 11
2693 Vilnius
Tel: +370 5 2603 779
Fax: +370 5 260 3813
Web: www.socmin.lt
Email: post@socmin.lt

Ministry of Transport
Gedimino pr 17
2679 Vilnius
Tel: +370 5 2393 911
Fax: +370 5 2124 335
Web: www.transp.lt
Email: info@transp.lt

Other government departments

Bank of Lithuania
Gedimino pr 6
2001 Vilnius
Tel: +370 5 268 0001
Fax: +370 5 212 1501
Web: www.lbank.lt
Email: lb_spauda@lbank.lt

Customs Department
Jaksto 1/25
2600 Vilnius
Tel: +370 5 212 6415
Fax: +370 5 212 4948
Web: www.cust.lt
Email: tara@cust.lt

Department of Statistics
Gedimino pr 29
2746 Vilnius
Tel: +370 5 236 4822
Fax: +370 5 236 4845
Web: www.std.lt
Email: statistika@mail.std.lt

European Committee under the Government of Lithuania
Gedimino pr 56
2685 Vilnius
Tel: +370 5 266 1700
Fax: +370 5 249 6178
Web: www.euro.lt
Email: mail@www.euro.lt

Lithuanian State Property Fund
Vilniaus 16
2600 Vilnius
Tel: +370 5 268 4999
Fax: +370 5 268 4997
Web: www.vtf.lt
Email: info@vtf.lt

State Patent Bureau
Kalvariju 3
2600 Vilnius
Tel: +370 5 278 0250
Fax: +370 5 275 0723
Web: www.is.lt/vpb/engl/index.htm
Email: spb@vpb.lt

Tourism Department
Vilniaus 4/35
2600 Vilnius
Tel: +370 5 262 2610
Fax: +370 5 212 6819
Web: www.tourism.lt
Email: info@tourism.lt

Lithuanian embassies

Austria
Lowengasse 47
1030 Wien
Austria
Tel: +43 1 718 5467
Fax: +43 1 718 5469

Benelux
Rue Maurice Lietart 48
1150 Bruxelles
Belgium
Tel: +32 2 772 2750
Fax: +32 2 772 1701

Canada
130 Albert Street
Suite 204
Ottawa
Ontario K1P 5G4
Canada
Tel: +1 613 567 5458
Fax: +1 613 567 5315
Email: litemb@storm.ca

China
3-1-11 San Li Tun
100600 Beijing
People's Republic of China
Tel: +86 10 653 244 21
Fax: +86 10 653 244 21

Czech Republic
Pod Klikovkou 1916/2
150 00 Praha 5 Smichov
Czech Republic
Tel: +420 2 572 101 22; +420 2 572 101 23
Fax: +420 2 572 101 24
Email: ltembcz@mbox.vol.cz

Estonia
Uus tn 15
Tallinn
EE 0100
Estonia
Tel: +372 631 4030; +372 631 4053
Fax: +372 641 2013

France
13 pl Charles de Gaulle
26100 Romans
France
Tel: + 33 4750 2225 0
Fax: +33 4750 2464 3
Email: psf2607@wanadoo.fr

Germany
Charitéstr 9
10117 Berlin-Mitte
Germany
Tel +49 30 890 681 0
Fax: +49 30 890 681 15
Email: info@botschaft-litauen.de

Italy
Viale di Villa
Grandzioli 9
00198 Rome
Italy
Tel: +39 06 855 90 52
Fax: +39 06 855 90 53

Japan
4F Pure City Roppongi
7-11-12 Roppongi
Minato-ku T
Tokyo 106-0032
Japan
Tel: +81 3 5414 3433
Fax: +81 3 5414 3434
Email: lithemb@gol.com

Latvia
Ripniecibas iela 2
1010 Riga
Latvia
Tel: +371 7 321 519
Fax: +371 7 321 589

Portugal
Av 5 de Outubro 81 Esq
Apartado 14160
1064-002 Lisboa Codex
Portugal
Tel: +351 1 799 01 10
Fax: +351 1 799 63 63

Russia
10 Borisoglebskij per10
121069 Moscow
Russia
Tel: +7 095 291 16 98
Fax: +7 095 202 35 16
Web: www.glasnet.ru/~unic13

Spain
C Fortuny 19
28010 Madrid
Spain
Tel: +34 91 310 20 75
Fax: +34 91 310 40 18

Sweden
Strandvägen 53
115 23 Stockholm
Sweden
Tel: +46 8 667 59 55
Fax: +46 8 667 54 56

Turkey
Mahatma Gandi Cad No 17/8-9
06700 GOP
Ankara
Turkey
Tel: +90 312 447 0766
Fax: +90 312 447 0663

United Kingdom
84 Gloucester Place
London W1U 6AU
United Kingdom
Tel: +44 20 7486 6401; +44 20 7486 6402
Fax: +44 20 7486 6403

United States of America
2622 16th Street NW
Washington DC 20009
United States of America
Tel: +1 202 234 5860
Fax: +1 202 328 0466
Email: info@ltembassyus.org

Municipalities

Association of Local Authorities in Lithuania
T.Vrublevskio 6
2001 Vilnius
Tel +370 5 231 3698
Fax +370 5 261 5366
Web: www.lsa.lt
Email: lsa3@vilnius.lt

Kaunas Municipality
Laisves al 96
3000 Kaunas
Tel: +370 37 425 088
Fax: +370 37 425 452
Web: www.kaunas.lt
Email: savivaldybe@kaunas.sav.lt

Klaipeda Municipality
Liepu 11
5800 Klaipeda
Tel: +370 46 396 066
Fax: +370 46 410 049
Web: www.klaipeda.lt
Email: bendras@klaipeda.lt

Panevezys Municipality
Laisves 20
5300 Panevezys
Tel: +370 45 501 360
Fax: +370 45 501 352
Web: www.panevezys.sav.lt
Email: admins@panevezys.sav.lt

Siauliai Municipality
Vasario 16-osios 62
5400 Siauliai
Tel: +370 41 596 200
Fax: +370 41 524 116
Web: www.siauliai.sav.lt
Email: meras@siauliai.sav.lt

Utena Municipality
Utenio 4a
4910 Utena
Tel: +370 389 61 611
Fax: +370 389 61 615
Web: www.utena.lt
Email: infosav@utena.sav.lt

Vilnius Municipality
Gedimino pr 9
2600 Vilnius
Tel: +370 5 212 6977
Fax: +370 5 262 9064
Web: www.vilnius.sav.lt
Email: savivaldybe@vilnius.lt

International business organizations

American Chamber of Commerce
Lukiskiu 5-204
2600 Vilnius
Tel: +370 5 2611 181
Fax: +370 5 2126 128
Web: www.acc.lt
Email: acc@post.omniTelnet

Austrian Trade Association
Kastonu 6/3-133
2600 Vilnius
Tel/Fax: +370 5 2616 732
Email: a80645@post.omniTelnet

British Chamber of Commerce
Fabijoniskiu 2
2001 Vilnius
Tel/Fax: +370 5 2301 731
Email: british.chamber@takas.lt

Canada–Lithuania Business Association
Gedimino pr 64
2001 Vilnius
Tel: +370 5 2120 853
Fax: +370 5 2120 884
Email: canambv@aiva.lt

Chinese Trade Mission
Blindziu 34
2004 Vilnius
Tel: +370 5 2722 375
Fax: +370 5 2722 161
Web: www.chinesecomoffice.lt

Commercial Office of the Embassy of the Republic of Hungary
Saviciaus 8-4
2001 Vilnius
Tel: +370 5 2690 930
Fax: +370 5 2314 021
Email: itdvilnius@vengrija.lt

Delegate Office of German Industry and Commerce
Algirdo 3
2006 Vilnius
Tel: +370 5 2131 122
Fax: +370 5 2131 013
Web: www.ahk-lit.lt
Email: info@ahk-lit.lt

Finish Trade Office
Dominikonu 5
2001 Vilnius
Tel: +370 5 2123 221
Fax: +370 5 2124 288
Email: vilna@finpro.fi

Flemish Trade and Economic Representative
Kalinausko 2B
2009 Vilnius
Tel: +370 5 2313 595
Fax: +370 5 2313 596
Email: vlev.vilnius@post.omniTelnet

French–Lithuanian Chamber of Commerce
French-Speaking Business Forum
Sv Ignoto 5-260
2001 Vilnius
Tel/Fax: +370 5 2127 040
Web: www.cci-fr.lt
Email: admin@cci-fr.lt

French Trade Mission
Didzioji 1
2001 Vilnius
Tel: +370 5 2123 786
Fax: +370 5 2123 898
Email: ambra-fr-vilnius@post.omniTelnet

German Business Mission
Kudirkos 6
2009 Vilnius
Tel: +370 5 2131 122
Fax: +370 5 2131 013
Email: info-ahklit@post.omniTelnet

Holland House
Didzioji 13-13
2001 Vilnius
Tel: +370 5 2124 085
Fax: +370 5 2124 084
Email: hollandhouse@eunet.lt

Italian Foreign Trade Institute
Universiteto 4
2600 Vilnius
Tel: +370 5 2123 744
Fax: +370 5 2123 449
Web: www.ice.it
Email: icevilnius@takas.lt

Norwegian Trade Council
Didzioji 25-20
2004 Vilnius
Tel: +370 5 2624 020
Fax: +370 5 2123 186
Email: vilnius@ntc.no

Polish Commercial Advisory Bureau
Kastonu 2/14
2001 Vilnius
Tel: +370 5 2617 960
Fax: +370 5 2124 084
Email: brh@takas.lt

Swedish Trade Council
Vokieciu 26
2600 Vilnius
Tel: +370 5 2126 155
Fax: +370 5 2126 697
Email: litauen@swedishtrade.se

International organizations

Delegation of European Bank for Research and Development (EBRD)
Seimyniskiu 1a
2600 Vilnius
Tel: +370 5 2638 480
Fax: +370 5 2638 481
Web: www.ebrd.lt
Email: grauzini@vil.ebrd.com

Delegation of European Commission
Naugarduko 10
2001 Vilnius
Tel: +370 5 2313 191
Fax: +370 5 2313 192
Web: www.eudel.lt
Email: eudelltu@delltu.cec.eu.int

International Monetary Fund (IMF)
Gedimino pr 11-207
2039 Vilnius
Tel: +370 5 2620 893
Fax: +370 5 2124 504
Web: www.imf.org/external/country/ltu/index.htm
Email: mhorton@imf.org

UNDP
J Tumo-Vaizganto 2
2600 Vilnius
Tel: +370 5 2107 400
Fax: +370 5 2107 401
Web: www.undp.lt
Email: registry@undp.lt

World Bank Group (IBRD&IFC)
Jogailos 4
2001 Vilnius
Tel: +370 5 2107 680
Fax: +370 5 2107 681
Web: www.worldbank.lt
Email: office@worldbank.lt

World Health Organization
Vilniaus 33-304
2001 Vilnius
Tel: +370 5 2126 743
Fax: +370 5 2126 605
Web: www.who.int
Email: ltwho@ktl.mii.lt

Lithuanian business organizations

Association of Construction Industry
Sevcenkos 19
2009 Vilnius
Tel: +370 5 2133 479
Fax: +370 5 2635 641
Email: scancem@post.omniTelnet

Association of Information Technology, Telecommunications and Office Equipment Companies – Infobalt
Vokieciu 28/17-6
2001 Vilnius
Tel: +370 5 2622 623
Fax: +370 5 2623 629
Web: www.infobalt.lt
Email: office@infobalt.lt

Association of Investment Companies
Seimyniskiu st 3
2600 Vilnius
Tel: +370 5 2790 601
Fax: +370 5 2790 530
Email: invalda@aiva.lt

Association of Lithuanian Banks
Ankstoji 5
2600 Vilnius
Tel: +370 5 2496 669
Fax: +370 5 2496 139
Email: info@lba.lt

Association of Lithuanian Chambers of Commerce, Industry and Crafts
J Tumo-Vaizganto 9/1-63a
2600 Vilnius
Tel: +370 5 2612 102
Fax: +370 5 2612 112
Web: www.chambers.lt
Email: info@chambers.lt

Association of Lithuanian Chemical Industry Enterprises
Vienuolio 8
2600 Vilnius
Tel/Fax: +370 5 2124 175
Web: www.tdd.lt/lchpia
Email: lchpia@tdd.lt

Association 'Lithuanian Food Industry'
Vienuolio 8
2600 Vilnius
Tel: +370 5 2627 022
Fax: +370 5 2124 447

Association of Retail Trade Enterprises
Vienuolio 8
2600 Vilnius
Tel/Fax: +370 5 2312 522
Email: zizysg@takas.lt

Confederation of Lithuanian Industrialists
Vienuolio 8
2000 Vilnius
Tel: +370 5 2125 217
Fax: +370 5 2125 209
Web: www.lpk.lt
Email: info@lpk.lt

Enterprises Association 'Praktika'
Vilniaus 137 A
2400 Siauliai
Tel: +370 41 502 730
Fax: +370 41 502 672
Web: www.praktika.lt
Email: praktika@siauliai.omniTelnet

Investors' Forum
c/o AB Lietuvos Telekomas
Lvovo 21a Room 303
2726 Vilnius
Tel/Fax: +370 5 2755 258
Web: www.investorsforum.lt
Email: investors.forum@takas.lt

International Chamber of Commerce Lithuania
Vokieciu 28/17
2001 Vilnius
Tel: +370 5 2122 111
Fax: +370 5 2122 621
Web: www.tprl.lt; www.iccwbo.org
Email: info@tprl.lt

Lithuanian Builders' Association
Vytauto 14
2004 Vilnius
Tel: +370 5 2734 676
Fax: +370 5 2125 901
Email: lsa@post.omniTelnet

Lithuanian Business Employers' Confederation
Rotundo 5
2600 Vilnius
Tel: +370 5 2498 345
Fax: +370 5 2496 448
Web: www.lvdk.lt
Email: lvdk@post.omniTelnet

Lithuanian National Freight Forwarders' Association 'LINEKA'
Verkiu 44-306
2600 Vilnius
Tel: +370 5 2779 036
Fax: +370 5 2779 036
Web: www.lineka.lt
Email: lineka@post.5ci.lt

National Regional Development Agency
Kalvariju 3-327
2005 Vilnius
Tel/Fax: +370 5 2731 254
Web: www.nrda.lt
Email: nrda@nrda.lt

Appendix 3

Contributors' Contact Details

Association of Financial Analysts
A.Goštauto St. 40, 5th floor
2001 Vilnius Lithuania
Tel: +3705 2362 714
Fax: +3705 2362 771
Web: www.finansai.lt
Contact: Ms. Viktorija Trimbel, President

AWS Structured Finance Ltd
Tel: +44 (0) 1892 667891
Fax: +44 (0) 1892 610891
Email: kevin.r.smith@awsconsult.co.uk
Web: www.awsconsult.co.uk
Contact: Kevin Smith

Deloitte and Touche
Aludariu 2, LT-2001 Vilnius
Lithuania
Tel.: +370 (5) 261 31 31
Mob: +370 687 39900
Fax: +370 (5) 212 68 44
Email: vramoskaite@deloitteCE.com
Contact: Violeta Ramoskaite, Executive Assistant

Lideika, Petrauskas, Valiunas ir Partneriai
Labdariu 5, LT-2001 Vilnius
Lithuania
Tel: (direct) +370 5 2681810
Tel: (switchboard) +370 5 2681888
Fax: +370 5 2125591
Email: LSkibarka@lpvp.lt
Web: www.lpvp.lt
Contact: Laimonas Skibarka

Lithuanian Development Agency
Tel: +370 5 2120776
Šv. Jono 3, LT-2600 Vilnius
Lithuania
Tel: +370 5 262 74 38
Fax: (370 5) 212 01 60
Email: lda@lda.lt
Web: www.lda.lt
Contact: Diana Miskiniene, Director of Information and PR department

Lithuanian Free Market Institute
Birutes St. 56, 2004 Vilnius
Lithuania
Tel: + 370 5 272 42 41
Email: asta@freema.org
Contact: Asta Tobuleviciene, Media Relations Officer

Prime Investment
S. Daukanto a. 2/5-12
2001 Vilnius
Lithuania
Tel: +370 5 231 4591, 231 4592, 262 6428
Fax: +370 5 262 8075
Email: info@primeinvestment.lt
Web: www.primeinvestment.lt

Prime Real Estate
S. Daukanto a. 2/5-12
2001 Vilnius
Lithuania
Tel: +370 5 231 4591/4592/262 6428
Fax: +370 5 262 8075
Email: info@primerealestate.lt
Web: www. primerealestate.lt

Suprema, Evli Group
A.Goštauto St. 40, 5th floor
2001 Vilnius
Lithuania
Tel: +3705 2362 770
Fax. +3705 2362 771
Web: www.suprema.com/ www.evli.com
Contact: Mr. Aidas Galubickas, Partner, Country Head

Index

References in italic indicate figures or tables

Index of Advertisers

Other international business titles from Kogan Page

Doing Business with Azerbaijan
Doing Business with Bahrain
Doing Business with China
Doing Business with the Czech Republic
Doing Business with Egypt
Doing Business with Georgia
Doing Business with Germany
Doing Business with Hungary
Doing Business with India
Doing Business with Iran
Doing Business with Kazakhstan
Doing Business with Libya
Doing Business with Oman
Doing Business with Poland
Doing Business with Qatar
Doing Business with Russia
Doing Business with Saudi Arabia
Doing Business with Spain
Doing Business with South Africa
Doing Business with Turkey
Doing Business with Ukraine
Doing Business with the United Arab Emirates